F. H Matthews

A Dialogue on Moral Education

F. H Matthews

A Dialogue on Moral Education

ISBN/EAN: 9783337218461

Printed in Europe, USA, Canada, Australia, Japan

Cover: Foto ©Thomas Meinert / pixelio.de

More available books at **www.hansebooks.com**

A DIALOGUE ON MORAL EDUCATION

By F. H. MATTHEWS M.A
HEAD MASTER OF BOLTON GRAMMAR SCHOOL
AND FORMERLY SCHOLAR OF
C.C.C. OXON

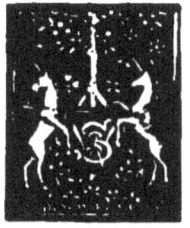

LONDON
SWAN SONNENSCHEIN & CO Lim
PATERNOSTER SQUARE
1898

BUTLER & TANNER,
THE SELWOOD PRINTING WORKS,
FROME, AND LONDON.

I

A MID-TERM holiday is a chance that a schoolmaster dare not despise. On one of them I had arranged to take a long country walk, accompanied by a doctor friend, both of us glad to be able for the nonce to shake off the cares of work and to reinvigorate ourselves, by drinking the fresh country breezes round us, for renewal of work on the morrow. We proposed to get rid of the smoke of our busy town by training it out to such a distance as would land us in the open country without fear of interruption, and were making preparations for the start when my neighbour, Reynolds, a clergyman, happened to drop in to borrow a book. Reynolds and I were very good friends, though our views were in many points most divergent; but divergence of views I have often found to be a strong bond of union among thinking men who are keen, as we both were, on argumentation, and alive to the fact that the last has scarcely been said on any subject of human speculation. Hearing that we purposed to escape "the smoke and stir of that dim spot which men call" Workton, but we in more familiar terms—though we breathe it not to others, the natives of the town—Smoke-i'-th'-Hole-cum-Filthton, Reynolds asked if he might join us, to which we gladly said yes. As he was well up in the district for many miles round, and was besides an excellent topographer and archæologist, I in particular was delighted; for I have a strong predilection for losing my way on the very least provocation—my friends are rude enough to say on none at all—and as Hindley had not been very long in the town, and during that time had been too busy with arranging his new practice to be able to make explorations, or even to study the maps of the district through which we proposed to tramp, the duties of organizer fell upon me, or rather would so have fallen had it not been for the opportune intervention of Reynolds, on to whose shoulders I gladly threw the, to me, unwelcome burden.

"I know you like it, so I will make no apologies; and if Hindley says, as he probably will, that it is most immoral and cowardly to back out of my undertaking in so brazenfaced a way, well, in the first place I do not care, as my education, I fear, was not sufficiently exalted to make me adopt the high tone in which he delights; in the second place, should he persist in his sermonizing and reproaches, you just leave, at the most ticklish point, the conduct of the walk to me, and I can assure you that, with the noblest intentions and the clearest map before me, I will lead him astray so far that he will not succeed in reaching home to-night, and then all those new patients to whom his court is so assiduous will have nothing more to do with him, because he has failed to pay the old ladies his due regulation visit at the expected time. So be careful, Hindley; no lecturing as you value your practice."

Hindley laughed and said:

"All right, I know you of old, that you are quite incorrigible; and whatever my sentiments may be about your natural laziness, I will suppress them till a convenient season, when I promise you they shall be delivered with all the expansive vigour which is generated by long bottling and good fermentation."

Reynolds for his part made no objection—very far from it; so off we started, and were soon landed in the train, wishing it would go a little faster and not waste so much of the valuable day. We had before us a long programme —to strike across country, by field as much as possible, over a mountain called High Fell, to descend the other side of it, mount a second height, Black Ridge, then stop at a little village for tea, and in the cooler part of the evening to trace the windings of the beautiful and wooded valley-road which led to the town of Windicombe, whence train was to see us home. Reynolds and I both knew the route, indeed Reynolds first introduced me to it; but to Hindley, who was a stranger from the level flats of the eastern counties, it seemed a true revelation, and though he was not given to violent expression of his emotions, I could tell by his look, and the occasional remarks he dropped, that he was enjoying it thoroughly. Perhaps I was wrong to say that he was not given to violent expression of his emotions; he certainly was given to violent expression of something very nearly akin to his emotions when his ideals were in any way touched. To tell the truth, I was rather hoping that I might be able to trot him out for the benefit of Reynolds, who had not as yet come to know him very well, but I was going to wait my chance; for I knew from old experience that when the conversation turned upon any social topic, as it invariably did with both of my companions, I should be sure to tread on Hindley's corns, who, though reluctant to confess it, was at heart a real Socialist. The chance, however, came much sooner than I expected; for, after we had gone some three or four miles, we came within sight of a well-known Roman Catholic College, about which I made use of a rather strong expression. Hindley at once pulled me up.

"You have no right to say that; I do not believe that any one—still less any body of men—is an utter hypocrite."

"No, I plead guilty; but I cannot get rid of the feeling that the directors of the system are aware of its glaring faults—at least, if they aren't they ought to be—and make no attempt to alter them, because they find the duping system better."

"There you are; even in your apology you beg the whole question. Why should they be aware of the glaring faults, as you please to call them?"

"How can any man of sense not be?"

"My good Trelawney, what is a man of sense? One who agrees with you, I suppose. But may I ask—you will forgive the question—if you are aware of your own glaring faults, whether personal, or in your system of education?"

"Well, I have a suspicion of some perhaps, but——"

"But you are not sure? Well, why don't you ask some particular friend to tell you quite candidly what they are, and amend them?"

"A friend I could not get to do it."

"Well, an enemy then."

"I'm afraid I haven't the moral courage."

"Precisely; nor probably have the Jesuits. The fact is you are the slave, partly of inherited, and, if I may coin a word, ineducated prejudices; partly perhaps—who knows?—of professional jealousy. Two of a trade never agree, and you probably are conscious only too much of the greatness of the work the Jesuits have done, and of the marked superiority of their closely-reasoned system over the system which is traditional in most of our schools, and of which you are now a professional exponent, to be able to judge in the question quite dispassionately."

"I think you are rather hard on Trelawney," said Reynolds. "I know he is alive, at all events, to some defects in our every-day round of working education, and tries his best to remedy them; but Rome, you know, was not built in a day, and education will hardly be perfected just yet."

"Oh," ejaculated Hindley, "I have known Trelawney long enough to be quite assured that he would not consciously reject anything that he recognised as better. I only say he is not in a position fairly to judge what is better."

"Who is then? Would you dethrone the specialist?"

"Most assuredly. The proper person to judge is an outsider, before whom the specialists should plead."

"Well, there," I intervened, "I think I agree with you, so long as it is not education that is in question."

At this my two friends burst into a hearty laugh, in which I joined, adding:

"I knew you would laugh; but, after all, I am afraid that is the position which, if pressed, I should finally have to confess that I believed in my heart of hearts to be the only tenable one, at least on education. And yet I have known officers in the merchant service object most strongly to the naval courts, on the ground that experts ought to be the judges, even while admitting that non-professional judges, helped only by special assessors and pleaders, constituted a system which worked well in every case save where their own business was concerned. I was greatly amused at the time, and now here I am doing exactly the same thing!"

"Never mind, old fellow, we doctors are more conservative than any one else when our own interests are attacked;

and as for taking lay opinion on a point of medical procedure or jurisprudence, why, I think if it were to be seriously suggested, the whole faculty would die in a fit."

"Dear me! what a terrible reflection on poor human nature!"—this from Reynolds. "Is there no one who has boldness and honesty enough to entirely cast away his prejudices?"

"I am afraid it is very difficult to find any one, and I certainly am not that being. Trelawney knows how often he has tried to convince me that I have a fatal twist in judging of social matters, and how little he has succeeded in altering my views, though I admit there is probably something to be said for his statements."

"Probably!—thank you," I replied. "It is the first time you have ever gone even so far as that."

"Oh, don't be alarmed; I made the admission for Reynolds's benefit, not yours. Please look upon yourself as an eavesdropper. So far as you are concerned, the remark is unsaid."

"Well now, what is the good of arguing with a fellow like this?" I said, turning to Reynolds. "*You* had better discuss with him, I'm sure I can't."

"I have been wanting," Reynolds said, "to find out what points in the Jesuit system Dr. Hindley considers so worthy of admiration. Of course," he added, addressing Hindley directly, "you will remember I am a clergyman of the Church of England."

"And therefore a biassed and incompetent judge, though doubtless you think yourself specially qualified to express an opinion. Well, my support of the Jesuits depends practically on two things: first, they have reasoned out a system of education and stick to it; secondly, to them the prime point is morality."

At this remark both Reynolds and I opened fire, but I managed to get the lead, and said that I admitted they had much to teach us in the matter of organization; but as for their moral training, I did not believe in it. However, as I saw that Reynolds was boiling over, I left off abruptly, and so gave free opening to the torrent that straightway came.

"Moral education, indeed! A system of spying and mistrust! Never a moment of freedom for the boy, never an act that is not watched and construed into the worst possible interpretation! Don't tell me that such a system can beget good results. Nothing but trust can lead to trustworthiness, and trust is the one feature which, if I read aright, is absolutely wanting to the Jesuit system. Of all things I hate hypocrisy, and hypocrisy is of Jesuitism the very keynote."

The Doctor looked amused and said,—

"I knew I should awake a lion. But, prejudice apart, don't you think there is something to be said for their view? Your Church also teaches the natural depravity of man."

"That is quite a different thing," ejaculated Reynolds.

"And I am sure," went on Hindley, without noticing the interruption, "that every schoolmaster"—looking at me—"will admit the truth of the indictment."

"Not at all," I rejoined; "it is a gross lie to say that the propensity of a child is by nature to evil rather than to good. The proper view to take is that children are, in inverse proportion to their years, non-moral beings; they do not know the difference between right and wrong, and are as well prepared to follow the one line as the other—of course with exceptions—if only the attractions can be made equal."

"Precisely; and that is exactly why I so much admire the Jesuits. They act upon the principle that children require to be instructed in morals as much as in lesser matters, and make accordingly a genuine effort to lay a solid foundation of morality. With all due respect to Mr. Reynolds, I think he has been trailing a red herring across the scent. I never said that I admired whatever the Jesuits did; my admiration is directed to the attempt they make to tackle one of the most difficult and important questions in the world, though I have my own opinion as to their methods and results. You must remember, too, that their system has been at work for some centuries, and was started at a time when public opinion held far more than at present that the end can justify any means whatever."

"Then what you mean is that you admire them for recognising that morality should be the aim of all education—a point which most other educational bodies, despite their own and the theorists' assertion of its vital nature, have in practice disregarded; and you pass no sentence at all upon their method of attempting to correct the defect?"

"Precisely."

"Oh, well, of course there I agree with you, and I do not suppose even Mr. Reynolds will fall foul of you any more."

"No, not till I hear some other opinion equally objectionable to rouse all my prej—no, they are not prejudices—my knowledge of what is right."

Neither Dr. Hindley nor I could altogether repress a smile, but we made no comment, and walked on for a few minutes in silence. At last I said,—

"But it really is a serious question, this of moral education; and I should be glad to know if you have any ideas on the subject. It is one on which I have thought a great deal, and read everything on which I could lay my hands—which, after all, considering the great bulk of educational literature from Plato downwards, is not much—yet my mind remains in absolute chaos. I wish some one would bring it into order."

"Let me recommend you to consider the Americans. They are perhaps at present the most go-ahead nation in educational matters—certainly they are the boldest in trying experiments; and they are beginning to tackle the problem in question in a notable manner. Have you read a recent book by Professor Felix Adler on the moral instruction of children?"

"Yes; and I found it very interesting and suggestive: but——"

"But what?".

"It is only instruction, not education; and that is the more important matter."

"True; but you remember he promises to tackle the larger question by-and-bye."

"Yes; but meantime we grovel in the dark. Still, I admit the book has been an enormous help to me, and that instruction must, if not precede, at all events run alongside of education."

Here Reynolds asked: "How does he set about the work?"

"He starts," I replied, "with stories and fairy tales — tales from the Bible, tales from the poets: makes a most careful and suggestive selection of those which teach forcibly and directly some simple moral lesson; and, carefully excluding every suggestion that is not in accordance with the highest possible morality, passes to practical suggestions on the matter of various duties—first of all the duty that comes closest to a child at school, the duty of acquiring knowledge; and then the other duties in order—duty to oneself, duty to one's friends, duty to one's country. Of course it seems tentative, but there is a great deal to be gained from it."

"Have you ever tried to carry it out yourself?"

"I have made half-hearted attempts, but you know, or do not know, how difficult it is to be a pioneer in teaching anything. But our hand is being forced by the elementary and continuation schools with their instruction in civic duty."

"It sounds all very nice," said Reynolds; "but why don't you leave the matter to the recognised bodies?"

"What are they?" the Doctor asked.

"Why, the different Churches and the clergymen."

At this Hindley pulled a long face and whistled, but, after a moment, said,—

"Well, I don't want to hurt your feelings, Mr. Reynolds; but in a discussion like this, where I feel so deeply, I must speak out. Now, do you as an honest man really consider that the parties you name have proved so efficient in the past that there is no opening for other bodies to take up the work?"

"No, I am not prepared to maintain that; but they are undoubtedly the right people for the work."

"Well, but when they have proved inefficient?"

"It does not follow that they will always be so."

"Granted; but I cannot see great signs of improvement. And what of the interim? Would you have the generations perish for want of all food, because the purveyors of the best either will not or cannot provide it?"

Here I interposed. "It seems to me," I said, "as one whose whole business is to discover the best methods of imparting knowledge, that in the matter of spiritual instruction the clergy go the wrong way to work. They preach from pulpits, where, so far from being answered, they cannot even be challenged, and then expect their congregations to develop as reasoned and lively a faith as if the congregations themselves were active participators in the lesson conveyed. In education we believe, perhaps too fondly, that the old pouring-in method is completely exploded: we have come to recognise that, if we are to do any lasting good, we must get the active co-operation of the pupils taught. If the clergy would pose rather as spiritual guides with wider knowledge and experience on special subjects than their flocks, and not claim to be, as often they do, authoritative and infallible exponents of a system in which development can find no place, exponents, too, to question whose statements is heresy—if, in short, like other teachers they would put feeling on one side and be guided only by regard to the best methods of instruction, they would have far more chance of influencing the most important beliefs and actions of the day, instead of, which I fear is happening at present, getting more and more out of touch with the spiritual desires and aspirations of the mass. I hope, Reynolds, I am not treading on your corns. I speak in all earnestness and with a sincere wish to see religion take that place which ought to be hers unquestioned and of right."

"No," said Reynolds, "you do not hurt me, though of course there are numbers of my fellow-clergymen who would be shocked beyond measure at the doctrine you lay down. But I am too broad for that. However, I must say that your remarks seem to me to have but little to do with the main question, which is, how best to teach morality."

"On the contrary, they seem to me to have a great deal to do with it. If you grant that the clergy of all denominations have failed, at all events as yet, to satisfy the demand for moral education, and that the demand is one which above all should be gratified as speedily as possible, then of course we have to consider what is the cause of their failure and who is to take their place. Now if I am right in saying that their failure is due in the main to defective method, and that they are not in a position to correct that defect, which also seems to me true—what do you say, Hindley?"

The Doctor replied: "For my part, I think you have hit the nail on the head, but I doubt if Mr. Reynolds will agree."

Reynolds merely shrugged his shoulders and said: "Well, never mind about me. I will not discuss at present the possibility of improving our methods. Go on."

"Then it follows," I resumed, "that the best people to take up the work are those who know something of teaching-method and who, being, like clergymen, in touch with large numbers, are able to produce the desired effect in quantity. And who are those people, if not," I added, with a smile and a bow to my two companions, "your humble servant and his compeers, the noble army of schoolmasters?"

Reynolds and Hindley both laughed, and the latter said:—

"Well, Trelawney, at all events you are not bashful nor cursed with too mean an opinion of your own importance. But, soberly, I agree almost entirely with what you say, other things, of course, such as personal influence and character, being equal."

"Of course, of course," I replied; "that must always be granted in an abstract discussion. But I should like to add one other point in favour of schoolmasters making moral education a regular part of their week's work, and it is this: they are, if worth their salt, regarded with a reverence—I may almost say worship—which is felt by the young for perhaps no one else, unless it be their parents, and then, alas! I fear by no means always. This half-worship which children often show towards their masters, and still more perhaps towards their mistresses, is a coign of vantage from which great work might be done. No one else seems to be in so favourable a position, unless we except in some cases the parents."

"Ah," said Reynolds, "I have been wondering how long the parents were to be left out of the discussion. It is all nonsense talking about school giving the chief part of moral education. Home and the Church are the proper places."

"That's all very fine," interposed Dr. Hindley, "but what about them when inefficient? It seems to me you will not face the real point. The Church is notoriously inefficient——"

Reynolds here interrupted coldly: " Of course, if you level insults at all that I hold most sacred, I can discuss nothing."

I saw we were getting on dangerous ground and was going to interpose in the interests of peace, but Hindley was before me.

" No, no, hang it all! I didn't mean to insult you; but I am rather a peppery fellow, and when I see notorious incompet—— No, bother! I will apologize once for all and have done with it. You must forgive me when my tongue runs away with me: I am afraid my own moral training never taught me to control myself. But you will at least allow me to start from this position—that the Church, for whatever reason, has not succeeded in satisfactorily covering the whole field."

" Well?"

" Well, all I propose is that it should be a recognised duty of our educators to supplement, if you will have it so, the teaching of our spiritual masters, bringing their high doctrines down to every-day life and the understanding of children. You surely cannot object to helpers in your work."

" There are professing helpers who are worse than foes. It all depends upon the attitude the helpers take up. How are you going to teach morality? Either religion must be its base or it must be left out of consideration. In the former case, I repeat the proper instructors are the clergy; in the latter, more harm will result than good."

" Ah, now," said Hindley, " we are getting to business. So morality is either a branch of religion pure and simple, or it is a deadly enemy to it. Is that your position?"

" You have put it rather strongly."

" Strong statements are best: you know exactly what is meant. I hate a man who never talks of a lie, but always of an untruth or a falsehood. Bah! They make me shiver, milk-and-water creatures! However, that is neither here nor there at present. But let us just look at your two positions. As to the first, I am at one with you in holding that morality must ultimately be the handmaid of religion,—and by religion I do not most emphatically mean theology,—but it does seem to me odd that you should be so jealous of any one else helping you in the work. It really looks as if you thought your influence were not securely enough grounded, and that every one except yourselves was your enemy. That I should be most loth to believe. I do think, and I repeat, that the clergy have in many ways fallen short, I do not say of what they could have done,—I am not judging their responsibility,—but of what we want, and if that is granted, it is surely desirable that other agencies should assist. Now those other agencies are *ex hypothesi* not religious. I mean they are non-religious—religion does not enter into the question at present. The religious teachers have been found unable to cope with the work and others come to help. Now you say that all teachers, so far as they are teachers of morality, must be religious workers, workers directly for religion? Yes? Well, how do you meet the difficulty—to start with an outside one—of the different religious sects and their divergent views?"

"Isn't that more theology than religion?"

"Ah, you are cunning. I might have raised that reply, but I hardly thought you would. Granted that it is; still, to the average mind, the two are inseparably mixed, and you will never get an ordinary parent to believe that in entrusting religious education to one of a creed that is not his own he is not entrusting his child's theology, and not merely those points of his child's beliefs in which all Christians practically agree. Ah! how wild it makes me that all the fuss about so-called religion is mostly a fighting about mere theology, wherein the true interests and aims of religion properly so called are not merely overlooked but actually impaired! But that again is neither here nor there. At present you will grant that theology and religion are inseparably mixed, more's the pity, and when a parent cries out that his child's religion is in danger, he mostly means nothing but his theology. Hence your reply will not overcome the objection. If moral training is to be confined to religious teachers only, does not that position imply that you believe in different morality in the different religious sects?"

"Not necessarily. It only means that I still maintain that religion and morality are so inseparably intertwined, and, from the practical side, in the world at present religion and theology are likewise so inseparably intertwined, that in handing over the teaching of morality to laymen you will, whether you mean and wish it or no, inevitably be handing over the teaching of religion too."

"Well, but, in the first place, I suppose, you would allow parents to have something to say in the matter of religious education; and in the second, if you admit, as you seem to, that religion and theology are two separate things, and that theology is of comparatively little importance——"

"I hope I never said that."

"But don't you imply it when you raise as an answer to my difficulty the fact that the difference between the different religious sects is chiefly a difference of theology, and therefore can be disregarded?"

"I don't think I ever said that."

"But you certainly seemed to imply it. What did you think, Trelawney?"

"I must confess," I replied, "that Reynolds's words seemed to carry the implication."

"Yes, I certainly took your meaning to be that it was no fair objection to leaving moral education entirely to the clergy that our schools of clergy are so divergent in their views."

"I certainly do not think it an insuperable difficulty, because no sensible man would deny that after all the main difference between the different sects is one either of discipline and procedure, or of such points of doctrine as among Christians—putting on one side perhaps the Roman Catholics—do not produce marked differences in actual practice. But I am aware that many think that the difference of belief is cardinal, though personally I do not share that view."

"Well, then I may take it for granted that for ordinary practical purposes you would place all religious sects on an equality in the matter of morality?"

"I would not say that absolutely: for instance, as I have already made clear, I have the strongest objection to the Church of Rome in regard to much of her actual inculcation of morality."

"Yes, but the cases of divergence are comparatively few."

"But any divergence at all upsets your position, which is, I take it, that there is such a common agreement on the points of morality that it does not require any special teachers to give the training in the subject required."

"If you understand by special, subordinating moral teaching to the attainments of other ends, that is my position, and I certainly do not feel that it is stormed by the objection that there is some divergence. In considering in the abstract any question whatever we are obliged to take the average of cases, or I should say the great majority, and legislate accordingly."

Here I interposed and said: "It seems to me we are rather wasting time. I sympathize with Reynolds's position very much, though I am a layman and certainly eclectic in my Church views: for I feel that in the long run morality must rest upon religion, and the great difficulty to me is how we are to teach morality to any satisfaction without the support of the chief prop. I wish, Hindley, you would go straight for that question, and when you come to it, no doubt Reynolds and I will both be able, if we feel inclined, to combat your position with rather more effect than at present. It seems to me now that we are simply beating the air."

"Well," said Dr. Hindley, "I will try, with Mr. Reynolds's leave, to tackle that problem, the really crucial one. If I can propound a method—and I feel by no means sanguine of doing so, as I have never thought out a scheme on the question which can claim to make even a decent approach to a satisfactory solution of a difficulty which leads to most revolutionary proposals—then I shall be satisfied. I only hope that Mr. Reynolds will not consider I am attacking either his personal predilections or the position of his class."

"No, no; a clergyman, especially of the Established Church, has to stand so much abuse as speedily to learn not to go out of his way to look for insults where none are intended. A thin-skinned man cannot better the world."

At this moment we reached the highest point on our route, and as we stepped upon the top, with a sudden cry of delight Dr. Hindley stood entranced. And well he might. We were pausing on the summit of the beautiful

Black Ridge,—a name drawn from the dark undergrowth of low furze which covered its flanks,—and on all sides from the pointed top the wide-stretching views were grand. The sun was lying to the west of south, and as the valleys on either side of us trended for the most part to the south-east and north-west, we saw one part of them in sunlight, the rest obscured in shadow. Far away to the south from which we had come, the mountains sank gently to lower and lower heights, until at last the country seemed well-nigh a level plain, bathed in June's warm glow and fresh with the glory of the coming hay. In and out we could see small streams tracking their delicate way, but so still was everything that we could have believed them as motionless as ourselves. To the north and east, whither we were bound, the mountains towered on high. Far as the eye could reach they folded one upon the other in calm repose, looking like giants resting on guard to prevent the sacrilege of intrusion on hallowed ground. Here and there clumps of beeches and stunted oak could be seen, mixed with the golden gorse, placed as it seemed expressly to be a focus for the glowing light. At one point in especial one valley doubled back, forming an islet of green meadow, from which we could hear faintly a tinkling cattle-bell, whose music only made the surrounding silence live. Peace was in the air: it was the very spot for a worn-out soul to come for quiet rest. Long stood the Doctor without a word, and even I, who had seen the view before, felt that it had never been more beautiful. At last Hindley turned and in a manner almost solemn said: "Do not speak, do not speak: I want to drink it in." He then lay down on the turf and gazed and gazed, till I could see that he was growing lost in a dream we would not disturb. Finally, with a long-drawn breath he rose and, turning to us slowly, said:—

"Do you know I think heaven must be like that—so rich, so varied, so calm. Here indeed one can feel the very presence of God; here one can indeed pray. But as we are at present everything palls; let us be getting on before I have time to feel that I have had too much."

I was surprised at this outburst, if an outburst so quiet a remark can be called, as I had never known Hindley so solemn before. I had indeed always felt that, like every man of strong convictions, he was essentially religious; but he rather liked shocking what he thought the narrowness of others, and hence would make comments on religious beliefs which even I could not think consonant with true religious feeling. But here, as often, I had to confess I had misjudged my man, and as we walked on for some time in silence, the thought came across me that perhaps our previous conversation had something to do with his state of mind, and that he had been more interested in it than he had chosen to say. When the conversation was renewed, I found I was not far wrong.

"I have been thinking," he said, after a long silence, "what an inestimable blessing the country is to man. How can we live in our hideous, soul-stifling towns? I would make it a cardinal point in any system of rational education that the young should be trained entirely in the country."

"The disadvantage is," I said, "that, apart from the expense, unless we are to have only small schools, the children must be shut up in barracks. This means the loss of the most valuable influence that can touch them in their younger years, the influence of mothers and sisters, or—in the case of girls—of their brothers, in place of which they only gain what are often questionable advantages indeed."

"I see you are no friend of our public schools. Well, I admit there is much in what you say, but am not sure that even on the whole I agree. However, we may break a lance on that question by-and-bye. You see, I am so convinced of the absolute unfitness of most parents to be parents at all that I would welcome almost any measures which would promise to bring an education, especially in morals, within reach of the young better than that which most parents now take the trouble to impart."

"I quite agree with you," I said. "Doubtless you know it is the fundamental article of a schoolmaster's creed that no one knows anything except himself."

"Yes. I have discovered it," replied the Doctor, with a twinkle, and Reynolds laughed.

"Well, you know," said the latter, "they must be forgiven. Headmasters and clergymen are nearly the only people left who can even approximate to absolute power."

"Don't talk of it," ejaculated the Doctor; "the term is a bugbear to me. If that is the position of schoolmasters, the sooner they are swept away the better."

"Thank you," I said.

"Never mind, never mind," replied Hindley; "let's talk of something else. You have almost driven out of my head the soothing effects of that recent glimpse of heaven. But I was dreaming, while lying there, of what the world might become, if only every man and woman did the duty that came to hand with full sincerity and full enlightenment."

"That will never be"—this from Reynolds.

"I am not so sure. I believe in the progress of man, slow though it be; were it not for that, my life would be but a dreary round."

"There come in the consolations of religion."

"Oh, now," began Hindley, but checked himself. I saw a storm coming, so intervened and turned the conversation in another direction.

"To return to the point you raised just now. Don't you exaggerate the deficiencies of the ordinary parent? Even I, though I said laughingly that I am always prepared to help to abuse the much-suffering parent, do not really consider them so bad as all that. Moreover, I am a parent myself and know something of the difficulties."

"My dear Trelawney," Hindley replied, and I could see by his almost solemn tones that he was now in deadly earnest, "when I speak on purely social topics you may be sure that I never to my conscious knowledge exaggerate. Believe me that a doctor sees more, infinitely more, than even a clergyman of the real insides of homes; and God forbid that I should represent them as worse than they really are. Your knowledge, of course, lies chiefly in the sphere of middle-class homes, where all specimens are to be found; but I assert deliberately that in every class of society, from the highest to the lowest, things are done and passed without a word of reproval which any good standard of morality must condemn, sometimes as absolutely vicious in themselves, sometimes as tending to produce vicious habits, even though in themselves comparatively harmless. Take, for instance, punctuality—a minor virtue, perhaps, but one which ought to be strictly enforced, not merely for a child's own sake, but also for the sake of others. Or a more serious matter still—the love of truth, the exact, absolute, unexaggerated truth. How many parents ever think of systematically checking all attempts at exaggeration? And once more—the practice and real love of true charity. Or, to go to a more extreme case still, how many parents are aware of the encouragement they give to that worst of all vices, impurity, by thoughtless household arrangements, meant primarily to spare trouble to themselves and their servants? How many, too, think of systematic instruction in regard to the different virtues? They deal with each question, perhaps, as it turns up; but who in any other branch of training whatever would think of being content to act so scrappily? No; the training must be regular and systematic from our cradle-days onwards, if we are ever to effect a radical improvement in public morality."

"From the cradle?" put in Reynolds. "That surely cannot matter. Is it possible to affect the morals of a child till he begins to show signs of consciousness?"

"Ah, Mr. Reynolds, you do not know what the researches of scientific men have proved. I lay it down as a maxim which no one who has gone into the subject will dispute, that the child is affected morally, as well as physically and intellectually, by everything which meets him from the moment of birth onwards. Nay, the thinking man who knows what we doctors know would probably go further still, and say that even before birth a child's moral development may be affected as strongly as his physical."

"Of course," I interposed, "every one knows that in one sense that is true. Our moral character is largely, and some people say wholly, due to those natural endowments which are with us from our mother's womb."

"But I mean more than that. I say deliberately that the unborn child may, through pernicious habits on the mother's part, have pernicious tendencies implanted which no amount of after-training will eradicate."

"What an awful responsibility you lay upon us!" said Reynolds.

"Did you think the question was one which could be dealt with offhand—a mere question of slight causes and slight changes of our usual procedure? If we are to go into the question thoroughly, we must be prepared to argue long and earnestly, and even then, unhappily, may arrive at nothing but tentative conclusions."

" Well, if we get some guidance from the discussion, I shall not hold the time as lost, though I still maintain that morality is but one branch of religion."

" It may be a branch. I have already expressed my own feelings on the matter, but you would probably not deny that in religion, as elsewhere, it is sometimes well to partition the subject."

" Yes, if you never lose sight of the fact, as for instance often happens to the devotees of political economy, that you are treating only a branch. As soon as you lose sight of the religious foundation you go hopelessly astray."

" Well, I am quite content to be judged on that point when you have heard all I have to say."

Here I broke in. " I referred just now," I said, " to the question how far nature and how far education are responsible for the finished product. That is a point to which I should like to recur before we make more advance. There are people who have maintained—whether seriously or not, I cannot say—that education can get nothing out of the child which is not already in him, as, indeed, the word seems to imply; while others hold that education is everything, and nature practically nothing. Of course, both views are exaggerations, but I should like to hear your opinion on the question."

" Nay," replied the Doctor; " I think you as a schoolmaster are best qualified to speak on that point."

" Ah," I said, " it is not easy to ensnare you. But I really do want guidance, for at times I feel almost in despair of doing any good. I sometimes say in my haste that education is useless, but in my saner moments, of course, admit that that is not so, and even go so far as to say that, given perfect education, we should have perfect men."

" There you certainly overlook inherited tendencies, as nowadays we call them; in older times people were content with saying the natural disposition."

" Yes; but logically I could overthrow you, for without perfect trainers, which, of course, includes parents, you could not have the perfect training, and perfect parents include perfect inherited tendencies."

"Not necessarily; there are still reversions. However, this is merely word-play; let us have your sober judgment on the question."

"It is not likely to be worth much. It is a question which is at least as old as Euripides, and it seems to me that we are scarcely nearer a solution than he was. You know the passage in the *Hecuba*?"

"Nay; my Greek was never much, and though, I suppose, every one who has read any Greek at all has read the *Hecuba*, yet I must confess that with me it is as rusty as an old door-nail in a brewery. Give it us, and, as you love me, translate."

"Well, ἆρ' οἱ τεκόντες διαφέρουσιν ἢ τροφαί, which being interpreted is: 'Do the parents make the difference, or the nurture?' Now, for my part, I think that the power of education is exaggerated; it makes, or seems to make, but little difference to the average boy."

Reynolds at once said: "You are surely too pessimistic. To begin with, you do as all schoolmasters are apt to do, you confound education with that comparatively unimportant part of it which goes on at school."

"Thank you," I said, with a laugh.

"Well, but don't you admit the charge yourself?"

"If you press me, I suppose I must say that I can well believe it to be the case."

"I see you will not even now wholly give away your *confrères*. But to pass on. Would you say that the general impression that the great advantage derived from a public school education in England is a moral one is wholly without foundation? If it is, I am sorry for the public schools."

"Emphatically," I burst out. "I should say that the impression is most grossly exaggerated. I believe that even still, with all the reforms of Arnold and Percival and Thring, the system is essentially bad, and introduces boys early to the knowledge of vices of which it would be well if they could remain ignorant all their lives; and that even where it does not bring such knowledge, it crushes all the gentler aspects of a boy's nature, producing a blighted, overbearing disposition for which the cultivation of other characteristics, such as manliness—which would always find sufficient development for itself—can never atone. But you know I am a bit prejudiced even still about public schools. So you must forgive my warmth."

"Well, I certainly did not expect to rouse such a tempest," Reynolds replied, "and am quite willing to give up that argument. I will give you the third point, which is that you are wanting in faith."

"How?"

"Because you cannot see the immediate result, you think there is no result at all. We clergymen have, at all events, that advantage over you laymen, that we have recognised faith as an essential principle in the moral order of the world, whereas too many of you refuse to see anything that you cannot handle with pincers and knife."

"I beg you will not rank me in that category," put in the Doctor; "to me the absolute necessity of faith is as clear as this glorious daylight."

"I am very glad to hear it," said Reynolds.

"Only," went on the Doctor, with a sly look and a wink at me, "you know there are different sorts of faith."

Reynolds gave him a quick glance, but was not sharp enough to catch his smile, so doubtless took it as a serious hit at his cloth, and, looking grave, said no more on the question. He turned instead to me and resumed:—

"Now, though you will not admit one of the arguments I used, you will admit one akin to it, which is that the whole world believes that education does something, even though it has not quite the power to make a silk purse out of a sow's ear. And again, just think what would happen if no attempt were made at all to train the young, in however imperfect a way, in the paths of virtue. I recollect a story which will confirm what I say. A friend of mine once told me that he was out one day with a very close friend of his, for whom he had a high admiration— an elementary schoolmaster, named Marin. As they were walking through the streets, a boy passed and capped the schoolmaster. My friend at once remarked: 'That is a queer customer, I should think, Marin.' 'Ah,' said Marin, 'it is a very sad story. One day there came to me at school a man who, just opening the door, pushed a boy violently in, and almost before he was himself visible, called out in rough and angry tones: "'Ere, Mr. Marin, 'ere's some'un for your birch rod. 'E's a reg'lar bad 'un, Oi can tell yer. Oi've flogged 'im an' flogged 'im, but 'tain't no good, nowt none; 'e's thorough, doonroight wicked. Oi thought as yer moight loike to try yer 'and on 'im, so 'ere 'a be. Doon't yer spare 'im, doon't yer spare 'im, that's what Oi sez; thrash 'im 'ard and then 'a mai learn t' obey 'is father when 'a speaks. Oi'll leave 'im wi' yer and doon't yer never moind; Oi'll never interfere, no matter what yer does—jest give it 'im stroight an' 'ot." I simply inquired the man's name and said I would do what I could, and was left alone with the lad; and he certainly, as you saw, was a rough 'un to look at. I was not going to commit myself in a hurry, so contented myself with asking his age. It was a long time before I could get anything more from him than " Oi ain't a-goin' to tell yer." But at last I found he was eight. Had he ever been to school before? No. He had managed to evade the officers, and when turned out of the house ran wild in the streets. And this poor youngster, eight years old, had been thrashed till I could see he was nearly covered with bruises, but had become so hardened to it that he did not seem to care. Well, I turned him over to a class, but it was not long before I found that he was utterly intractable. He was sullen and noisy and flatly disobedient, and at last I kept him out of any regular class, and always had him by me. I could see what he expected, and no doubt wanted, for the purpose of showing how little he cared; and that was a good thrashing. But that was just what I made up my mind I would not give him. Whenever he got peculiarly intractable I always invented something for him to do—to clean the board, run an errand or something of that sort; or else, if possible, turned his attention to something else, or left him absolutely alone. I sometimes trembled for my discipline with the others, but found that they looked upon him as quite outside the ordinary run, and so I did not fear any feeling of injustice arising from their different treatment. But I can assure you that I was often sorely tried, and it was with the greatest difficulty that I could keep myself under control. But at last my reward came, though it was many and many a week before even a sign of a change appeared. But when the change did come, it was thorough. Badly dispositioned as you see the boy is, and infamously as he had been reared at home, that boy now absolutely worships me, and will do anything or go anywhere, if I express a wish. It was a terrible struggle, but my instinct told me I was right, and thank God it proved so.'

"When my friend had ended his story, he added that within a year after that his friend, Marin—a noble schoolmaster, if ever there was one—died, and he went to his funeral, and of all the boys at his school, where he was extremely popular, that boy was the only one present, and to see the way he cried made his heart bleed. Now that I can vouch for as a perfectly true incident, and it is sufficient to prove that in some cases, at all events, training can overcome even the greatest difficulties."

"Yes," said the Doctor, "it illustrates what I always maintain must be the basis of all effective education—treatment by kindness, not by punishment. Especially in moral education must that be the fundamental principle—kindness, kindness, kindness."

"Ah, Doctor," I said, "a greater man than you discovered that principle long since. It was the guiding star of that noblest of schoolmasters and yet saddest of men—the dreamer of dreams of a golden age of which he gave the world too brief a taste—the poor old stumbling, grandly-scheming, yes, and grandly-acting, Pestalozzi."

"I know nothing of Pestalozzi, but if he made love the keynote of his system, I honour him with all my heart. But one thing we must recollect, there is such a thing as a criminal disposition, which no training on earth can turn to good. The cases happily are rare, but of their existence there can be no doubt."

"Yes," I rejoined, "but we cannot treat exceptions, only the normalities at first. If we do not now put some limit to our enquiries, we shall never reach any conclusions at all, though, mind you, I am not sanguine that under the best of conditions we shall ever attain to a result worth having."

"Well," replied Dr. Hindley, "you have commissioned me to undertake the job, so I will see if I can go on, disregarding for the present outrageous cases. Now I have already reached incidentally my first principle—love,—a principle, indeed, without which I should say that all moral progress is absolutely impossible."

"That is putting it rather strongly," interposed Reynolds.

"But surely a clergyman would say the same thing? Wherein do you consider that religion differs from morality, if not in love for a personal God? It is one of the great points which differentiates Christianity from all other religions, so far as I know, that it makes love for Christ the motive of all action."

"True."

"Well, then, that granted, what steps are we to take to assure love's predominance in the whole training of the young? To begin with, it is obvious that love is not now the regulating factor even of many homes, still less of all school life."

"Pestalozzi and Arnold went far to show that love can become, at all events, very nearly the ruling factor even at school," I said.

"Ah, you have an advantage over me in your knowledge of educational history: I speak merely as an outsider. But I am truly rejoiced to hear that even in a field so unpromising as a school, love has been tried and worked with success. I do not see why it should not always be so."

"There you do speak as an outsider, indeed, Hindley. Had you been in my position you would have known soon enough why it is not possible to make love the guiding principle, or perhaps I should say, the main support, in trying to govern character."

"Well, instruct me then. Why is it?"

"Simply for this reason, that a schoolmaster has to deal with so large a number that he cannot make himself a centre of direct love to all under his control. Were schools, as with the Port-Royalists, always limited to a few, taught and teacher could get into the necessary *rapport*, but as it is a master, especially in day-schools, frequently knows next to nothing of his pupils beyond their power to work."

"More shame to him," said Reynolds; and Hindley at once chimed in with :—

"I quite agree. Surely the first duty of a schoolmaster is to provide such opportunities for gaining knowledge of his pupils that he will be able to influence them even when they are completely unaware of it. How did your friend Pestalozzi manage matters? How many pupils had he?"

"About eighty, I think; sometimes more."

"And Arnold?"

"Oh, some hundreds, I suppose."

"Then you give up your case?"

"But they were exceptional."

"And therefore good for types. Schoolmasters should always be exceptional men."

"Oh, well, if you wish to go in for Utopias, of course I resign. I thought we were discussing what was most feasible at present."

"Hardly; but the possibility of moral education, its conditions and methods of procedure. And surely I am quite justified in saying that the schoolmasters ought always to be the most exceptional men; for, as Plato you know thinks, to choose the trainers of the young is the most important task which a State can discharge, and in considering the abstract, I may surely lay down such conditions as I please. We can, when we have arrived at a satisfactory theory, supply the qualifications needed to reform modern practice. So then I say that for due training of children we want special gifts of observation and love, and that to love, in all that they do, the trainers must endeavour to give the predominance."

"A difficult matter and likely to lead to quagmires."

"Doubtless; but are there no quagmires at present? I wonder whether you, if quite candid, would pretend that the difficulties on my method are greater than those with which you and all schoolmasters must needs be familiar? You know you schoolmasters get more entangled, if I may say so without offence, in the paralyzing meshes of tradition and routine than any other body, at all events in England, of professional men. You want an outsider to waken you up; now don't you?"

"You're a sanguine man, Dr. Hindley," said Reynolds, "if you expect any man would, on a bare question like that, consent so utterly to malign his professional brethren.

But I think I can get the confession out of our friend indirectly; so look out, Trelawney, here goes. I happen too, you know, to have read something on education, and I should just like to ask our schoolmaster here how many reformers and theorizers on education have been schoolmasters in the ordinary sense of the term. Neither Plato nor Quintilian, neither Rabelais nor Montaigne, neither Locke nor Rousseau; Pestalozzi and Comenius you can perhaps half claim, and Froebel with more show of reason —though he too was far from being always in practice; Herbart was no schoolmaster by original profession; and Spencer, so far as I know, has never tried the work. Whom have we left to match these great lights? The Jesuits, who had ulterior aims, the Port-Royalists, Basedow, Arnold,—though he too was formed largely apart from school,—Percival, Thring, together with such men as Sturm and Milton, who can hardly be considered at present. Now I should like to ask Trelawney whether, after such a list as that, he does not think outsiders the more effective of reformers."

"I am afraid I must admit that outsiders' views are fresher—that suggestions more frequently come from them which are of benefit to the whole world. That we fall readily into a groove I should be the last to deny, and it is one reason the more for basing moral instruction chiefly on the home. The fact seems to me an inevitable result of the conditions under which a schoolmaster has to work and of the material with which he is supplied. But I should like at the same time to utter a protest against the formidable array of names you have drawn up, and to say that among some wise suggestions these wonderful men have uttered a vast deal of impossible nonsense."

"Never mind about that—your admission is enough," resumed Dr. Hindley; "it is clear you will allow that even an outsider may light upon a happy and far-reaching suggestion. Now, I am an outsider, and I venture to repeat that teachers should in all things let their pupils see that their guiding motive is always love."

"But how are you to do it? The greatest of love-workers, Pestalozzi himself, found, when his numbers were much above eighty, that his family theory was unworkable."

"Then don't go above the eighty. I really cannot see the advantage in these big schools. I know something of both kinds, and I say deliberately that there is no gain in the big schools which sufficiently counterbalances the loss of direct influence. What is your opinion, Trelawney?"

"I am at one with you. A hundred to a hundred and fifty is enough for any school."

"But surely," said Reynolds, "the system of houses and house-masters quite counteracts the evil effects of such large numbers."

"I don't know about quite," rejoined the Doctor, "though I grant it does something. But my theory is that every master ought to have a reasonable chance of getting fairly intimate with every boy, and the first duty of the head-master should be to know all. Why, at present, it is the commonest thing for even the head-master to be unacquainted by sight with many of his boys. And yet we expect moral influence! No doubt with grown people we can produce moral influence apart from personal knowledge, but with children it is hardly the same; they are so largely governed by their present sensations that any one who attempts to rule them without personal contact puts unnecessary difficulties in his own way. Hence I would limit the numbers in a school, and primarily choose my masters by their ability to exercise moral influence upon the young. It is really very easy to gain a child's love, and that once done, the worst is over and you can mould him almost at your will."

Reynolds here referred to the widespreading effect of a good as well as of an evil tone, adding that in a small school the tone could change more rapidly; while I, though in my heart I could scarcely help assenting, at all events in the main, to what Hindley said, yet found the schoolmaster instinct too strong and broke out with:—

"It is all very well talking, but you do not know the difficulties. I will grant that much may be done by love, but you cannot rest everything upon it."

"Yet you yourself admit that up to a certain point Pestalozzi succeeded, taking for his rule just what you now condemn. He could succeed; why should not we?"

"We haven't the time to give to sufficient study of the children."

"Ah, you are leading me farther than I thought at first, into a complete scholastic revolution. Well, in for a penny, in for a pound, and I may as well go the whole hog. As for studying the children, that must be done in part before teaching is begun; teachers must be properly trained, not merely to impart knowledge—the least important of their functions—but to make the proper psychological observations. In moral education this is by no means easy, and yet it is a prime condition."

"Why so?" said Reynolds. "Surely we can all note the manifestations of morality and fashion our training as they require."

"You know in medicine," said Dr. Hindley, "it is the small indications which escape the untrained that often lead to a correct diagnosis, on which depends the proper method of treatment; and it is just the same, as I believe, in treatment for morality."

"Yes," I chimed in, "there I back you up, and not merely for morality, but for all training whatsoever. The observation of minute details is the surest guide to success. There are stages in a child's life when he is secretive or reticent, and will suppress, if he can, all outward indications of his exact mental attitude. In such cases our main guide is the observation of those small, unconscious revelations of his inner self, of which he probably does not know and which he cannot suppress even if he would."

"But surely those revelations are very small and rare. If common we all notice them without special training."

"Unhappily, if we notice, we do not infer from them," I said. "The most obvious signs are before our eyes, and we often remain absolutely blind. How much more are we likely to pass over the slighter ones which in many cases are our only guide! Here, as so often, the Americans are ahead of us, and that in a wonderful way. I saw quite recently just the kind of thing. It was drawn up by a man who has got a great name in America—Dr. Stanley Hall—and was called 'A Topical Syllabus for Child-study—Anger.' It was a series of suggestions for systematically noting whatever phenomena might be expected to appear under the influence of the passion in question, and ranged from purely physical or unconscious manifestations, such as the action of the vaso-motor system, to overt acts, and enquired also into the degrees of proneness to anger in different subjects, the difference of sex, temperament, and the like, and the attitude of children themselves towards anger, when once the angry fit is past. I remember one point which struck me especially as a proof that the observations were to be scientifically treated: 'Describe the intensity curve of quick and slow children' was one of the injunctions laid down. Now it is the mass of observations which are thus suggested that makes me object to Dr. Hindley's proposal and say that we teachers have no time."

"Well, imagination is fetterless, so I will make another demand: the hours of teachers should be limited."

"There you may be sure I shall be with you," I said.

"No doubt; every one is lazy if he gets the chance."

"What a pessimist you are, Dr. Hindley," put in Reynolds. "I know plenty of people who would not be lazy, even with the most favouring chances."

"Oh, you must not take me too seriously. All I mean is that most people like to give as little time as possible to gaining their livelihood, for in every profession there is a great deal of drudgery, and whatever our liking for our own special line, in course of years the drudgery grows uppermost, and anything comes as a welcome change. But an industrious man is industrious always, though he may naturally dislike being so tied down by the necessities of life as to have no time to give to other pursuits than the grinding one of his profession. And that is all I meant. But, seriously, I do consider that a conscientious schoolmaster is very much overworked; at least, if we hope to get from him the maximum of good. In his, as in my own profession, it is above all things desirable that the agent should be fresh, and freshness is impossible where the school hours are so long, at least when conjoined with evening work, as to leave him no time either to recruit himself fairly or to think over his difficulties, digest his notes on children, and devise better methods of treatment."

"But," Reynolds said, "the same argument applies to all engaged in education—mothers, nurses, governesses, and University tutors, as well as to schoolmasters. Can you carry it out in all cases?"

"We must try."

Here I said: "I think that shows the impracticability of your proposal. But of course I do not complain. I only say you give us schoolmasters a large task; I fear you would not think much of the way we usually discharge it."

"Well, humanity is frail, and for my own part I am prepared to find fault with anything at a moment's notice. But after all, I am talking not of what is, but of what should be. And I say deliberately that until you give schoolmasters—and I would, *mutatis mutandis*, include the other classes Reynolds named—such leisure as to allow them to take ample notes of their work and to digest them, and equip them, moreover, with the desire to profit by that leisure and the training to enable them to do so, so long will your education be but a halting thing, especially on the moral side. Here, then, we need another reform—the shortening of a schoolmaster's working hours, coupled with that insistence on the paramount importance of moral qualifications to which we referred some time ago."

"You attach very great importance to a schoolmaster's functions."

"And am I not right? Have I not the high authority of Plato? No doubt your practical man is content with a makeshift, and if schoolmasters do not uphold the banner of the ideal in face of the overwhelming difficulties, who, pray, is to do so? I may be sketching a Utopia, but it is a Utopia to which an approximation could be made, if we would but try."

"Well, Hindley," I said, "'tis not for me to find fault, though I fear the world would have laughed had I made the proposal. I can assure you that I should take good care to have a high old time."

"Flippancy is not argument," Hindley gravely replied, and I felt rather crushed. "But," he went on, "I know you too well, Trelawney, to accept your self-disparagement. I know you would have nothing like what you are pleased to call in such vulgar phrase 'a high old time,' unless it is a high old time to throw yourself heart and soul into your duties, for the one simple reason that your duties they are."

"Well," said Reynolds, "that possibility may hold of our friend here, and it would be rude to suggest the opposite; but I have a wide and varied acquaintance among schoolmasters, and I must confess that, despite many noble exceptions, I have not as yet seen reason to believe that they do their duty from any deeper conscientiousness, taken as a class, than any other body of men."

"That may be so now; but you remember I laid down as an express condition that the trainers were to be the exceptional men, and surely a keen sense of duty is one of the chief points which in such matters go to form exceptional men."

"True; but you will have to make it worth while for men thus exceptionally endowed to enter the profession."

"That naturally."

"And then comes the further difficulty, how would you test them? They would have to be tried as schoolmasters before you could know all their qualifications, and meantime the harm would be done."

"I do not expect to arrive at perfection all at once. But if schoolmasters and all trainers were so paid, and received such social honour as to attract into the profession always the best men, and above all into those parts of it which require the best men most—I mean, of course, the elementary stages—instead of drawing them, as at present, in the main to the universities, where students can be more trusted to look after themselves, then you would start with such a pick that it would not be difficult to get rid of the less competent, provided only that you had at the head of all a man so strong as to be guided solely by merit, and not sacrifice, as is so often, alas! the case now, the interests of the children to his own personal likings or the supposed claims of long work. Of course a pension scheme is involved, at least till the days of communism; but to perfect education I grudge no expense."

"I grant the desirability of your end, but I fear it is utterly and entirely impracticable."

"Do not say entirely, but only at present. We must, of course, approximate by degrees; but the first mercenary step taken we should have gone a long way towards the end which I hope to attain. However, let us pass on, for in any reconstruction of society I grant that the suggested schemes seem at the outset hopeless. A real reconstruction requires parallel advance along all lines at once. But here at least is a point which is feasible, and easily feasible—we must have mixed schools, and mixed teachers for every school—boys and girls studying together, and men and women teaching together."

Reynolds burst out laughing, and exclaimed: "Well, really, Dr. Hindley, you must excuse me, but you go from bad to worse. When you said something quite feasible was coming, I little expected so startling a revolution. But the farther you go, the more hopeless seems your case."

"What a fine lot of amusement we should have, both among pupils and teachers!" I said.

"Now there you are again, Trelawney, flippant as usual. If I did not know you I should really think you did not care one iota for educational problems at all. But I do not know why you should consider it so hopeless. Surely you will admit, Mr. Reynolds, that even at present the mixed system among pupils and teachers at the elementary schools works well."

"I have known some object."

"But not, I think, the majority. And in America the mixed system is in vogue, among the children at all events, and in very common vogue too. What I have seen about it seems to prove that it leads to excellent results. Do you know if this is so, Trelawney, if your flippant mind has ever condescended to note such amusing details?"

"All right, Hindley, I shall have you some day, I guess, as the Americans say. I know something more about their system of education than you do, and I am bound to confess that so far as I have been able to find out, every one almost without exception is deep in admiration of the system."

"I suppose," said Reynolds, "I must acknowledge that my laughter was but the crackling of thorns under the pot——"

"Well, if you choose to be so uncomplimentary to yourself," said Hindley, with a wink at me, "of course it is not for me to gainsay you."

Reynolds laughed and went on: "But I could not help being amazed at your calm disregard, in speaking of a feasible project, of all the ingrained conservatism and prejudices of the British parent. Why, your proposal would turn the British matron's hair white. My work lies extensively among what we, like snobs, call the middle classes, and while I do not think that the lower or upper classes, for different reasons, would raise very great difficulties in the way, I am convinced that in the middle classes the opposition would be uncompromising."

"Oh, if that is all, I have not much fear. If the two extremes of society set the fashion, the middle class will not be long in following, partly because they are very fond of aping those who are so unjustly called their betters, partly because, when they see the lower classes doing well under the system, they will be too jealous not to follow suit."

"You are not very complimentary to them, and yet I think both your arguments are mistaken. As regards the first, I should say that the middle classes, who have so long resisted, in blind contentment, the system of the public schools, are not likely to take up rapidly with such a revolution as you propose; and as regards the second, do you think it is worth anything at all, when you consider the amazing fact that for twenty years and more the middle classes have been contented with an education really costly, yet in many points inferior to that which those whom they consider so far below them have been obtaining for their children for next to nothing? It is to me an almost heart-breaking proof of the narrowing effects of shop-keeping and social prejudice. Of course there are exceptions, but I think in the main my sketch is true. And if so, how are you going to convert them?"

"Either by disregarding them, and leaving them to work out their own salvation by being hopelessly worsted in the race of life, or, better still, by drastic measures on the part of the State."

"Hurrah! hurrah! here is your socialism at last!" I exclaimed. "I have been waiting for it to turn up, as I knew when it did you would be thoroughly warm to your work, and likely to make a good stiff fight. So now, then, set to. I will form a ring and hold the stakes, and, further, will bet ten to one that neither of you will be beaten!"

At this both my companions laughed, and Reynolds said:—

"Though our subject is near it, we are not discussing socialism at present, so I utterly decline at this point to be drawn into a pitched battle. I would rather hear the rest of these very startling views. I will content myself with saying that interference by the State I simply loathe, and consider that in education it has done a vast deal of harm."

"I am glad that you do not say more harm than good. I suppose you are interested in a voluntary school? Ah, well, then I can forgive your heat: it is not pleasant to be driven against one's will. But let us abandon that question, if you please, and return to moral education. It has always seemed to me that the separation of the sexes in education is at the root of most of our grievous social evils, especially when combined with what the Bishop of Chester has well called the barrack system of education as applied to boys, and to a less extent to girls also."

"Well, you are certainly a revolutionist," said Reynolds. "What advantages, pray, do you expect to accrue, then, from the mixing of the sexes at school?"

"To put it briefly, this: that each sex will develop some of the virtues of the opposite. At present we brutalize boys, and make them still more empty of the gentler virtues by separating them from the influence of women, while we rob girls of all chance of shaking off the timidity and want of self-management and independence to which they are by nature so prone, as we give them no opportunity of seeing anything of a world where these virtues are held in high regard. You know the old story of the preacher who, in his sermon, urged the young women to be brave, and the young men to be chaste? A member of his congregation remonstrated with him afterwards, and wanted to know whether he had not misplaced his words. 'Ah, no,' he replied; 'Nature has taken care that young men should be brave and young women chaste. Our aim must be to cultivate in each sex precisely those virtues in which they are deficient.' And so I say now, that those virtues which are the birthright of each sex require in education comparatively small regard: what should claim our chief attention and our most unstinted efforts is the cultivation of those which are not likely to grow strong of themselves. And I cannot think that a more refining influence can be brought to bear upon boys than the constant presence among them of womanly and girlish delicacy and grace, or, on the other hand, a more bracing and stimulative influence upon girls than the healthy masculinity and self-reliant courage of boys and men. This, indeed, is chiefly from the side of the children mixed, but from the mixture of teachers also similar results will follow. In boys' schools I think we shall especially see this change; the frequent uproariousness and want of proper self-restraint will be more advantageously and easily curbed through a boy's feeling of chivalry for a lady-teacher than through the awe which he may feel before a man. It is easier for a woman to gain a boy's love, provided, of course, she has the power of command. And a like feeling on the other side will probably take possession of the breasts of those girls who have masters over them; in fact, I do not believe that our hopes of gain could ever be excessive. In the case of the very young, say up to ten years of age, I hold that boys should never be left entirely to men, unless, indeed, they be men of most unusual endowments; though as regards young girls, the most striking lesson I ever saw was one given by a master at a school in Prussia to a class—or rather two classes—of little girls, aged respectively five and six. And what do you suppose the subject was? Arithmetic —the elementary numbers up to 10 and 100. Still, this was at a day school, and the object was mainly intellectual; it would be a different matter to hand over the children to men alone for months together. No doubt we could find cases to prove that a man is capable of taking quite young boys, or even girls, with great effect from the point of view of moral advance as well as, for instance, if I understand aright, our friend's great champion, Pestalozzi; but in the main I think our chief guide should be the principle I have already laid down. Young children to women entirely: from about the age of ten onwards, in the main, though not exclusively, to teachers of the sex opposite to their own."

Here I interposed. "But you are laying down an impossibility. You say schools are to be mixed, and unless you are going to keep the classes separate, when practically the schools will not be mixed at all, you will not be able to give the boys to women chiefly and the girls to men."

Dr. Hindley laughed a moment, and then said, "Well, I am a fool——"

Reynolds at once broke in slily with "*I* did not say so; but if you choose to be so uncomplimentary to yourself, of course it is not for me to gainsay you."

Hindley recognised his own words, and laughing, said : "A very fair retort. But what I was going to say was this, that it is very difficult in sketching an ideal to keep oneself free from present conditions, and I am afraid I let my thoughts carry me back to our usual practice without considering what I was doing. Of course, if my original plan were carried out, that boys and girls should always be educated together, the last stipulation—to give children to teachers of the sex opposite to their own—is unnecessary, nay, more, an impossibility; if only we add the mixing of teachers as it occurs, I know, often in German girls' schools, the whole thing is done. Of course I am aware that a great deal of prejudice, so ably expounded by our friend Mr. Reynolds, has to be overcome; but it is surely worth while to try. It will indeed require some boldness to make the start—though I hear it has already occurred—as it would probably mean bankruptcy at first. If, however, we could find two sets of people—first some wealthy and charitable person to finance the scheme, and secondly a number of enthusiastic parents willing to let their children be the *corpora vilia*—I have no doubt the fashion would spread, as the goodness of it would soon be apparent."

"Doctor," I said, "the scheme has been tried, not only in America, but also in London."

"And what has been the result?"

"The school goes on well, so I understand, and has certainly met with the cordial approval of more than one educational expert."

"I am heartily glad of it," said the Doctor, "and wish the experiment every success."

The afternoon was now growing late, and the cooler air, moistened by the river on whose banks we were walking, was a welcome refreshment to our tired spirits—tired with both physical and mental work. The sun was striking low just over the top of a beautiful fir-clad mountain ridge, tinging with a richer colour the long grass in the meadow through which our path now lay. Cows were peacefully grazing, or, a commoner case, lying the picture of calm contentment, lazily chewing the cud. Not a sound could be heard save our own steps and voices and the placid murmur of the gentle river gliding over its smooth-worn bed. Occasionally we caught a bird's light call, or saw one flit past us on hurrying wing. The lengthening shadows and faint freshness of the grass seemed to bid us lay by our toils and rest, at least so long as would give our minds time to revive their energies for further work. But for our bodies, we were now in so good a swing of walking, and were, to boot, so alive to the calls of the inner man, that when I suggested we had better postpone the rest of our discussion, the more so at this most convenient breaking-point, my companions readily agreed. So we trudged along in happy heart the remaining mile or two, till we reached at last the fishing inn, where we knew we could obtain a healthy tea, and take the joyful rest of a pipe and complete repose—not the least of the enjoyment on an all-day's tramp. Long we sat by the river's brink, watching at times the growing shadows and the declining sun, at times marking listlessly the fish as they rose, or the birds as they flitted home, or still more listlessly brooding in thought or chatting in broken spasms on anything and everything that came first into our minds. At last we rose to make for the nearest town to catch the train home, but we did not separate without agreeing that the discussion must be finished; and so, as I urged that if our wives could join us it would be an advantage to have the woman's point of view, we decided to meet at my house for dinner three days thence, and discuss the remaining points under the placid conditions of a good meal and an easy chair.

Thus we parted, each, no doubt, with food for thought; and I, in especial, wondering whether after all it was not true, as Reynolds had said, that most of the great reformers in education were outsiders, because schoolmasters were too narrow to know their limitations, and whether that view had not received confirmation in the past day's astounding proposals. For astounding I felt them to be, although a socialist is, by the very law of his being, nothing if not astounding. For, to say nothing of the question of mixed education, tried already with success in various parts of the world, the theory that schoolmasters should be the picked men and should have large leisure abundantly guaranteed, though I had often heard it propounded before, I had never heard laid down as a fundamental proposition, at least in recent years. And then, again, the point that the whole of education must be based on love, love consciously given and consciously received, was to me a great stumbling-block, for I could not help smiling as I thought what havoc it would make of the ordinary school routine. In theory it was beyond question excellent, and Pestalozzi had shown that under certain conditions it could be made to work; but those conditions —when were they likely to recur? And, after all, Pestalozzi seemed, except at Yverdun, to have had mainly to deal with the class of children to whom love is almost a stranger, and in whom, therefore, any show of it, no matter how slight, would be likely to call forth a vigorous response. Would the same result follow its bestowal on those who had a liberal allowance of it in their own homes? I could not but have doubts, though I admitted to myself that I should be glad for some one to try the experiment. For myself, I lacked a reformer's nerve, and, indeed, was so placed that I could not risk failing. That difficulty I fear prevents many of us trying to carry out our theories in actual practice; a hero would be wanted to accomplish the work, and not every one, alas! is so noble and so brave as that hero of heroes, the wonderful Pestalozzi.

II

WHEN the evening we had appointed for our next discussion came we sat down to a quite informal dinner, we three and our respective wives. As I said at the beginning, it was a good thing now that we were to take into consideration the woman's view, for women see education with different eyes and with more regulation, perhaps, from the feelings than we sterner men. And our wives were as different as we ourselves. Mrs. Hindley was steeped in social philosophy—an ardent advocate of women's rights. So well read was she that I never could suppress trepidation when I ventured to dispute any of her dicta. And yet I had to do so not unfrequently, for of dicta she was very fond, and, indeed, would have been regarded as a formidable instance of the evil effects of a woman's education had it not been that throughout all discussions she never lost her true womanliness and the grace that was but heightened by her extreme ardour. Mrs. Reynolds was of a different type, quiet, unpretending, yet gifted with a shrewd insight into practical matters—a firm believer in all that is good in this world, and possessed of a strong faith in the next, a woman whom no one could meet without admiring for her gentleness and simplicity and characteristic kindness of heart. She was for a clergyman an ideal wife. My own wife again varied from them both: she was enthusiastic and largely influenced by her feelings, yet from her training as a schoolmistress was also well aware that her feelings were not always her best guide. Her impetuosity would often lead her into mistakes, which she was ready to detect and admit at once. She could always see the right, but did not quite always manage to do it. In a discussion such as that which we were going to resume, I knew where her sympathies would lie, but I also knew that so long as the question was in the abstract, she would detect, despite her sympathies, mistakes on any side. Such were the six, then, who were met to discuss the all-important topic of moral education. I knew the discussion was likely to be long, so lost no time in introducing the subject.

"You know," I said, "ladies, that we three here present, your legal lords and husbands, have already had a long talk about moral education, and Dr. Hindley has laid it down as a fundamental proposition, from which, of course, Mr. Reynolds and I dissented, that the chief end of such training should be—now, what do you suppose?—to turn boys into girls and girls into boys."

Here there was a general laugh, and Mrs. Hindley at once said:—

"If I thought that my husband had ever said anything so foolish, I would apply for a divorce on the spot."

"'Oh, mighty Cæsar, dost thou lie so low?
Are all thy conquests, glories, triumphs, spoils,
Shrunk to this little measure? Fare thee well!'"

murmured Dr. Hindley. "I should be sorry to be so lightly dispatched, but am rejoiced, my dear, to find that you still have left a gleam of faith in your husband's common sense. Really, Mrs. Trelawney," he went on, turning to my wife, "you ought to keep your husband in better order. All the time during our walk the other day he was coming out with some flippant remarks on the least possible provocation—a course of procedure naturally not conducive to the philosophic mind; and now, on once more introducing the subject, he is not merely flippant, but grossly calumnious. Certainly his own moral education must have been in some way grievously defective."

"Oh, he is always like that," my wife cruelly replied; "if he does not lead the talk himself, he will never let any one else speak."

"My dear!" I expostulated, but met with no sympathy, for after the laugh was over, Mrs. Hindley turned to Reynolds and asked him as the third and trustworthy party to say what her husband had really propounded.

"As far as I remember, what Dr. Hindley said was this, that an educator should make it one of his chief aims to develop in each sex those qualities which constitute its own leading deficiencies, and at the same time the chief glory of the other half of the race. He urged, what seems undoubtedly of force, that boys and girls may be trusted to develop of themselves, at least in the main, those peculiar virtues to which Nature has made them prone, but that they require special care in order to secure the adequate development of certain other qualities which are in danger too often of disappearing altogether."

"Well, Mrs. Hindley," said my wife, "I think after that the divorce should be for me. To think that I should be wedded to a man who is either unable or unwilling to carry in his head so excellent a proposition! There is only one word to express my feelings, and that is the German abscheulich—abominable!"

"I pity you, my dear," replied Mrs. Hindley, with a would-be withering look at me. "But now I should like to ask my husband whether that account does fairly represent what he actually said."

"Yes, very well."

"Good; I am proud, my dear, to think how apt a pupil I have had to all my teaching, and to see that you can carry my principles into spheres to which I have never brought them."

"Oh," replied the Doctor, "there might be two opinions on the question who was the teacher and who the taught."

"Well, husband and wife are one, so we will regard ourselves as both teacher and taught. But now, I think, Mr. Trelawney ought for a penance to tell us what else my husband said, in order that we may see exactly how far the discussion went. And this time, if you please," she added, turning to me, "quite seriously: the matter is too important for joking. And, Mr. Reynolds, will you be kind enough to pull Mr. Trelawney up as soon as ever he oversteps the line of strict truth? So now, Mr. Trelawney, begin, if you please. General principles first, details afterwards."

"Well, for my sins I suppose I must do my best. The propositions which Dr. Hindley laid down were, I think, these:—

1. "That all school life must be based on the principle of love."

Here I saw my wife rather open her eyes, but in a moment she nodded her head, and I went on without stopping:—

2. "That in choosing our schoolmasters, and, indeed, all trainers of the young, we are to choose men the most exceptional to be found."

3. "These trainers are to be most highly paid, which, indeed, follows from 2, and, oh joy!——"

Mrs. Hindley looked stern and shook a warning finger at me. "They are to have unending leisure."

"Hardly unending," put in the Doctor.

4. "All schools are to be mixed, and the teachers are to be both men and women in the same school, with the proviso that children up to ten are not to be committed, save in the rarest cases, to any one's hands but a woman's."

"Good, indeed," ejaculated Mrs. Hindley.

5. "There is to be a stern censor, whom neither fear nor favour can influence, to weed out remorselessly all the incompetents, and not sacrifice the claims of the many to the one for whom he may happen to have special regard."

6. "The best teachers are to be given to the youngest children, the less good to those next in years, and so on regularly as we climb the tree, until at the Universities we no longer find the pick of the profession, as usually now, but, of the body whose members are all largely competent, those who are the least competent of all."

"What an odd proviso!" said my wife.

"Surely not," replied the Doctor. "I stipulate that simply on the ground that the older and more advanced a student is the better he can be trusted to make good of himself defects on the part of his master. Your own experience surely will confirm that view."

"Yes, now I see. But what a revolution your theory would cause, a revolution not confined to moral training alone!"

"That, I think," I said, "brings the main positions to an end."

"Excuse me, Trelawney," said the Doctor, "but I really think you must be trying to intentionally represent me as a hopeless idiot. Else why should you leave out the great stipulation which explains the provision at which you expressed such joy: the stipulation, I mean, that teachers are to be trained so as constantly to make scientific observations on children's psychology and moral characters, and so as to be able to digest their notes and work them into something like a rational scheme, as the basis for proper training? That is the reason why, above all, I say that schoolmasters should have abundance of leisure. And if this point is to be number seven, there is yet an eighth, which has completely escaped you, that education, so far as possible, is to find its home entirely in the country; and that if this cannot be, from collision with that other, yet more important, law of keeping the child in touch with his home, then, at all events, the country must be visited often, and this not chiefly for health, but above all to purify the weary little soul and to cultivate the sense of freshness and beauty—influences which bear more directly upon morality than many who have thought but little on the subject would at first be willing to admit."

"I am glad, Dr. Hindley," said Mrs. Reynolds in reply, "that you have made some mention of the home at last. I was afraid we poor mothers were going to be disregarded, left out in the cold altogether."

"That I assure you was merely an accident of the circumstances under which our discussion took place. I knew we should have to come to home at last."

"And there is another point, if you please," my wife put in, "which has still to be considered. It is all very well to lay down fine principles of vague breadth and great generality, but where are your details? Details alone can supply the test of any scheme, however ambitious."

"I do not agree with you, Mrs. Trelawney," said the Doctor's wife. "I grant their importance in the proper place, but in any scheme for the reconstruction of society main lines come first, details afterwards."

"I know many people say that, but to me it seems the very reason why many schemes are of so little value in this our makeshift, work-a-day world. From my own experience in the management of school, I know that the details are the deciding points; from them comes the possibility of carrying out the principles, not *vice versâ*. And I am sure my husband agrees with me, don't you?"

"With this reservation, that it is no good attempting to rearrange details unless you have in your mind the guiding principle to begin with."

"Ah," Mrs. Hindley cried with joy, "that gives the case entirely to me."

"No, no; I cannot admit that," rejoined my wife; "but we will not theorize on theory at present, as we have something much more important to discuss. I daresay when we come to talk the matter out, we shall find our divergencies mainly verbal."

"I hope so; but now I should like to ask what the general public here assembled thinks of the outline so far? Do you agree that the outline is a good one—suitable, that is, for filling with details of a really good scheme of moral education?"

After a slight discussion we seemed pretty well agreed that, though the project might not be in all points very feasible, there were some to which an approximation might be made, and that it would at all events be worth our while to retrace our steps and go into detail, considering moral education from cradle-days onwards.

"Only," Mrs. Hindley said, "I would have you please observe how, even in a matter which by their own confession the three gentlemen here consider to be chiefly a woman's sphere, they have shown their sex's domineering propensities, and have laid down, without even asking our advice, the main lines of our procedure and the conditions of our work, and only now solicit our help when deductions are to be drawn and no initiative is left. The kings have issued their royal mandate—'Such is our will and pleasure; obey, or be thrust out,' and we, their subjects, have to comply. Truly, women are a feeble folk!"

At this sally we all laughed, and the Doctor said: "I do not think, my dear, you need be afraid that there will not be abundance of opportunity for initiative when the time comes for details to be faced; for they are, indeed, the most difficult matter, and may still shipwreck the whole scheme. Indeed, though I have had a few days to consider what is to be said on this part of the subject, I fear it far more than the original discussion on which I was launched quite unprepared. However, I must, I suppose, begin.

"First, then, as a doctor I lay down this maxim, that the primary requisite of all is health; physical education claims precedence as the condition on which all else depends."

"But surely, Dr. Hindley, you are not going to maintain that a person cannot reach a high degree of morality without good health."

"My dear Mrs. Reynolds, do not mistake me. I am going to make no assertions which I do not think I can prove. I have, and doubtless you have too, known far too many cases of wonderful character in very ailing bodies to leave me the chance of maintaining that bad health and morality are inconsistent. But remember we are discussing a problem of education, and I say that the more perfect the body, the more easy is it to perfect the moral character. Not that I look for perfection in either, at all events for a long time to come; but no one, I think, would utterly deny that health has much to do with, at least, some sides of morality. There is said to have been once a Catholic Archbishop, who, when any of his flock complained to him of wicked thoughts, instead of imposing penance, simply told them to look to their digestions. The ancients placed the seat of many passions in the liver; and though modern medical science does not exactly bear out their theories, still there is no doubt that the state of the liver has a very direct bearing not merely upon our happiness, but, what is more important, upon our character too. Therefore I say that we must look to health first of all. If any one indeed is so unfortunate as to be gifted with an ailing constitution from the beginning, then we must recognise that in trying to train him we are working at a certain disadvantage; but this disadvantage in our abstract discussion we must for the present disregard."

"But what do you say, Doctor, of the discipline of suffering?"—Reynolds was thus supporting his wife.

"We shall have to deal with the question of pain and punishment in its proper place. For the moment I will only say that I know the influence of physical suffering is often to refine, though, sometimes, I grieve to say, its effect is the opposite. But does it not stand to reason that the man whose bodily functions work with least effort and resistance is likely to have more energy to spare for moral growth—for which energy is required as for every other part of life—and that the cheerfulness which results from unimpeded health is a most valuable ally to morality? Indeed, I often think that people do not sufficiently weigh the importance of cheerfulness in the moral order of the world. I look upon it as a primary duty, not merely to oneself but above all to one's neighbours, to try and cultivate a habit of cheerfulness. Many sacrifices should be made with that object in view, and great care must be taken that by regular and well-ordered exercise and training all the natural organs perform their functions well. Most of the more grievous moral faults of children may be traced to one or other of two causes—want of forethought to estimate the full effect of their actions, or some physical infirmity, temporary or permanent. And in this connection their feeding requires especial care. By unsuitable diet, which leads to bad nutrition, we permanently injure not merely the physical but also the moral well-being of the child. This is a point in which parents require most careful instruction. In the main a child's likes and dislikes will be a safe guide, though we must not, of course, be led into absurdities, and give them anything for which they may choose to ask, no matter how injurious it may have been shown to be. But if children have not had the opportunity of noticing that their elders have preferences and likes and dislikes, there is little chance of their developing to any serious extent the vices of fastidiousness and Näscherei. If they do show signs of them, they can easily be checked, partly by giving variety of food, partly by cutting off all opportunities of getting dainties, though for this latter end we may have to deny ourselves, in order to avoid exposing our children to temptation."

"Ah! that is all very well," I said; "but how many parents would you find willing to practise such self-denial?"

"We know, Mr. Schoolmaster, that you are the parents' sworn decrier. But I venture to think that if you make enquiries you will find parents are more ready to practise self-denial, with the hope of doing their children good, than you are at present inclined to believe."

"The real difficulty," my wife said, "is, not in getting them to forego pleasures for their children's sake, but in getting them to admit that certain indulgences of their own do their children any harm."

"Precisely. And in order to instruct them on this

head, we want, first, a better general education, and, secondly, specific instruction in morality, particularly as regards our duty to others, one special branch of which must be the direct instruction of future parents in parental duty."

"It is a large course you are sketching," I said.

"Not too large for the end in view. For we aim at nothing less than the production of a perfect man, and to attain that end no effort can be too great. We shall not attain it all at once, but we can approximate. However, the proper method of specific instruction is rather beyond our purpose at this moment—I am afraid I am always being led off the point. We will consider it in due time, but now, with your permission, I should like to return to the earlier stages. Will you allow that care for physical well-being is one of the most important structures of morality?"

"Important, yes," said Reynolds; "but hardly essential."

"Surely essential in the abstract, though a higher height may be scaled under less promising conditions. I think I need hardly detail in full the requisites for a healthy physical training; I will content myself with mentioning such points as the ventilation, especially of bedrooms, good lighting and warming, constant baths—if possible, cold—the avoidance of overcrowding, nutritious and varied, but, in the main, simple food, attention to teeth and clothing, in particular of the feet, daily physical exercise in the open air, and occasional change of scene. Nor must the influence of companions of a like age be forgotten; the younger the child, at least after the first few weeks, the more important is this association. It belongs, perhaps, rather to the domain of morals and the intellect than to that of physical education, but even in this sphere the force of example has great results. With the necessity of a healthy and systematic physical training thus premised, not a mere haphazard trusting to chance, we may go on to consider in its stricter sense the aims and meaning of ethical training.

"Now there are two main aims which, it seems to me, the educator ought always to keep steadily before him. The first is the development of a sense of far-reaching, one may almost say unending, responsibility—the recognition of the fact that any action of ours, no matter how trifling, may continue to produce effects for centuries to come, and that our actions, if wrong, may not be punished immediately, but that the punishment, though long delayed, will come at last, borne not always by ourselves; and the second, the recognition of the importance of our neighbours, I will not say society, in contrast with ourselves. Self-negation and responsibility are the pole-stars of morality; by them all training must be guided. Were we gifted with a higher sense of our vast responsibility and a greater power of forecasting the outcome of our actions, the world would be far better than it is. I beg you then, through all that I shall say, to see if I conform to my own principles, and to try to bring my practical precepts under one or other of these heads.

"Now the development of morality begins from the cradle, perhaps even before. Every impression made on the sensorium of a young child leaves an impression for better or for worse, and many even of those acts which seem quite non-moral may have an indirect influence upon a child's way of regarding things. If a child is brought in contact—and what child is not?—with debasing sights and sounds, sights and sounds which are completely severed from all ideal of beauty, the child's ideals of beauty will also be debased, and so debased, it may be, that of a true ideal no trace will remain. And how large an inlet to high morality, yes, and how pleasant a one, is here closed, perhaps for ever! Did art but furnish us with merely innocent forms of pleasure, that would be a vast deal in this world—for the mass of evil is done in pursuit of pleasures that are but grovelling; if all the world had hobbies to occupy their spare time, evil would be much less. Let us then strive, when we bring a helpless infant into this world, to accustom it unconsciously to beautiful sights and sounds; let it from the first have round it nothing but what ennobles; there is then some hope that even unconsciously it may grow in mind like what it beholds. Such a requirement demands not only beauty in surrounding objects, but also moral beauty in surrounding persons. Here, you will say, impossibility comes in. But I would beg you to think a little. It is possible for even servants to have ennobling characters; no pains are surely too great to acquire them."

"Yes, Dr. Hindley," was Mrs. Reynolds's rejoinder, "in theory it is no doubt very nice; but have you ever had the trouble of getting your servants? What does Mrs. Hindley say to your proposal?"

"I say that much more might be done than is; but you must be prepared to pay high."

"But"—Mr. Reynolds once more came to his wife's support—"you have not always got the means to pay."

"I am surprised, Mr. Reynolds, that one of your profession should raise that difficulty. Self-denial is not unusual with you, I am sure."

"It seems to me," my wife said, "that you are making good moral education the privilege of the rich."

"Ah," burst in Mrs. Hindley once more, "now, perhaps, you see why I am a Socialist. I would have no one debarred from the best the world can offer; and if Socialism means loss of much of external art and beauty, yet the counterbalancing gain to morality far outweighs it all."

"It is true," Dr. Hindley went on, "that my plan is not feasible in full detail at present; but you know my Socialistic views are like my wife's, and if much that I suggest can only be carried out by the help of Socialism, well, I say, take Socialism with morality rather than the present constitution without. We have undoubtedly from the first to face the difficult question of allowing children to have contact with servants at all, and the remedy I would suggest will, no doubt, be too heroic for you—the mother should have the sole charge of her children and never leave them to a nurse."

Now I could see the storm was coming. My wife at once impetuously said, "Quite impossible!" while Mrs. Reynolds asked, "But what is to become of the house?"

At this question the Doctor smiled, as he answered:—

"Leave the house to servants and your children to yourselves. It is entirely a question of comparative values: if the house is of more value, choose that; if the child, choose that."

"No, Doctor," I put in, "the question is not so simple. You evidently are biassed, filled with an unjust suspicion of all save those who have had as good a bringing-up as you have yourself. I fear at the bottom of your proposal lies, if not class-hatred, at all events a certain amount of class-suspicion and contempt."

"I pray God not," said the Doctor earnestly, "though it is impossible for any man to fathom his own mind. But I do most urgently plead for more personal attention on the part of parents to their children—more self-sacrifice, more direct study of their characters and interests."

"But," went on my wife, "no woman can do everything. And if the eye of the mistress is not over all, nothing but confusion and misery will result. How would you like it, pray, yourself, if Mrs. Hindley gave up her whole time and energy to washing, teaching, playing with your children, and left the house alone?"

"I am proud to say that my wife does very nearly that now."

"And do you enjoy it?"

"I am proud of my wife beyond measure, and as for the lesser things—my own comfort, to wit—well, I can put up with much in what I know is a good cause."

"I think you are rather giving me away, my dear," said Mrs. Hindley. "Really, Mrs. Trelawney, I think you would not find much amiss in our house. Of course it is harder work for me, and deprives me of a good deal of social pleasure; but I would far rather that should happen than feel I was not doing my very utmost for my children. People are so unreasonable, not to say inhuman; they offer from £14 to £20 a year for a servant, and expect a paragon to undertake the most dull and slaving work that can, perhaps, be found in the world. And how many mistresses ever think at all of the interests of their servants, physical, mental, or moral? I am talking now, you will understand, of ordinary middle-class people who have no money to throw away. What I say is this: if, instead of keeping a nurse, you would put some of her wages into the pockets of a good housekeeper, you would get a valuable servant to whom you could without fear entrust almost all the household affairs. One other pair of hands to relieve yourself, if so it must be, of the more menial duties in connection with your children, and the task is solved; you will have your house in perfect order, and your own energies to spare for those to whom they are due.

As it is, we women spoil our husbands, leading them to regard themselves as the very lords of earth, and making them into dissatisfied brutes if they have not every luxury they might expect in a palace. Till women maintain that they also have souls, we can expect nothing better."

We were all rather amused at this sally, and Mrs. Reynolds was clearly puzzled. I laughed and said :—

" There, Hindley, now we know your character ; you are a dissatisfied brute. My dear," I said, turning to my wife, and holding up a threatening finger, " don't you ever let me catch you at such tricks ; I am not a Socialist. A schoolmaster expects his bread and butter cut for tea, whether there are children with claims or not."

" Don't you trouble yourself; if ever I do let the house run itself, you are none the wiser."

At this the others laughed, and I went on :—

" Well, I am not a schoolmaster at home, and so cannot be sure of obedience. But, seriously, I do think you ask too much, Doctor Hindley. To begin with, a woman, if she is to keep herself fresh, wants a holiday from her children, and then what is to be done with them ? But even apart from that, the conventions of society cannot be entirely over-ridden——"

" Why not ? Every reformer is met by the same answer—It is impossible ! Have but the courage of your opinions and try. We suffer so much because we are all cowards. Some one must start a reform, and why not you as well as another ? And in the interests of our children it is vital to keep them out of our servants' way ; they harm them alike physically, morally, and intellectually."

" I grant the harm, especially the intellectual harm," I said. " That often seems to me the most serious, because the moral harm, which is chiefly encouraging disobedience or preventing a punishment having its full effect, can be easily counteracted where the parents possess, as should always be the case, the real love of their child. Servants seldom have a direct interest in deliberately fostering the worse traits of children. But the intellectual harm of implanting in their minds all sorts of foolish ideas, especially idle and dangerous superstitions, which often, too, run into the moral domain, takes years of eradication, and is often not eradicated at all. The danger has long since been noticed: Locke, for instance, is full of it. But still, I do not see how you are to conquer it."

"The first and better way is that which I have already laid down—take the care of your children out of your servants' hands entirely."

"I would it were possible," said Reynolds, with a sigh; "but I must confess I agree with the majority here that it is impossible."

"Don't talk to me of impossible," said the Doctor, with a sudden display of warmth; "nothing is impossible."

"Not even to make a man into a woman, or *vice versâ*?" I asked slily.

Here the Doctor smiled, and he resumed more calmly:—

"Well, if you will not follow the better way, take the other."

"Which is——?"

"To educate and pay your servants properly, and show some human interest in them, even though they be but servants."

I was resolved not to notice the sneer in this remark, the more so as I knew it to be in general justified, so rather turned the conversation in another direction, saying:—

"That brings me, Doctor, to a consideration I want to urge, namely this—you yourself the other day said something like it—you cannot get progress along one line alone. We are supposed to be discussing moral education, yet constantly we are diverging into other branches. It is one of the lessons I have to be preaching daily, that everything one does affects everything else. Boys will not believe it, but so it is. And hence it seems to me that your endeavour to lay down a clear line of advance for moral education is liable to be upset, if by nothing else, at least fatally by this—that you do not allow sufficiently for the requisite advance in intellectual development and power, and, above all, for the necessary concomitant—I will not say quite equal—advance of all sections of society at once. You seem to have an ideal for the middle class before your eyes, but forget how much depends upon the action of classes who will be quite shut out from participation in the benefits you sketch. These two difficulties go far to make shipwreck of your whole scheme."

"I heartily trust not," was the Doctor's reply, "though I grant that difficulties, great difficulties, they are. Not difficulties, however, in the way of the theory as a theory, but merely as a project that is feasible at once. That my proposals could be carried into instant practice without a violent revolution, I do not claim; but I do claim this, that they are worth consideration, and that some of them, at all events, might be adopted without such great dislocation of the social machinery as you all seem to fear. I, though in theory a Socialist, in one at least of the senses of that much abused term, yet should hold myself to be as a scientific man disgraced if I did not know that changes are most effective when gradual; and were a cataclysm to come and carry out my reforms at one sudden stroke, I should do nothing but tremble for the permanence of the new arrangements. None the less is an ideal valuable because it is impracticable. We are so immersed in the ordinary aspect of things around us, that it requires a violent shock to make us lift up our eyes and see—to turn from the darkness of Plato's cavern, where we but watch shadows, to the full light of the real sun. This, then, must be my excuse for laying before you a series of propositions which you all unite in condemning, though of this one point I certainly feel proud: that well-nigh all your objections, so far, have rested upon the fact that my proposals are impracticable, not upon their intrinsic undesirability."

"Yes," said Reynolds quietly; "and I, as one who looks for a nobler world to come than any we have yet seen, will at least say this, that your ideal in most respects seems to me a grand one, and that even an approach to its realization would do much to help forward Christ's work upon earth."

"But to return to our point," resumed the Doctor. "I abandon all hope of converting you to the feasibility of at present getting mothers to do their primary duty—for primary duty it surely is. What business have women to be mothers at all if they cannot discharge their maternal duties? There is an old and admirable saying,—'No rights without duties,' and when we consider what the rights and privileges of a parent are, can we look upon any duties as too heavy to undertake in return for that great honour? It makes me wild to see how young men and women rush into marriage and make themselves parents in the blindest haste, without a minute's thought of their power to discharge the most sacred and responsible duty in the world—without ever from their birth to—I had almost said—the day of their death giving one real, conscientious moment's thought to what is the best way to meet the awful responsibility every parent will incur. But I must not dwell upon this or I shall never end. Let me only repeat that I still hold, whatever you may think to the contrary, that a mother's first duty is plain—to sacrifice everything for the sake of her child. However, I will proceed.

"I think we have now surveyed sufficiently what I may call the outside of a good moral training. Let us now turn to the child himself and see what we can make of him. But here I would beg you to look upon my remarks as far more tentative than the foregoing; for I have not made, I am sorry to say, that direct and personal study of childhood from its earliest hours, which is really essential to an adequate attempt to devise a scheme of moral training. My reading too on the point has been desultory, and several of the books I have taken up do not seem to me of very much profit from the point of view of actual practice."

"There I can bear you out," I said. "Works expressly treating of moral education are comparatively few, and those which I have read—and I have read all that I could lay my hands on—are in many cases merely vague dilutions of well-known precepts, old, I had almost said, as the hills. The most striking I have found is a recent work to which we have already alluded, that by Professor Felix Adler, which is certainly of very great use. Still it is fair to remember that almost every work on general education treats more or less of the moral side. This treatment, it is true, is sometimes indirect; but in the great writers you may pick up many valuable thoughts, albeit their suggestions are not always systematic."

"Ah," said Dr. Hindley, "it is clear I shall have a shrewd critic in you. But you must be merciful, for I am but an untrained novice trying his hand at a work beyond him."

"Oh, never fear me, I am only too glad to learn. My forte does not lie in suggesting new ideas, or even in criticising old; what I like is to try to improve my methods in the light of suggestions from any source."

"That is good; I shall work with less fear. Now the first thing that strikes me is this: We can learn far more from badly-trained children than from those whose rearing has been more fortunate."

"That sounds odd," said my wife.

"It is a well-known fact in science that an experiment which fails often teaches you more than one that succeeds. Now if we look at what we call with such truth a spoilt child, what feature should we say is the most prominent?"

"Self-will," suggested Mrs. Reynolds.

"Precisely. The will is everything. But as we cannot manipulate the will all at once—it is a very complex factor—we must go deeper and enquire what is the essential ingredient in the quality we usually call self-will—what has been neglected so as to produce the result we so often see. I wish I knew psychology better; it would simplify our enquiry so much. Is there no one here who can lead the way? Surely, Mr. Trelawney, you are an expert in psychology, being an Oxford man first and then a schoolmaster."

I could not help smiling as I replied:—

"I fear my Oxford psychology is rather rusty with age, and as for my profession of necessity involving a knowledge of psychology, why, my compeers would think me utterly daft if I studied the science because I teach."

Dr. Hindley opened his eyes and said:—

"Do you really mean to tell me that you schoolmasters do not hold psychology to be essential to your knowledge of your profession?"

"Certainly I do. We in England are above such things—so most of us say—though for my own part there is nothing I regret so much as that when I left Oxford I could not go to a training college where I might have made practical my abstract knowledge of psychology. But at that time such a place was not in existence save for the teachers of elementary schools; and even now, I believe, there is only one * of them, and that dragging on but a feeble life. Women, however, are better off."

"Well, I can only say I am amazed. Now I understand why the elementary schoolmasters seem to do the mere teaching so much better than you. No, I cannot get over it. It seems to me like a man setting up for a doctor whose knowledge of anatomy is the surface of his own person. You know I pursued my studies for a long time in Germany, in a town which, though small, had a good University, and I know that there such a confession would have awakened the surprise, not to say scorn, of every teacher in the place. To the Germans a thorough training in psychology as applicable to education is essential before a man is allowed to teach at all. But here it seems I must rely upon myself, though I hope, Trelawney, that even your amateurish knowledge—though I really suspect it is better than you admit—will serve at times to keep me straight.

"To return to the point of self-will once more. What defect has there been in a child's training whose most prominent characteristic is self-will? I imagine there will be no hesitation in the answer—he has not learnt obedience. Yet here is the cardinal virtue of all. Without obedience what were man? Man who is born to suffer and to die can only make life endurable by self-renunciation; to attain that end he must learn obedience even from his first breath. Obedience is well-nigh the only virtue which a child can learn from the very beginning. The youngest child has desires and commands; woe to the mother who cannot tell when those commands are lawful, when they are not! Through all her after-life her present joy will be her curse. Even the infant can become imperious and exact obedience more servile than any king. It may be hard to refuse one seemingly so helpless, but the lesson must be learnt. And here once more we face nature's terrible complexity: if the parents are not wise with moral wisdom, their children will not be well brought up; the evil will spread from age to age, only to be checked by influences brought to bear from outside—influences which must be fortuitous, more or less. Let us then insist, as at the proper time I propose to do

* This remark now no longer holds good.

in detail, on the training of the young in a parent's duties, hoping to avoid by this means the worst of elementary blunders.

"For methods of enforcing obedience it is impossible to lay down perfect abstract laws. One caution, however, may be of use—command as little as may be and forbid as little as you can. Let the training to obedience come rather indirectly by way of suggestion, by appeals to a child to act from love for you."

"But," interrupted my wife, "surely that cannot do with quite young children; they cannot realize love for their parents."

"That, Mrs. Trelawney, is a hard saying. I do not think we any of us know the full extent of a speechless infant's love for those around it. But I understand your position, and admit that I have run on too far and confused distinct points. I was thinking at the moment of children with intelligence appreciably developed, who could understand, if they refused to act for you, why you refused to act for them. Such an appeal would be lost on the very young, to whom I ought to have confined my remarks. For the very young then, say those of less than two years, I would propose that we should act by suggestion, not directly, taking trouble to keep them, so far as we can, out of the reach of wrong desires; and where that is impossible, as often it will be, diverting their attention to other things. Here nature has been merciful and helps us greatly; for a young child is so constituted that he can easily be led by appropriate objects to forget a thing even of keen desire. 'Prevention is better than cure,' is a maxim of more weight in matters moral than in any other sphere of human life."

"I remember," said my wife, "a case which Locke relates of a mother who, on her child's return from nursing, had to whip her no less than eight times before she would obey. Whenever I read the passage my heart bleeds."

"And mine too, Mrs. Trelawney, for I know the place you mean. Yet for all one's suffering one must not flinch."

"Does it not often seem to you that one is readiest to punish those for whom one's love is greatest? I know," I said, "for my own part that I am severest upon those boys who are my favourites at school, however much I try to keep an even hand. It is so much greater pain to see those whom one loves do wrong than those about whom one is comparatively indifferent, that I fear we act from a sort of blind revenge, to return the pain we have been made to suffer."

"That is a curious theory," said Reynolds; "but after all the mere fact is very near that grand old saying of the Bible—to my thinking one of the greatest sources of consolation to be found in the whole of it—'Whom the Lord loveth He chasteneth.'"

"I am afraid the theory or the practice does not hold good of all, or indeed of the majority," said Mrs. Hindley.

"No, alas! no," the Doctor resumed; "otherwise my hatred of even necessary punishment would not be so strong as it is. But whether painful or not, insistence on obedience is for a parent the supreme necessity."

"Would you say so even when a rule is absurd?"

"I wonder that you as a schoolmaster can ask such a question. You must know too well the results of neglecting to enforce a command, even though it is injudicious or wrong to begin with. Of course I am not considering the case where the commander has changed his opinion before the command is carried out. I remember an instance which well illustrates the difficulty into which a man may put himself by an unwise command. At a large day-school, just before the Easter holidays, a father applied for his boy to leave school on the Tuesday in Holy Week instead of on the Thursday, the day fixed for breaking up, because he was going to Rome for Easter and was anxious to take his son with him. The boy was in the top form but one, and bore an exceedingly good character; yet the head-master refused the leave. As an outsider, I think he was extremely injudicious, but that is not to the point; doubtless you would decide otherwise. What followed? The father took his son all the same, and as a natural and inevitable consequence, the boy was not allowed to return to the school—was, one may say, practically expelled. What would have happened to that head-master had he let the boy return? After his first refusal no other course was open; and so it is with a parent who gives a young child an order, even though that order be not a wise one. And here once more comes in the need of a wise training on the part of the parent. I have often and often seen stupid orders given which have directly fostered disobedience, through the difficulty, and in some cases the real impossibility, to a conscientious child of carrying them out. And not merely must we avoid such impossible orders, we must further be quite sure that the child understands exactly what he has to do. Often and often this is not the case, and then when we punish we are considered—and really are—cruel and unjust. We cannot be too careful to think all round a question before we take an irrevocable step. These dangers occur more in the case of children of some growth, but there is an analogous danger with those quite young—that of being capricious, now forbidding and now allowing precisely the same thing. We must school ourselves to keep the even tenor of our way, turning neither to right hand nor to left. And we must remember to make allowance for the natural instincts of childhood—I am thinking in especial of what is a great torment to us elders, but inevitable in a healthily developing child—fidgetiness, restlessness, and a constant desire to be experimenting on something new. If we forbid movement and a change of occupation, we are not training the child by healthy discipline, but are inflicting on it a torture which makes it resent our rule, and besides sometimes hindering the free development of the body, we may also permanently mark the mind with the curse of peevishness or nervous irritability. And the folly of it is that this tendency to restlessness dies—without execution—as the years go on. This is, in fact, a feature too often neglected, that a vast number of faults eliminate themselves as the child matures, so that we are often wasting time to less than no purpose in trying to eradicate them before nature has ordained it, to the sore trial and sometimes permanent damage of the tempers of our children as well as of ourselves."

"I am afraid, Dr. Hindley," put in Reynolds, "that your millennium recedes as we go further. You expect us poor parents to be perfect—surely too much to expect of any one."

"Yes, I am like Plato, and expect that my guardians shall be perfect, to secure which end I shall spare no pains in their training. But now that we have dealt with the primary virtue of obedience and recognised that it must be emphasized even in minute particulars from the cradle onwards, let us turn to the next point which is most convenient to discuss—habit."

"Your order is peculiar, Doctor," I interrupted. "Why should you take habit now? Does it not apply equally well to obedience? For my own part I should have thought one of two courses was open to you—either to take it first as the general aim of all our discussion, or to treat it last, as a focus for suggestions already made."

"I admit the justice of your charge," the Doctor said; "but you remember I disclaimed being a systematic philosopher. I only utter my thoughts as they happen to occur, and I do not think it matters much where habit comes in our discussion. But I really had a reason for treating it just here, which was that obedience can begin when the child is almost unconscious, whereas consciousness seems required to co-operate to some extent in the true formation of moral habit."

"Surely not," I said; "habits may be reflex and automatic—not consciously formed at all."

"True, but you remember I said 'seems to be required.' And though I admit the spontaneous formation of many habits, still in morality, our special subject now, the cooperation of the will is so imperatively required for healthy development, that I think we may leave out of view this unconscious formation. But even my language is, I feel, to a certain extent ambiguous. I mean by conscious formation of habit, not that we necessarily set ourselves to watch every step in a habit's growth, but that our general development is such that the reflecting powers can, if needful, be, and indeed frequently are, brought to bear upon the formation of the habit, so that the child being trained can be made to see, only vaguely perhaps at first, but more and more clearly as time advances, both that a habit is being formed and how it can itself help or hinder the process. And I would say this, that it is a good thing to enlist as much as may be the child's active cooperation, by explaining to him the desirability of the end and the best method of its attainment. People are much too afraid of explaining why they give particular orders,

Sometimes I believe they really think that blind obedience is preferable to obedience with knowledge, against which I can only urge that if their law had been always followed we should still be slaves to savage chieftains; at other times I think they refuse to give reasons because they have a half idea that, if they came to argue them out, they would find their own positions untenable. But whether they have such a feeling or not, at least they save themselves a great deal of trouble if they lay down a law without reasons assigned. But think what a revolution in practice we should have if every one, before giving injunctions or advice, were really to thoroughly go over to himself the grounds on which he would base his procedure! This step alone would go far to raise the moral tone of the world; we should no longer be 'like dumb, driven cattle,' but should each be using for its noblest purpose the gift that shows closest our affinity with God."

"Do you know what George Eliot says somewhere?" said Mrs. Hindley:—"'Reason about everything with your child, you make him a monster, without reverence, without affections.'"

"Very true," I chimed in, "and I may say that I have tried the principle at school, but am by no means satisfied with the result. Often I have secured a more willing obedience, and the special fault in that boy has vanished for ever; but at other times I have met with casuistical answers, and I have dreaded to expose the whole basis of my action for fear of encouraging the spirit of casuistry and unsettling, by failing to convince, the whole foundation of a boy's morality. Hence I have dropped my argument, appearing to be defeated—with what results I leave you to conceive. Children are not as grown men; the latter you can sometimes make recognise their bias and allow for it accordingly, but children are so full of their own wisdom that this, combined with their self-interest, will lead them to stifle the voice of reason which in an older person might perhaps be heard. And if you ask me, I would say further that it is precisely this difficulty which seems to me the most serious that can be brought against the attempt to teach morality at all—so serious, indeed, that I am by no means yet convinced that it is wise even to make the attempt."

"That is a large question which I will not argue now. Doubtless it will crop up again in the course of our discussion, so will you allow me to postpone it for the present? If the answer does not suggest itself as we go on, I think, at all events, we shall be in a better position for considering it when I have set forth my project in full. If a lengthy discussion should then be needed I will not shrink; but I hope and trust none will be required. Meantime I would say in reply to what I grant is a weighty objection, first, that if George Eliot says, 'Use reason always, and you make your child a moral monster,' we can retort, 'Use reason never and you make him a moral idiot'; secondly, that the difficulty lies entirely in the method after which you deal with your subject in hand. And, further, it is greater in the present attitude of teachers towards the discussion of moral questions than it would be if the reforms I am now suggesting become part and parcel of their daily work. For then, with moral problems carefully chosen and adapted, the children would take them as a matter of course, and being accustomed to deal with moral difficulties would not be so ready to believe themselves infallible. By the time they were of age to discuss any of those points where at first they might think their own view really weighty, they would have come to recognise that morality was part of a vast complex whole, and that if they disturbed even one small particle of it there was likely to result a disturbance to the whole, ending perhaps in incalculable harm. And I should like to ask you this, Trelawney, whether you do not exaggerate the likelihood of children developing the casuistical spirit. My own experience—limited, I grant, to my own children—has led me to believe that the young are in the main very ready to accept those views of morality which they find habitually held by those around them, especially when they are urged by one for whom they feel true love and respect. Have you not found that to be so too?"

"At times, yes, and indeed not unfrequently; but then you must remember that a schoolmaster's position differs essentially from a parent's: you cannot expect him to be loved by his boys as a parent is loved and revered by his children."

"Really, Trelawney, if I thought you always spoke the genuine beliefs of members of your craft, and were not often playing *advocatus diaboli*, my opinion of your profession would sink to low depths. I do not see at all why a schoolmaster should not be as much beloved and revered by his boys as a parent, albeit the love and reverence differ in kind. You will remember that I had this point in view when from the first I laid down that the school must be only of such a size as will allow each master to have something of this feeling developed towards him by every boy. The Port-Royalists tried this and achieved a mighty work; why should not all? And surely a schoolmaster can compensate for disadvantages by the greater awe which he inspires as compared with a parent. That the schoolmaster has often a greater influence than the parent I will not urge, because you may say I am taking exceptions and not the rule."

"But I still think that the danger of evoking the casuistical spirit in however few is sufficiently great to make it unwarrantable, even in the interests of the majority, to give any opening for such a result."

"That is a serious argument, but there are two answers. First, we are laying down a law for the general mass. I debarred myself from using an argument just now because you might retort that it was based on exceptional cases, and I think in fairness you ought to renounce the same advantage. But inasmuch as your argument is based upon a moral danger, I will not press that point, but give my other reply, which is this, that whoever teaches morality must be alive to all the dangers, and if he sees any likelihood of so undesirable a result accruing as you fear, he must change his line of attack and show the wisdom of an able general combined with the loving care of one whose whole interests are a pure morality. In this point, as in every other, the result will depend upon the individual; and though mistakes unhappily cannot always be avoided by us imperfect men, we must do our best in all honesty and love and be content to leave the result to God."

"Doctor," said Mr. Reynolds, "I think your position shows that you quite leave out of account in the moral world what to me is the most important factor in it—the necessity of faith."

"What do you mean by faith? If you mean by it the assurance that there are more things in heaven and earth than are dreamt of in our philosophy, then I should be sorry indeed to admit your accusation. If, however, you mean that we must be prepared to believe many things for which no evidence can be produced and which are entirely contrary, I do not say to our knowledge of nature at present—which is a poor argument—but to our very moral sense, even the moral sense of those most highly gifted with it, then most certainly I leave out all reference to faith, and with the greatest joy. But that faith in the sense of taking some things on trust is essential to any real morality of character, I most fully admit; but what things are to be taken on trust is another matter altogether."

"You are on dangerous ground, Doctor, talking of the moral sense," I said. "If you had a professed philosopher here I fear you might be pounded into dust."

"Let us be thankful then that we have no such dangerous foe at hand. But we shall see later in what sense I consider faith to be essential, and then I hope Mr. Reynolds will raise his question again. Has any one else anything to say about giving children reasons for rules before I proceed to other points?"

"Yes," said my wife. "It seems to me that your insistence on the necessity of reasoning and being able ourselves to explain our grounds of action on every occasion itself does away with the necessity of forming habits, on which you were so strong a short time ago. If we are always to fall back upon reason, why try to form habits at all?"

"It is clear," said the Doctor, laughing, "that the country is most unfavourable for the even and steady flow of the stream of my argument; but I must not complain. Till now it has had a fairly smooth course; little rocks have appeared here and there, just serving to give picturesqueness to the scenery. But now I have met with such a combination of obstacles that my waters must either rest and collect till they rise to such a height as to flow over them—a course undignified for a noble river—or, despite their apparently immovable mass, they must sweep them away altogether; or finally, they must, to their great sorrow and loss of labour, turn aside and find a smoother channel."

"No, Doctor, I should think you ought not to complain indeed," said Reynolds; "you talk of slight obstacles—I should say your current had swept through awful gorges without swerving one hair's breadth."

"Well, I suppose I must address myself to this last of impediments. So you think, Mrs. Trelawney, that I am self-contradictory. It is a serious charge even against one who does not profess to be a philosopher, but I hope to show that it is unfounded. In the first place I would say that you cannot yourself be sure of your moral position, unless it is based on a habit of right acting; secondly, because you, when full-grown and responsible, ought always to be able to give the grounds on which you act, does it therefore follow that your pupil may not learn through habit first, and only develop later his reasoning faculty? And, moreover, the fact that to reason is in your power does not necessarily imply that you are to have your moral arguments explicit in your own mind at every turn; time may not always allow you to reason—habit is there for use in emergencies. The mass of life consists of routine, and the mass of morality consequently is the same. The value of habit, in short, is twofold: it saves waste expenditure of thought and labour, and it secures far greater certainty of aim. It is like a machine as contrasted with a man; the former will work with perfect precision towards the end for which it was made, the latter is liable to hesitate and blunder—to break out suddenly into irregularity."

"But," my wife went on, "is not that precision itself a danger? In cases which differ from the normal type to all appearance only slightly, the force of habit may be so great as to obscure the difference and lead one astray."

"And therefore it is that I put a check upon habit by insisting on the proper cultivation of reason. If we are accustomed to apply our reason to every problem as it appears, however unconscious the process may become, we shall still have two principles balancing each other—habit always wanting to do as of old, reason always arising to justify or condemn. In morality, in fact, we shall get a habit of reasoning, than which nothing can be more valuable. Now this process I say you cannot begin too early."

Here Mr. Reynolds interrupted. "I would rather say, Doctor, that you might begin too early. The best maxim to lay down, I think, would be this: Begin to reason with your children when they have begun it, never before."

"That principle is good in one way," said the Doctor, "but often we do not know when they really begin. They do not say openly all that they think. Hence, if only you adapt yourself and your arguments to the particular stage of the development of the child, I still maintain my view is the right one—you cannot begin moral reasoning too soon. If a child is first taught to perform his duties mechanically without understanding their reasons and aims—save only in the case of those virtues which, like obedience, rarely conflict with any other, and which, if they do, as a rule show clearly what is after all the right course to adopt—one of two evils is likely to happen when at last the child reaches the independent years: he will either, from not understanding the grounds on which he finds that, while some acts are still tabooed, others he may now do, come to the conclusion that morality is conventional and kick over the traces altogether; or, which is perhaps the commoner case, remain all his life the slave of others' opinions, with no light by which to trace his own path. The latter is the state of the world at large, but of the former I have marked a rising danger where perhaps you might least expect to find it—in our public schools. In the hope of checking other serious evils the modern theory seems to be that it is good to provide some forced occupation, not in itself of necessity unpleasant, to cover the whole of a boy's time. This result follows: the boy, not having time for reflection and self-development, goes out into life without a compass to guide, or else he becomes a mere hall-marked commodity, one of a pattern with no stamp of his own. One of the most famous of our younger public schools seems to me especially to tend in this direction. I grieve deeply to see it; for to sap the independence of a growing spirit leads to infinite harm to the whole State. This, indeed, I regard as the most serious evil which threatens our modern educational system."

"Doctor," I said, "I must take exception to one remark

you made in passing—that obedience rarely conflicts with other virtues, or that if it does the right is easy to discern. Surely all history is against you. Still the question is trivial for our present purpose, and I will not press the point. It would probably lead us too far astray."

"I am glad you are merciful, for I find thorns enough without going out of my way to seek them. I grant I may have put the remark too strongly, but you know an advocate to make an impression has always to exaggerate the points of his case. But having undergone so severe a heckling I hope I may now have a little peace; may I ask if there is any other objection any lady or gentleman still wishes to raise? Come, Mrs. Reynolds, all have attacked me, I think, except you; have you not got something to say? Or am I so lucky as to have made one convert?"

"I cannot quite say that," replied Mrs. Reynolds with a smile, "but I have nothing to add to the objections already urged, and to my mind, I must say, only half answered."

At this we all laughed, and my wife, saying: "You see, Dr. Hindley, silence does not always show consent," rose to leave, followed by the ladies. We settled ourselves down to wine and a smoke, and after a minute's pause the Doctor resumed.

"You know I do feel most strongly on that question of absorbing a boy's whole time. I know it is done from noble objects, but it seems to me, though you may think me reckless in saying so, too heavy a price to pay."

"But what would you do?" said Reynolds. "Surely nothing can be more than it is good to pay in order to master the demon of impurity. And what other remedy would you suggest?"

"Ah, that is the difficulty. But you know the evil does not always begin at school. It is often fostered by bad home arrangements, due to mere ignorance or the thoughtlessness of parents. It arises in the first instance from the inquisitiveness of children, and in the case of the very young might be left to cure itself, were it not that the passion roused, being one of the strongest, tends to gather strength with enormous rapidity and is fed by the least thought which runs that way. In this respect I think it is unique among our passions; there is no other,

I believe, which can be excited so thoroughly by mere thought. Hence the peculiar difficulty of treatment, and hence, too, the reason why many noble men have held that the best way to conquer it is to keep mind and body for ever occupied. But one may urge as against that view that, apart from the arguments used before while the ladies were still in the room, it cannot be said of hard physical work at all events, work even almost to the point of exhaustion, that it prevents the development of the vice in question—and I am not sure that the same does not hold of mental work as well. It is true that, if the body and brain be already in a state of exhaustion, indulgence in this vice will enfeeble the body to a very great degree, and it might be hoped that any one indulging in it would observe the effects and refrain, from the fear of what might follow. But this presupposes that the child has already reached such an age and is of such a disposition as to be able to trace connection between cause and effect; whereas the seeds of the vice are often sown very early, and have taken firm root before such comparative maturity is reached. Moreover, even supposing the inference is drawn, we cannot be sure of the desired result following. And further, by relying upon this position, we are in danger of undermining the stamina of the race, owing entirely to the ignorance of the individual and our faulty system of attacking the foe. No, I cannot approve the method, though for their motives and courage in facing the problem, its upholders deserve the greatest respect."

"You trace the evil to home, Doctor," said Mr. Reynolds; "can you give any cases where you think harm is done by thoughtless domestic arrangements?"

"Certainly I can. Nurses often directly and culpably foster the passion in quite young children."

"In what way?"

"The details are not pleasant, and if you do not mind, I would rather not go into them. Every medical man knows much of this subject that he would only too willingly forget if he could. But to proceed. Two children should never be placed in the same bed, and if possible not even in the same room; or if this is unavoidable, then they should not be left except when they have gone soundly asleep. And I am by no means convinced of the wisdom of bathing even young children in sight of one another. But I feel that all such measures are more avoidance of temptation than real training to pure morality."

"I think," I said, "to avoid temptation is the chief thing in the cultivation of purity. It is the countless provocations to which the passion is exposed that lead to its enormous and hideous growth. You have yourself, Doctor, suggested how at home we may remove some of the provocations. I could easily add others from the school point of view. It is at boarding-schools that the temptations are most rife, and to me this fact seems one of the most serious charges that can be levelled against them, even with all due allowance for the improvement undoubtedly made. But as you have already condemned these schools, I will not traverse the ground again. But at day-schools, too, unless teachers are vigilant, there are many incentives and opportunities for impurity. First and foremost stands the undesirable mixture of boys who have passed puberty with boys who have not. Above all things one has to be careful to prevent a big boy taking up with a small one, often with innocent motives at first, though I always fear the result. Again, brief spells of unoccupied time are a fruitful source of harm. There is more of unclean talk during the few minutes in which a master may have either not yet arrived or perhaps quitted the room than in the larger lapses of time when there is abundant opportunity for the boys to start something serious. Finally, the reading of unclean books is the wellhead whence flows an unfathomed stream of evil. For much of the harm that has been done in the past, classical literature is to blame. It is unfortunate that much of what scholars assure us is essential for a good knowledge of the classical languages should be so utterly steeped in foulness. Under this condemnation must come even works whose whole result is a lesson in morality, as, for instance, is the case with the Greek tragedians; for it is, I fear, but too true that a boy, while he may miss the moral lesson ultimately conveyed, can hardly fail to understand the filthiness of the tales on which the plays are so often based. As the subjects are beyond the experience of the young, but represent a sphere which the grown can comprehend, a grown man may read them and take no harm; but can we therefore say that they will not permanently stain the innocent mind of a poor child? I look upon it as one of the great incidental gains which a deposition from their supremacy of the classics would bring, that we should have as the staple of a cultured education literatures that could be limited wholly to what is good."

"But," said Reynolds, "I do not see that either of you has done anything except to point out what we have to avoid. You have not laid down any educating principle, nor can I see what motive power you will ever get save the one great principle Christ enunciated, 'Be ye perfect, even as your Father in heaven is perfect.'"

"You know religious arguments are for the present excluded," I said; "but I admit that this subject would give the fairest chance for maintaining that religion is essential to morality. Still I think some suggestions of active measures may be made. I was very much struck by a remark of Dr. Abbott that we are not frank enough in attacking these questions; less reticence, he argues, would win more results. The reticence is natural, but after long thought I have come to the conclusion Dr. Abbott is right. And the same view is taken by Mrs. Josephine Butler, who shared in the work of her husband at Liverpool, and from many points of view is an authority to be respected. The matter should be tackled in early days at home by father or mother, or even by both. It is partly the feeling that children have that the subject is a forbidden one that makes the fascination. We know that the same principle applies to grown men too; owing to some unaccountable perversity we often conceive our first desire for a thing when we have learnt that we cannot have it. And with children the tendency is even stronger, owing, I suppose, to their love of experiment; were we therefore at times to discuss the matter openly, we might kill at least one incentive to impurity. Wholly exclude our children from a knowledge of it, we cannot, unless we cut them off entirely from all intercourse with their fellows, a course for many reasons undesirable; but if we encourage them to lay open their feelings on the matter we shall have means of guidance ready at hand. For this further fact must always be borne in mind, that children are most ready to take tone from their elders; if we show them how much we abhor such things, and as they grow older set forth to them to some extent the serious harm done by indulgence in evil passions, we shall probably touch springs which once set at work will continue to move for ever. At present we are like ostriches; we put our heads in the sand, and, blinding our eyes, say the danger is past. It is nothing short of moral cowardice, and that on a point most vital to our children's welfare. No father should ever send his child to a boarding-school, no matter how young the child may be, without serious warning in the plainest language on this very point. Proper supervision of dormitories is essential, and by proper I do not mean an unexpected visit at casual moments on the part of a master, but the presence in the room without intermission of some one who can be made really responsible. I am happy to believe that in most cases our monitors can be thoroughly trusted to do their duty; but exceptions, alas! I know occur. The mere occurrence of such exceptions leads me to say: Sweep away the whole system. Separate rooms many authorities condemn, on the ground that the vice may still occur in secret; but better in secret and alone than as a bad example to others. Impracticable, no doubt I shall be told, the suggestion is; but I would reply, as you, Doctor, have done before, that the matter is one entirely of cost, and where education is already so costly, the difference cannot be vital. It is the question of purity beyond all others that makes me agree with your chief points: first, that day-school education is preferable to a boarding-school; and secondly, that joint education of the sexes is one of the greatest and most desirable of reforms. For in the mixing of the sexes there is not the same incentive to what is at the bottom of the whole mischief—filthy talk. It would take a bad boy indeed to raise the subject with girls, though he might have no hesitation with those of his own sex. And this alone would mean that we should guard from evil the vast majority—those, namely, who, not being specially prone to vice, are yet not over strong to resist it, those who would be safe if shielded from temptation, but who fall before the force of attack."

"Yes," said Reynolds, "that is a strong argument; but I should like to know a little more fully how you would definitely approach the subject—what kind of arguments you would use to a child."

"I should base myself first on what I think must be our starting-point in all our moral education of children—the fact that impurity is wrong in itself; and then as the years of the child permitted, I should start from the analogy of plants and animals, explaining in this way the reproductive process. Then I should point out that misuse of our powers leads to serious physical harm, apart altogether from the degrading influence exercised on the character of the whole man. What would you say, Doctor?"

"You would have a most unpleasant task."

"Unpleasantness and duty are not contradictory. But of course I should not go into all the details of physiology, general statements would suffice."

"I am by no means sure," said the Doctor, "that that would not be the wisest way of tackling the difficulty. Still, even then you would have to allow for the fact that men know the right and choose the wrong."

"Ah, Doctor," I said, smiling, "I could bring that same argument against all the moral training you are proposing. We do not look for perfection all at once."

"There is another point, Trelawney," said Reynolds, "on which you, as a schoolmaster, ought to give us a good opinion. Would you discuss the matter individually with the children, or take them altogether as a school or as a class?"

"I think individually."

"Why?"

"Because it is so unpleasant to deal with the subject before a large number."

"That is surely rather a cowardly reason."

"Well, I think you can get a boy to open his heart to you better——"

"No doubt."

"And you have more chance of working upon him effectually than if you are dealing with a large mass."

"Is that always true?" asked Hindley. "Certainly one knows that sympathy or common feeling will sometimes intensify itself quite wonderfully, where an individual would be left almost cold."

" And," added Reynolds, " there is another danger. If the boy is talked to individually, he is likely from mere curiosity to discuss the matter with his schoolfellows outside, and they, not having shared in the serious nature of the discussion, will be more or less unimpressed by the whole proceeding, and tend to erase the good effect you may have produced upon the mind of your one boy; whereas if you deal with the subject in class, all will go away with more or less of the same feelings, and no one will care, in all probability, to raise the subject again; while if anybody does, scarcely one will dare to treat it with flippancy, owing to the solemn feeling which a good master will have been able to introduce into the whole matter. Boys are easily impressed, and though we often think the good seed thrown away, I am confident it fructifies in the majority of cases. The same thing holds of families with the due qualifications."

" I must confess," I said, after a moment's thought, " I think you are right. At the same time," I added, " I am firmly convinced from personal experience of the good of discussion with individuals."

" And I as a clergyman too. But why should that not be supplementary to the other? It seems to me that if the whole school knows that you have no hesitation in dealing with such matters quite outspokenly and before them all, they will have such a tone on the point in question that there will be no fear of any one, from mere flippant curiosity, prying into anything you may say apart. Hence you will gain the advantage of both methods."

" Yes," said the Doctor, " I think that would be the wisest way to deal with the matter;" and I assented.

After a minute's pause I resumed:—

" Can you tell us, Hindley, if the same difficulty occurs in the case of girls?"

" Girls, too, require instruction in these matters; but they are much purer-minded, and the instruction for them should aim not so much at safeguarding them against impurity, of which the risk is comparatively slight, but at giving them proper physiological knowledge of the different bodily functions. Yet those who have charge of them should still be very careful in all their arrangements."

"A point occurs to me. How could one treat the subject in a mixed school?"

"You mean that you would not like to do so, and I can quite understand. But here again I think, as you yourself were saying, the level of purity would have risen from the mere presence of both sexes. Our feelings on these matters are largely due to custom, and though at the first set-off it might seem strange, I feel convinced both boys and girls would in time come to regard it in the same light as they regarded their other lessons together. After all we have analogies. A clergyman would deal with the subject from his pulpit before a mixed congregation."

"Hardly," said Reynolds, "with the same frankness that he would use in dealing with the subject before men alone. He could not so well bring home the special faults of each."

"That is true, and therefore I would say that the general talks to a mixed class require supplementation—the masters speaking specially to the boys, the mistresses speaking specially to the girls. But there is another case very much in point which will give us a clue to what would happen. When the medical schools were first opened to women great fears were expressed that it would tend to lessen the thoroughness of the teaching from the dislike of the teachers to handle certain subjects before a mixed class of young men and young women. There are still, I believe, to be found professors who shrink from that part of their subject with dread; but the evidence of the mass of those who have tried it seems to prove that so far from having proved a difficulty, it has helped, if anything, to raise the tone of the teaching. That is a fairly close analogy, and I think may be taken as conclusive."

"It seems, then, that we have come to this conclusion on this most difficult of all subjects," I said: "we are to take as watchful and large precautions as possible, but are never to shrink from handling the subject openly or in private whenever it seems that good may be done."

The other two assented, I went on :—

"I suppose, as we are aiming at an ideal, we need not raise the question what parents would say if they knew our method of procedure."

Hindley smiled and said:—

"Why, you always seem afraid of the parent. Of course not. My belief, however, is that he would rather rejoice at our tackling the subject at all than fear further harm. But of course all depends upon the tone we adopt."

"I think we have already agreed that it is only the men of highest tone in morality who are to handle ethics, at least in schools."

"Yes, that is my cardinal principle."

"You have a great many cardinal principles," I said, smiling. "However, as we have managed to get to something like an agreement on this unpleasant question, happily in the absence of the ladies—which, by the bye, is against our own principle—shall we go and rejoin them?"

III

WHEN we arrived we found ourselves in the midst of a hot discussion, a battle royal on the question of truth and social conventions. Mrs. Hindley was saying in her dogmatic way :—

"It is absolutely wrong; nothing can justify it."

My wife urged in reply :—

"Surely it is an instance of your own maxim—in a choice between two evils choose the less. Would you rather give your friend mortal offence by sending down word that you did not want to see her, or gain your purpose and yet avoid quarrels by sending a message known to be fictitious?"

"If you are so uncharitable as not to wish to see your visitor, you have enough iniquity to answer for without increasing it by an uncalled-for lie. And further, if the message is known to be fictitious, what is the good of sending it at all?"

"In a given case your visitor is in doubt."

"Then you admit a deliberate lie."

"But what would you do? Take an instance which I know actually occurred. A lady having been left alone one afternoon, thought, as it was getting rather late and she was safely protected from further interruption, she would put her time to a good purpose, and so proceeded to wash her hair. Just in the middle of it all a visitor is announced. What was she to do? She sent down word that she was not at home. You would have liked her to say, 'I am washing my hair and cannot see you'!"

At this there was a general laugh, and Mrs. Reynolds, who had hitherto remained silent since our entrance, turned to us and said :—

"I am so glad you have come; I hardly feel competent to keep the peace. Here is a furious discussion raging, and has been for a long time, and both combatants are as convinced of the rightness of their position as when they began—nay, I rather think more so! For my own part I agree in theory with Mrs. Hindley; but our hostess, I fear, is quite unconvertible. However, as you gentlemen are at last here, we may perhaps get the matter settled."

"You forget, Mrs. Reynolds," said the Doctor very gravely, "that my wife is an ardent advocate of women's rights. It would be as much as my peace for a week is worth to interfere without appeal from one of the two combatants."

"Oh, well, then," said Mrs. Reynolds with a sigh, "I give up. But I leave you to answer for the consequences."

"It is all your fault, my dear," said my wife, turning to me. "What business have you to throw such an apple of discord among us as theories of morality? We were so in love with the subject at dinner that we went on with it afterwards, and now you see, having diverged fatally on a crucial point, are more in love with it than ever."

"Ah," I said, "Thackeray speculates somewhere on the mystery of the conversation carried on by the ladies while the gentlemen are eating and vapouring in smoke. Now we know all about it. They are so short of originality that they continue the gentlemen's subjects—and quarrel."

"All right, Mr. Trelawney," said Mrs. Hindley, "I will remember that remark and have my revenge some day. Who was it, please, if my husband speaks truth, who wanted to finish the discussion on moral training in the evening at home, because, as he said, there were points in education which women could settle better than men?"

"It is not fair, Mrs. Hindley, to avail yourself of knowledge gained behind your adversary's back."

"That is all very well; but to show you that we women are capable of propounding matters which are too great even for your mighty intellects, I will lay the subject of our dispute before you. Are society lies justifiable, and if so, on what ground?"

"Certainly they are, as the smaller of two evils."

"And would you teach your children so?"

"When they are the proper age to grasp the distinction."

"And what age may that be?"

"That depends upon their development—say about seventeen."

"Well, and if you indulge in them, are you so sanguine as to believe that your children will not discover your habit before the proper age to grasp the distinction?"

"You will, of course, have to show very great care."

"Of course," repeated Mrs. Hindley, with a touch of sarcasm.

"And do you hope to succeed?"

"I should try."

"Don't evade my question, if you please. Do you in your heart think you will succeed in escaping the notice of those all-observant eyes?"

"No, perhaps not; but——"

"But what? Why hesitate? You are only dealing with a woman."

"You must run some risks. The code of morality cannot be quite the same for children as for grown men and women."

"Ah, now we have come down to the arch-heresy that morality is conditional. George," went on Mrs. Hindley, turning to her husband, "I beg you to take due notice that Mr. Trelawney's morality is very far from perfect, even in theory, and therefore when you see your way to carrying into practice your ideal of perfect schoolmasters as the proper trainers of the young, you will take care to give him a very wide berth. So, Mr. Trelawney, you think that codes differ for young and old. Pray on what ground?"

"On the ground of the prime rule of method in all education, that you must teach wide principles before you take exceptions."

"That may be true as regards teaching; is it equally true as regards practice?"

"Certainly; the master would be a fool who, after laying down such a rule, we will say, for the *oratio obliqua* in Latin, as that historic tenses always take historic tenses, should promptly lead his boys to passages with primaries. Those should only be pointed out to them when they have the broader rule thoroughly imbedded, so thoroughly that they can even apply it unerringly."

"And now, Mr. Trelawney, may I ask whether the same rule of practice does not apply to morality? And with even more imperativeness in proportion to the vastly more important results that depend on it?"

The laugh, I was bound to confess, was fairly against me, and when Mrs. Hindley added, "Oh, you need not be afraid of me; I am only a woman, you know, and no doubt if my husband or Mr. Reynolds had used the argument you would have been able to answer them," I could only reply:—

"Spare me, Mrs. Hindley, spare me; I confess myself fairly worsted, and will pay whatever penalty you like, even to the extent of doing what is most unpleasant to me—recanting my opinions and recalling the ungallant remark I made a few minutes since."

"Upon my word, sir, you make matters worse. You recall an ungallant remark and say that you find the duty most unpleasant! You are like the famous member of the House of Commons—do you know the story?—who, on being ordered to apologize for calling another member a liar, did so on this wise: 'I called the hon. member a liar. It is true. I am ordered to apologize. I am very sorry.' It will be impossible to have any dealings with you if you go on in this wise."

"No, I assure you I did not mean that——"

"Then why did you say it? I would certainly recommend you to say no more; it is clear that you do not know the proper use of language, so that even a woman can set you right. So now, Mr. Trelawney, be careful in future how you disparage women's conversation; you see they can score a good revenge. But, dropping chaff, to be serious again: this question of truth, how are we to teach its supreme importance to the young as long as we ourselves are so shamefully lax?"

"I am very pleased, Mrs. Hindley, to hear you take so strong a view," said Reynolds. "Even if among ourselves these white lies, as they are called, do no harm, they cause incalculable mischief in the minds of our children by preventing a clear notion of the real essence of what I think I may style the most important of all altruistic virtues—truthfulness. It is no answer to urge that we cannot possibly hope to banish them. That I sorrowfully admit to be true, at least in the present condition of the world; but we can surely do something to improve our own conduct."

"I am convinced that the only proper standpoint to take, especially in education," said Mrs. Hindley, " is the one I have already expressed rather vigorously,"—and Mr. Trelawney assented,—" that there is no justification for a lie except to avoid some greater evil."

"But I say in answer," replied my wife, " that the wound you inflict on other people's sensibilities by speaking the exact truth is often far greater than the harm done by telling such a lie as I have supposed. You have never yet answered the problem I raised—what should the hair-washing lady have done?"

"She might have sent down word that she was unfortunately engaged for a long time to come. And after all, when we consider it, why should anything have been needed beyond the bare truth were it not for the absurd conventions of society, whose tyranny is as overbearing and killing as any of the dread superstitions of savagedom? Of course I know we cannot quite disregard them, but why comfort our souls with the thought of doing right, when really we are guilty of infringing the moral law simply through cowardice, because we are afraid of that far mightier law, social convention? It is just like tight-lacing, which comes under the condemnation of that supreme rule which forbids you ever to injure your health."

"How, then, would you set about instructing children in truth, and when would you begin?" I asked.

"Let me answer the latter question first," Mrs. Hindley said,—" the time. Begin from the very earliest days when a child can speak or even indicate by signs truth or a lie. There is no vice to which young children are so prone as telling falsehoods, a statement I am sure both Mrs. Trelawney and Mrs. Reynolds will support. It is not always exactly intentional: it is as often as not due at first to imagination and defect of memory. A child will readily confuse one event with another if there happens to be a superficial resemblance. But this tendency must be checked from the very outset, and on no account must the stories, often told for mere effect, receive the meed of laughter. They must be taken quite seriously, and in a short time will be abandoned. This is the only way to form a habit of truthfulness, as indeed to form any habit at all, by constant, unremitting practice, never letting a single chance escape. And this first of social virtues has one great advantage, it is easy to prove its importance to quite young children. They can by one or two crucial instances be easily brought to see that the whole continuance of society depends upon this virtue. It is an excellent introduction to a series of lessons on our duty to our neighbours. But there is one thing about which we must be most careful—never to show that we suspect an untruth unless we are clear in our own minds that we can bring the fault home to the real offender. And another point is this: we must never encourage lying even unconsciously to ourselves, as I fear we often do."

"Ah," I exclaimed, "I know what you mean. It is one of my standing difficulties when I have to enquire into offences at school. By putting leading questions one often suggests a lie to a child's mind, even where, if left to himself, he would probably speak the truth. It is so much easier to say yes or no than to invent a whole statement of one's own, and to a child, I expect, the guilt does not appear the same. I am convinced we often unintentionally induce to lying, especially by suggesting excuses or motives which never entered the child's head at the time he committed the given offence."

"Quite so, and your last remark calls up two other points, both of great importance. The first is excuses. Many excuses, as you say, are mere lies, making the matter worse instead of better. Yet one is bound to give a child a hearing."

"One master I know," I said, "has an ingenious method of getting over the difficulty. When he asks a boy if he has any excuse to give, he always says that if it is a worthless one, he will inflict a special punishment for that alone. The consequence is he never hears an excuse save such as are really valid."

"But the matter would be rather more difficult to handle with quite small children than with children of some growth. However, the chief point in all moral training is to be alive to the possibilities of going wrong and misleading unintentionally. If we know of the difficulties we shall probably get over them. The second matter to which I wished to refer was the matter of exactness, where common opinion would call it harsh to speak of lying. But the more I observe children, the more convinced I am that a great portion of lying arises from mere exaggeration through a desire for the picturesque. It is very difficult to get a practised observer even to give exactly an account of what he saw and nothing else, how much more so with children! And it is here that ordinary intellectual education comes perhaps most closely into touch with moral: both of them develop, if properly managed, an extreme and scrupulous love for truth. Wanton exaggeration and unconscious misrepresenting through a defect in training in observation are two of the commonest sources of lying. What a vital effect they have on after life in the fostering of prejudices and unwillingness to look facts fairly in the face I need hardly pause to say."

"Very often, I think," said the Doctor, " the misrepresentation is due to confusion, as you just now hinted, at least in the minds of very young children, of two perfectly distinct yet similar events. There is no intention not to speak the truth, but the children have not learnt to distinguish. With proper care as the mind develops, this fault can easily be corrected. But we must be alive to it. Those who are engaged in bringing up children would get many hints from published studies, such as the book by M. Perez, called *The First Three Years of Childhood*. Instances of various kinds of untruthfulness are given there, and M. Perez says, what is quite true, that lying is a perfectly subordinate vice: it usually springs from some different cause, which cause must be ascertained if we would check it."

"That is very true," said Mr. Reynolds, "but it only illustrates what is a well-known fact, that one defect usually conduces to another, and that it is not possible to raise one part of character without at the same time raising the whole. But," he went on, " I do not quite understand how you are to get your concrete instances of lying.

If I understood aright what was said some time ago by you, I think, Trelawney, while we were on our walk, we must give specimens from tales and other sources, and treat the subject largely from the intellectual side. That was so, wasn't it?"

"That is the method Professor Adler recommends."

"Could you give us a little more in detail a specimen of his way of proceeding?"

"Well, if you will allow me to fetch his book, we shall see what can be said on the question."

In a minute or two I reappeared, and turning over the leaves said,—

"You must remember this point first, that Professor Adler is dealing with school education, and only runs over very briefly the education which can be imparted at home. He impresses upon us the vital necessity of insisting from the first on regularity—a check upon impulse, he calls it —and obedience, and says further that by the age of six —bear in mind, please, that the book is written by an American—there will be a development of conscience and self-consciousness,—not in the bad sense as equivalent to shyness,—and, more important perhaps than anything, of reverence, which he regards, quite rightly, I think, as the mainspring of the child's whole moral growth. The recognition of himself as a separate entity brings to the child a notion of property, and with this outfit at the age of six the child enters school. Then Dr. Adler sketches a course of moral teaching, of which you will gain a fair idea if I run over rapidly the headings in his index. I do not propose to enumerate all the virtues he has tackled in detail, as it would take too long. I can only say that his method seems to me so good that every educator must be ready to work on his lines, not in every detail, perhaps, but at least in the main. If you wish, then, to go into the question thoroughly, you should get the book and read it for yourselves. I will only ask you to assume that, in any remarks I may make as to the actual intellectual instruction in morality, I accept everything he has said, and will only add such points as he may have omitted for different reasons, except in those cases—rare, if any—in which I may expressly indicate dissent. His headings, then, are these: First, in the primary course, till the children are about twelve, he makes two main divisions, the use of fairy tales and the use of fables. This he follows by additional remarks on fables and a detailed exposition of special stories. His stories he takes in the main from the Bible, and after specimens of his suggested method of treatment, he turns to tales from the Iliad and Odyssey, or perhaps I should say gives us a sketch of the whole outline of these poems. Next comes the grammar course, from twelve to fifteen. This portion of the book receives a sub-title, 'Lessons on Duty,' and having classified duties earlier, Professor Adler now treats them in accordance with his arrangement in the following order: the duty of acquiring knowledge, a very happy beginning; duties relating to the physical life and the feelings; those relating to others, more specially defined as filial and fraternal duties; duties towards all men, *i.e.* justice and charity, and the elements of civic duty. Then follows a chapter on the use of proverbs and speeches, and another on that most important point, the individualization of moral teaching. The book is closed by an appendix on the influence of manual training upon character."

"Why is that in an appendix only?" asked my wife.

"Oh, that," I said, "seems to be more or less of an accident. The subject is mentioned in the text, but as Professor Adler had dealt with it separately on another occasion, he refers his hearers to the address then given. In that address he is dealing chiefly with children of one type of criminality, that of moral deterioration arising from weakness of will; but he emphasizes for every one the immense moral gain that results from systematic manual education. His remarks, however, should not be treated as final, for he says the theory of the subject is only beginning to be worked out; but as far as they go they strike me as admirable. I suppose though he would claim, and to my thinking rightly, a greater degree of surety for his conclusions on training generally, and that is, perhaps, one reason why he has kept the two apart.

"But to proceed. I have given you an outline of his underlying principles. I now want to show you, if possible, in brief, how he would attempt to carry them out. I do not propose to consider how far his different choices of material are the best that could be made, but will give you a summary of his method in detail. In the first place, the fairy tales he says must be told—the response is more living than if they are read. Secondly, we must not elaborate the moral; if the tale is distorted to serve such a purpose all its life will have disappeared: the point should be emphasized only incidentally. Next we must avoid anything that is merely superstitious, and anything, too, of an evil tendency. By observing this last pair of points, a great many tales will be ruled out. From the instances given of useful lessons we may take as an illustration of the duty of keeping faith the story of the 'Frog King,' and among the fables that of the 'Traveller and the Bear.' At the same time, a warning is given that the fables are wanting in a really moral spirit—the appeal is to the auxiliary motive—self-interest. But Professor Adler thinks this is no disadvantage, provided the defect be constantly borne in mind. He says the motive of self-interest has to be developed also, though it must always be subordinate to the moral motive. But self-interest, he says, ' serves the purpose of strengthening the weak conscience of the young,'—a very searching remark. The fables, in particular, are useful as isolating one moral fact, and they can be taken as types of certain virtues and vices, the names serving afterwards to classify any acts we may have to notice among the children themselves. For the way of handling them, Professor Adler shows that he is well versed in the theory of method when he says, ' Relate the fable ; let the pupil repeat it in his own words, making sure that the essential points are stated correctly. By means of questions elicit a clear-cut expression of the point which the fable illustrates, then ask the pupil to give out of his experience other instances illustrating the same point.'

"At this point, the author passes to stories from the Bible, which he handles in what, to an Englishman, seems a very odd way. He dwells upon the fact that the stories, both in the Bible and in the Homeric poems, are full of the 'lucid expression of primary motives,' and so are admirably fitted to teach the outlines of moral truth. The former especially dwell upon filial and fraternal duties in a way which cannot be matched elsewhere, but they are of a more advanced type than fairy tales or fables, inasmuch as 'a succession of acts and their consequences are (*sic*) presented to the scholar, on each of which his judgment is to be exercised.' I will just give you the sketch of the way in which he treats the story of Adam and Eve; it will be an excellent illustration of his method. He takes the outline of the story, and develops details, as he would in telling the tale to little children; he changes Adam and Eve into a boy and a girl, who had every advantage that children could desire, for they lived in a garden in company with their father, to whom they went every morning for a loving look, who came to them every night before they slept. There was only one tree whose fruit they might not eat; that was hurtful their father told them, though they could not then understand why. They must, however, trust him, as he loved them and would give them no command save for their good. But one day as Eve was passing near this tree, she heard a snake's voice talking to her; she stopped to listen, and was at last persuaded to take one of the fruits and eat. As soon as she had done so, she ran off to Adam, and he, too, was tempted and ate the fruit; but at night they were afraid and hid themselves. When their father found them and asked why they hid, they stammered forth all sorts of excuses, and at last, when he drew the confession from them, they tried to throw the blame on others. Punishment followed, the natural punishment. Next morning they had to quit the garden, but were told that some day they might hope to regain it by dint of hard work and much suffering."

"I think," said Mr. Reynolds, "he would be a bold man who, in England, would venture to treat Bible stories in this way. It seems so curious that it should be possible to retell the tale to children of apparently something more than six years of age without their at once recognising the source, especially as he keeps the original names. It does not say much for the knowledge of the Bible possessed by the average American."

"There are two things," I replied, "which you must remember: First, that the stories are for children of all classes, and many, surely, of the working classes, would have no knowledge of them; secondly, my experience as a schoolmaster has shown me how shockingly ignorant of the ordinary Bible narrative are children of even well-to-do parents who have been in the habit of attending church regularly. I feel sure that, if you were to ask the examiners at Oxford in the pass Divinity schools, they would quite bear out what I say, that even young men who move in good society and have been for several years at a boarding-school, where they hear four lessons in chapel every Sunday, to say nothing of the others they hear on week-days, often know practically nothing about the Bible. Hence, I do not think we need be much surprised if children show great ignorance on ordinary Bible subjects, though I grant that the simpler tales, such as the one I have given, might reasonably be expected to be known to all."

" Does Professor Adler," Mrs. Hindley asked, " clearly bring out the various moral points involved in the story ? He seems to omit much of what is of primary importance, as, for instance, the serpent's characteristic exaggeration of the hardship of the command laid on the children."

"I am afraid the omission is mine, Mrs. Hindley. That is a point on which the author expressly dwells, with others which I have passed by for shortness. Thinking it would take too much of our time if I gave the account in full, I contented myself with merely a summary, but shall be happy to lend the book to any one who would like to go further into the matter. Of course, the main lesson in this story is obedience."

"I do not like," said Mrs. Reynolds, "taking sacred stories and dressing them up just as you please, with all the reference to God left out."

" Yet surely," said Mrs. Hindley, " as for dressing them up, that is what we all do when we tell children the stories for the first time, and I do not think many people would raise an objection to our bringing them within the measure of a child's understanding."

" Would it not be better to read them just as they stand in the Bible ? "

" It hardly follows, does it," said my wife, " that children would understand every point ? They constantly ask questions for further explanation. We must adapt our teaching, religious and moral, as well as intellectual, to a child's capacity to understand it, and you know how much greater hold a decorated story has over children than a bald narrative. It suits their imaginative turn. I do not think I should object to the method of treatment on the ground of departure from the original version."

"And as to the other point," I put in, "I should like to read you a note which Professor Adler gives: 'I would add to what has been said in the text, that the pupils are expected to return to the study of the Bible, to read and re-read these stories, and to receive a progressively higher interpretation of their meaning as they grow older. If in the above I have spoken in a general way of a father and his two children, it will be easy for the Sunday-school teacher to add later on that the father in the story was God.' I think that meets your objection, Mrs. Reynolds, does it not?"

"In one way, yes; but why should not the religious side be taught from the first?"

"We discussed that question with your husband the other morning, when we first fell on to this topic, and our aim was to try and find out whether it was possible to do anything for morality apart from religion, religion to be the natural outcome of moral teaching, but instruction in it left in the main to different hands from those which concern themselves with morality pure and simple. And Professor Adler begins his book with a discussion of the reasons for and against the possibility of unsectarian moral instruction, and assuming himself to have proved his position that such instruction is not only possible but desirable, at all events under the educational conditions prevailing in the United States, he treats the questions throughout purely from the moral side, leaving, as I have shown you, the religious aspect to be developed by the proper and professed religious teachers; but he is very far from being antagonistic to religion.

"I will now resume my analysis of the book. Professor Adler treats a number of other stories as he treated that of Adam and Eve, some in detail, others in suggestion; and then points out that, in the legislation ascribed to Moses, there are a number of simple rules fitted for children which should be drawn up in the form of a regular table, and committed to memory and recited in chorus. They are far more extensive than the Ten Commandments. But he warns us especially that the rules must be quite simple, and what he proposes in his course of instruction is to content himself at first with moral pictures, and only get on to deducing moral rules when the children are advancing in their store of moral facts. And there is another very wise caution that he gives—chiefly, indeed, in connection with the fables—that we must study the conditions under which the tales had birth, so as to grasp their exact spirit and thus be able with more decision to reject those which may be unsuitable. Many, for instance, of the well-known fables, coming from the servile races of Asia, inculcate passive obedience to tyrants—a doctrine it is certainly not desirable to teach under present conditions in the West. I would only propose that, when the children have begun to feel their legs to some extent in the matter, these stories might be taken in order to exercise them in detecting the faults of morality involved. They would thus serve instead of every-day instances, which are not always ready to hand."

"Ah," said the Doctor, "I am glad of that remark, as it leads on easily to an objection I want to raise. This teaching of stories and exposition of their morality is all very well, but does it go beyond intellectual knowledge? Our aim is practice. It is true we cannot have a perfect practice without scientific knowledge behind it, but then, I fear, it is even more true that knowledge without practice is of no avail at all. Now will you tell us what means—for I have forgotten—Professor Adler suggests for securing to the children opportunities of practice? Instruction after all is not education."

"That, my dear Hindley, you surely remember, is one of the points on which Adler himself is very strong. But he regards the practice, or some of it—the habits—as coming first, and the instruction as following on. His words are these: 'The function of moral instruction is to explicate in clear statements fit to be grasped by the intellect the laws of duty which underlie the habits. The value of such intellectual statements is that they give a rational underpinning to moral practice, and, furthermore, that they permit the moral rules to be applied to new cases not heretofore brought within the scope of habit.' Now I am not quite sure that I personally should agree with the order of precedence which he suggests. Of course, it is only a logical precedence; in practice the two must go on together. Thus far, however, I will grant that he is right: that in most cases the child must have some experience of the duty in hand before a course of lessons on it can be of use. But his statement seems rather to imply that the habit must first have reached a high development, and, if so, I disagree. It seems to me that only a very rudimentary conception of the duty is required, and that the habit will grow all the faster and more securely if at once enforced by arguments in support. The arguments, of course, must be adapted to the powers. If they are deferred, we may get defective habits firmly rooted by imperfect trainers, and our work will be doubled, if it is not killed. Yet, I have no doubt that, were we able to discuss together cases as they arise, we should not find much divergence in our actual practice. So you see, Hindley, Dr. Adler, like yourself, is alive to the fact that instruction is not the sole thing or the chief; he makes it subsidiary to education and practice."

"Yes, but still you have not got my point quite fully. You know that in science, as well as in education, one is constantly testing to see if the pupils are able to apply their knowledge. Now, where are you going to test like that in morals? You dare not invent test cases—the avoidance of temptation is the great rule in morality: how, then, can you know if the knowledge is really practical? Professor Adler, I think, hardly tackles just this point."

"No, I think not; at least, I cannot recall it at present."

"Then, after all, his moral education—— "

"The express title of his book is *Moral* INSTRUCTION *of Children*."

"Well, then, his moral instruction is moral instruction, and not practice, and, much as I admire his book, I am disappointed."

"I do not know why you should be disappointed at a book not containing what it does not profess to contain."

"I am not exactly disappointed at the book, but disappointed generally. I hoped we were going to be saved the difficulty of worrying out for ourselves what is really the cardinal point—how to practise children in the virtues. But I suppose we shall have to set about it, and meantime I think the plan you suggested, that we might use the morally defective tales and fables as a kind of intellectual exercise on the application of rules learnt, a very happy one."

"It certainly corresponds to a common practice in intellectual education, that of setting faulty examples to be corrected. I am aware that many high authorities condemn the practice altogether, on the ground that the learner should see only perfect models; but I think the objection is overstrained."

"Would you think it overstrained in moral education, which is on a different footing from intellectual?"

"Yes, I think I should call it overstrained even there, provided we use the faulty examples as I proposed, taking care that the children found out the faults and knew what was to be avoided. After all it is impossible—and for their future well-being perhaps undesirable—that children should be led by their rearing to suppose that the world contains nothing but good. They must learn early to know and to fight the bad. Of course I should take care to bring before their notice none but such defects as they might easily meet in their own career at their given age."

"Oh, Mr. Trelawney," put in Mrs. Hindley, "do you remember some time back a certain remark about not showing boys any cases of the breach of *oratio obliqua* rules till those rules were thoroughly imbedded? I think you applied a strong term to any master who chose to go on a different line. You even called him a fool; and pray, what are you doing now?"

Our friends all laughed, while I said:—

"Now, Mrs. Hindley, you are both merciless and vindictive. *Is* this a right spirit in which to discuss so sacred a subject as moral education?"

"Ah, yes," Mrs. Hindley replied, "it is all very well, but you cannot get off so easily. Pray, what about consistency?"

"Oh, consistency is a scarecrow made to frighten politicians. I ought to have been more careful in my former statement and put in a qualification, that it was necessary to warn pupils against the apparent breach of the rules at times. This done, to make the passage conform to regular rules would then be valuable practice. And it is just the same with the proposed fables. But if you do not mind, I should like to defer this question till we have been over the whole ground; for it seems to me we shall see as we go along more clearly where the mere instruction requires supplementing by practice. So if you have no objection, I will return to Dr. Adler.

"The next point, you remember, to tales from the Bible was tales from the Iliad and Odyssey. Of his method of treating the latter, Professor Adler gives us several beautiful specimens; but I will not go into them at length, as my illustration from the Bible is sufficiently typical of his whole proceeding. With the Iliad he contents himself with throwing out suggestions, and then, stimulated as we are by the beauty of his sketch, he takes us out next beyond the range of the primary into what he calls the grammar course, and lands us in the midst of lessons on duties.

"Now it is clear that in order to be thorough it is necessary to have a classification of duties. I have already given you, in brief, the classification Professor Adler adopts, and do not intend to criticise it now. We may have to return to the point later on. I shall at present only summarize his actual proposals.

"The new part of the book opens with theory. In the primary course the aim, says the author, was to lead to the formation of moral percepts; in the grammar course we advance to concepts—from observation, that is, and collection of instances we now are to pass to generalization. But the generalizations we are at present concerned with are not the largest and most comprehensive, those which are the business of moral philosophers; but the smaller and secondary generalizations on which the world is practically agreed. He illustrates his meaning by the virtue of truthfulness. He says that on quitting the primary stage the child will have grasped the general maxim against untruthfulness, but room will be left for the multitude of doubts arising under exceptional conditions. Hence what we want is a general rule fitted to cover those exceptions too. How are we to get it? The author starts with a case where the children would condemn without hesitation a statement as a lie, and emphasizes, in passing, the importance of getting the children themselves to take part in the discussion. After several instances he suggests as a definition that the statement does not correspond with facts. Were then the old astronomers liars when they declared that the sun went round the earth? Certainly not. Yet their statements did not correspond with facts. Suppose we take, then, conformity to fact. Still there is the difficulty that a statement may appear to be in literal conformity with the fact, and yet be nothing but a contemptible lie. Cases in point, too, are mental reservations. A further alteration then. Shall we say, 'Intend that thy words shall correspond to the essential facts'? But even this is not enough. We are sometimes justified in telling a lie, to the insane, for example, or the sick. For this we find justification in the fact that language as a means of human intercourse must further the rational ends of life. Details in proof of this statement are then given, and finally we arrive at some such formula as this: Intend to communicate the essential facts to those who are capable of making a rational use of them."

"Surely, Mr. Trelawney," interposed Mrs. Reynolds, "you cannot approve of laying such exceptional cases before children. It will upset their belief in truthfulness altogether."

"Professor Adler himself refers to the danger, but he points out—and I can support him from recollections of my own childhood and from a pretty extensive observation since—that children know well that there are some cases when no one tells the truth save a moral fanatic, and that this knowledge, if we admit no exceptions to our rule, will lead to the very result you fear—a disbelief in the imperativeness of truth altogether. It is no good shutting our eyes to facts and pretending not to know of the sharp-sightedness of children. Honesty is imperative in all our dealings. To illustrate the difficulty a child may have in reaching a satisfactory criterion for himself, may I tell a story of my own younger days? You will certainly be amused, but it will show you how one who is very conscientious—a fanatic, perhaps, to use our author's term—may make the rough maxim into an idol, whether its effects be good or bad. When I was at college, just beginning ethics, one of my tutors put to me this question: 'Suppose you were in a wood and had just parted from a friend, when some robbers came up and asked where he had gone. What would you do? Would you speak the truth or not?' I thought for a little time and decided for the truth. Well do I remember the force of the reply and the shock it gave me: 'Then if I were a judge, I should not hesitate for a moment in sentencing you to several years' penal servitude.' Of course, in argument, the case is not uncommon, but my rearing had been strict in notions of truth-telling, and though, when asked the question, I felt a slight hesitation, I had never got hold of any ground on which to justify disregard of truth. Now I say that it was absolutely wrong that I, brought up as a boy at a public school, and not then fresh to the University, should, at the age of twenty as I then was, be unable from nothing but overconscientiousness to see my course clear along the right path in a case so simple as that."

"I quite agree with you, Trelawney," said the Doctor; "but it was just like you."

"Is that a compliment or the reverse?" I asked, with a laugh. "However, I do not know that that matters much at present. I simply give the case in answer to Mrs. Reynolds as an illustration of the need of proper training. Of course, it is all-important that the difficulty be not raised till the children have grasped firmly the main principle,—please note, Mrs. Hindley, how I can learn,—and until they have reached such an age or such development that they are likely to begin to ask the question themselves. Indeed, that is a point which is always fundamental: we must suit our teaching to the children's capacities, and never begin subjects till nature suggests them. In all things nature must be our guide."

"Is that in Adler, too?" asked Reynolds.

"Most assuredly, though I hardly imagine that any thinking man will question the truth of it. And yet I do not know; on the side of the intellect the analogous rule is constantly violated."

"In fact," said Dr. Hindley, "as I urged some time

ago, right knowledge does not guarantee right practice."

"No; but for the present we put that question aside."

"It seems to me," said Mrs. Hindley, "your present is for ever."

"Now really, Mrs. Hindley, I call that unkind. But sarcasm, no matter how cutting, shall not stir me from my path. So I will return at once to our friend Adler.

"Taking the duty of acquiring knowledge first, he starts by telling stories in illustration, choosing those of Cleanthes and Hillel; and, if I may add a parenthesis, I should say the average boy would be greatly taken by the story as such, but afterwards would be found reflecting to himself, 'Catch me being such a fool——' "

"There you are, Trelawney," interrupted the Doctor, "flippant as usual. Really, Mrs. Trelawney, you must teach your husband better. There may be some excuse for flippancy when a friend is propounding a theory; but when he is propounding it himself—— I shall really have to hold an investigation *de lunatico inquirendo*."

"Be calm, be calm, my dear fellow," I replied. "You forget I am here merely giving Adler's views."

"But you said that where you did not express dissent we were to take it that you agreed."

"And did not my flippancy, as you heartlessly call it, expressly show my dissent? I am not prepared to bow down to all Adler's instances, though with his main lines I am in hearty accord. And my remark I did not mean to be flippant in spirit, whatever its expression may have seemed. I do really believe that what I said would represent the attitude of an average boy, at least to these illustrative tales. It is fortunate they are not essential to the scheme. But to proceed. After the tales, Adler takes the points raised—the value of knowledge for various reasons—and gives headings for what we may roughly call a topical lecture. He adds one very practical suggestion, that the teacher, after going through the points in the abstract, should take the various school subjects and explain the value of each. That is a procedure, as he says, far too commonly neglected. Were it adopted more, we might perhaps hear less of the many unreasoning arguments urged against the classics. He says, too, we should make clear how various other school virtues are contributory to this one, and so reduce our moral knowledge to an organized correlated whole.

"Next come the duties relating to the physical life, such as avoidance of suicide, and practice of cleanliness and temperance, closely related to which he makes those which concern the feelings—fear, anger, and the like. I could go through the whole list, but it is unnecessary, especially as we may have to make a scheme for ourselves. After these are placed duties relating to others, under the two great sub-divisions of filial—covering especially reverence —and fraternal duties. Then drawing what seems an awkward distinction, Adler proceeds to treat of duties towards all men. Under these he puts justice and charity, into which he enters in some detail, the duty of gratitude, duties to servants, and, oddly enough, duties as regards animals, where, I must confess, I felt rather a shock; for his first words are, 'I cannot admit that we have duties towards animals.' My impulse was at once to reply that I should rather say our duties towards them were from one point of view even more imperative than our duties towards our fellow-men, for the latter can defend themselves and force their rights to be recognised —an impossibility with the brute beasts. Moreover, I am even inclined to go further, though you may think me a mere sentimentalist, and say that we have duties to the vegetable creation also, for

> ' 'Tis my faith that every flower
> Enjoys the air it breathes.'

That, however, is to raise an unnecessary question now, and I will only say that Professor Adler's distinction ends rather in logical subtlety than in any practical difference. For he continues thus: ' We cannot very well speak of duties towards creatures on which we in part subsist; but there are duties with respect to animals.'"

"It is a good thing," said my wife, "that Professor Adler does not live in a cannibal country."

"Yes," I replied; "and, indeed, I do think in treating this subject his ardour rather cools."

"Perhaps he is a vivisectionist," said Mrs. Hindley, "and is afraid of being posed."

"I am sure I cannot say: I only give you the impression he leaves on my mind. He falls largely back on what Froebel recommended—the keeping of tame animals—no, I beg his pardon, not quite that; he merely says, 'Get your pupils interested in the habits of animals. Familiarity in this case will breed sympathy.' He then refers to bees and beavers. Now, for my own part, I would say this: that just as the highest test of a thorough gentleman is his treatment of those who are socially his inferiors, so much so that he would, if he must show discourtesy, be discourteous to an equal rather than to them, so the highest test of a man's moral development is often to be found in his treatment of dumb animals. I do not mean those which he may have brought up, or which may belong to him,—for in that case many brutes might claim high morality,—but especially of those creatures in which he has no direct interest, on which, in fact, he may look with a certain amount of loathing."

"Bravo!" cried Mrs. Hindley; "then you are a Socialist after all."

"Does Professor Adler take any notice of the use of animals for food?" asked Reynolds.

"Yes; but not at great length. He says, with apparently some hesitation, that 'the highest point of view to take is this, that man is, so to speak, the crucible in which all the utilities of nature are refined to higher spiritual uses,' and that, as he puts all nature to his service—trees, metals, clay, flowers—so 'he may actually absorb the life of the lower animals, in order to transform and transfigure it, as it were, into that higher life which is possible only in human society. But it follows that he is a mere parasite and an interloper in nature, unless he actually leads the truly human life.' A very curious and, to me, an unsatisfactory argument. I wonder how it would seem to us to be transformed and transfigured in a similar way?"

"Don't you think," said Reynolds, "that the Divine purpose is to transform and transfigure us in some such way?"

"Perhaps; but according to the ordinary theory, we shall enjoy a conscious immortality and be able to estimate the gain that has resulted from our sufferings here on earth. Animals, however, have no such compensation."

"I think it monstrous," said Mrs. Hindley, "that any one should believe he is destined to attain immortality himself and be quite content to leave his loved pets and dumb friends to an endless death—a death without a hope."

"Well, Trelawney," said the Doctor, "you are very strong against Adler. How would you justify the use of animals for food?"

"Ah, there you have me. I really do not know."

"Then why are you so hard on poor Adler?"

"Surely I may criticise a feeble argument, without being able to produce a better."

"Yes; but I think the question, as well as that of vivisection, may have to be solved before we stop, and I must confess I expect you as our guide to choose distinctly one side or the other."

"Oh, dear!" I said, "I really did hope I should not have let myself in for these questions. They seem to me to be cases where practice contravenes every moral consideration, and yet where we can hardly abandon the practice. But I will do as I always do—postpone them!"

"No, no; let's have them now," they all cried, and Mrs. Hindley added, "We know you too well to let you off this time."

"No, seriously, I positively cannot tackle the question now. In the first place, I do not know why you should expect me to stand up here to be criticised. It was the Doctor who was going to give his views on things, not I."

"But you pushed yourself forward," Mrs. Hindley put in, "just in accordance with the character your wife gives you—that you can never be silent when others are talking and take the second place."

"Doctor, you really must intercede with your wife, or else use your husbandly authority. Because I offended her once, she is most remorseless. However, even if I have thrust myself in——"

"You may be sure," said the Doctor, "I do not resent it, especially as we are discussing methods of instruction, on which you, as a practical teacher, must be far better qualified to speak than I."

"Yes, perhaps there is something in that. But I was going to say as my second reason, that the question is really out of place now, for our present object is to review a complete method of moral instruction. Whereas later on, when we have left Professor Adler and are suggesting our own views on various topics, this and similar questions will come in naturally and in their proper logical place."

"Yes, that is a point certainly," said Reynolds. "Well, if we let you off now, will you promise us not to forget what we have postponed?"

"Oh, never fear," said Mrs. Hindley. "I will remind him."

At this there was a laugh; but I said, "Well, after all, I will just give my opinion now and let the matter slide. The only justifications I can find for vivisection and taking life to supply ourselves with food are, first, analogy from the arrangements of nature, which has produced many a flesh-eating animal; secondly, the fact that we are masters of the earth, and if our interests and those of our inferiors come into conflict, our inferiors must give way. Might, in fact, in this case, seems to give right."

"Well, Trelawney," said the Doctor, "I don't think your second point worth a moment's consideration. It is merely Adler's argument in other words—altered very considerably for the worse."

"Yes, I feel that myself, but cannot help it," I said. "I give you my view for what it is worth, and shall be only too glad to let the subject drop. I still think that in this case morality and practice are incompatible, and yet practice cannot give way. But let us resume our analysis of Adler.

"We have been over nearly all the different heads of duty. There remains, however, one very important branch, newly discovered, or rather re-discovered, that aspect of duty called the duty of a citizen. Here Professor Adler proposes to emphasize three political ideas: the idea of the supremacy of the law, the true idea of punishment, and the idea of nationality. The school, as he shows, affords an excellent starting-point for developing the two former ideas. Incidentally he makes a good remark—that school government should rest as far as possible on the willing consent and co-operation of the governed—a thought which would have almost turned grey with horror the hair of some good old pedagogues of the past, though now, happily, if not always carried out to conscious thoroughness, the maxim has become almost an accepted rule, at least in this country. Further, he dwells on another point we all admit now—the value of the discipline of games. As to the development of the idea of nationality, that should be done through the history of our country, the different periods being so treated as to bring the different moral ideas which swayed the nation at each point into high relief. At the same time he warns us against Chauvinism, and as an antidote proposes universal history, taught in such a way as to throw into prominence the contributions made by different nations to the history of the whole human race. Further, there should be a brief exposition of the various functions of government, but this is to be subsidiary to the other point."

"In that respect," said Reynolds, "he differs widely from the enthusiasts on this side of the water, who are turning instruction in civic duty in the direction which we English find so hard to avoid,—the purely practical,—so that the teaching is in danger already of becoming merely another subject for intellectual mastery—and examination."

"You are surely rather hard," I said, " though I admit the danger. But you know how difficult a task it is to keep clear of cram and confine oneself strictly to the developing side of a subject, when examinations are looming ahead. But to return to our muttons, as the saying goes. Professor Adler concludes his book with two short chapters —one on the use of proverbs and speeches, and another, consisting merely of a few cautions and recommendations about the collection of evidence for each child's character, on the way to individualize moral training. As to proverbs, he regards them as mines of wisdom not easily to be exhausted, and compares them to pegs on which the memory can hang long chains of moral reflection. For speeches, he would like some of those which are full of high moral sentiment, such as parts of Isaiah, and the speech of Socrates before his judges, to be carefully explained, and then recited by the pupils. The mere recitation, he truly says, makes one for the time assume the character of the speaker, and so retain a permanent mark. This is a profound truth which other nations, and notably the Americans, seem to have realized in their ordinary curriculum. I have long wished that we applied it more.

"Thus, then, save for a brief summary and the appendix I have mentioned on manual training, the book ends. I am afraid I have kept you a very long time, but it seems to me a contribution of such high value to the part of moral education which it considers that it could not well be lost labour to go over it at some length. It will, at all events, be needless for us to propound a new method, so that in the long run we shall have gained time rather than lost it."

IV

FOR a minute or two there was silence; we all felt that we had come to the end of a long and difficult stage on our journey. At last Mrs. Hindley broke the silence by saying:—

"We are not a society, but I think we owe thanks to Mr. Trelawney for introducing to our notice so valuable a book. I for one shall get hold of it, and study it closely as soon as ever I can."

"I must confess that the general impression left on me," said Reynolds, "is that there is very great danger of the development of casuistry. You remember we referred to this point some time ago. You said then, Trelawney, that you looked upon that danger as one of the most serious that could attend moral training; yet now you seem to defend it."

"No; I still maintain that the danger is very grave. But on further reflection, I have come to the conclusion that I rather overstated the strength of my views, and I think that is valid which Dr. Hindley urged in answer, that the responsibility rests with the teacher. After all, whatever our methods, a good man will produce a good result, and a bad man a bad result, though method may help either to attain a higher ground. And if, as the Doctor said, the teacher is alive to the danger of evoking a casuistical spirit, then he must when needful change his procedure. And really, at bottom, all this moral instruction, valuable as I admit it to be, I cannot help regarding as quite subsidiary to the influence—largely intangible and unconscious—which a man of high moral ideals will produce without perhaps direct teaching at all. I grant the value of knowing what is right, but for practice, in the long run, we must rely upon example. If that is bad, no amount of good instruction will ever produce the effect we wish."

"But you are rather evading the point," replied Reynolds. "I gather that you abandon your previous position, that the danger is so great as to require us not to run any, even the slightest, risk of incurring it—no, not though great advantages accrue to the individual, or even to the mass?"

"Yes; I should prefer to safeguard myself by securing that only those were allowed to instruct in morals who were both of exceptionally high character themselves and greatly experienced in other teaching—who to a special knowledge of the theory of morals added great success with children in other subjects. Not every tyro should attempt the work. Training would be essential in this subject above all."

"You have then come round to the Doctor's opinion, and quite leave out of sight the great value of faith?"

"Will you define faith?"

"For the present purpose I mean a willingness of learners to accept a declaration that something is wrong without always wanting the why and the wherefore."

At this Mrs. Hindley fired up, and exclaimed passionately:—

"Oh, yes, our old friend obscurantism. Of the two I would rather have a casuistical spirit than the dulness of unreflecting right action which never leads you any further."

"Then I think, Mrs. Hindley," said Reynolds, in a graver tone, "you are likely to be almost alone in your opinion."

"But what would you do to secure progress?"

"Let men of ripe years lead the way."

"But on your proposal you will only have one, where, if moral instruction were imparted to all, you might have a hundred."

"The world has waited many thousand years, and can, no doubt, wait thousands more. As Christianity grows and spreads, morality will advance."

"I really cannot in the least understand," Mrs. Hindley began again, "why so many zealous Christians are afraid of others helping on their work. But I think we had better drop the argument; it is quite clear that Mr. Reynolds's position cuts at the very basis of the system we are expounding; I am afraid we shall never convert him, and I am quite sure he will never convert me. On this point it is manifest we shall part company."

"Is not the divergence," my wife said, "more a matter of degree than of principle? I suppose we should all admit that it is not possible to explain everything to a child at once. Some things he is bound to take on trust."

"No doubt," said Mrs. Hindley; "but I am morally convinced that is not all Mr. Reynolds means."

"No; I say quite openly I mean a vast deal more than that. I mean that it is, considering the dangers, far better that a child should not be taught to reason on morality at all, but look upon moral law as irrevocable, unswerving, to be obeyed at whatever risk. On the religious ground I do not touch."

"There I must dissent," I said. "As a schoolmaster I am bound to hold that the best action is the most intelligent."

"Yes; but you have already confessed yourself a renegade, so we shall not value your opinion too highly. But does not Adler himself touch on this question?"

"Oh, yes," I said. "It is one of the difficulties he clears —perhaps in deference to you I should say, tries to clear— out of the way. In a searching passage he points out that he suggested for the first period only *Anschauung*, or, roughly, observation leading on to habit, and reserved analysis till the grammar stage. Then after referring to the limitations of custom, that it is quite powerless in presence of a new set of circumstances, he says at the same time that moral rules must not break the force of habit. Hence he says this: 'He—*i.e.* the teacher—should always take the moral habit for granted. He should never give his pupils to understand that he and they are about to examine whether, for instance, it is wrong or not wrong to lie. The commandment against lying is assumed, and its obligation acknowledged at the outset. The only object of the analysis is to discern more exactly what is meant by lying, to define the rule of veracity with greater precision and circumspectness, so that we may be enabled to fulfill (*sic*) the commandment more perfectly.' And then he insists on the helpfulness of externals—moral earnestness in the teacher, pictures of noble men and women on the walls, and perhaps songs, but above all instruction by word of mouth, for the due flow of the desired moral influence is hindered by the use of books. On the whole he does not seem to think the difficulty so great as we have feared. But the spirit of the instruction is the essential point."

"One thing struck me about the suggested plan," said Mrs. Hindley, "and that is that Professor Adler draws too hard and fast a line between the elementary and more advanced stages—the primary and grammar stages I think are his terms."

"And," added my wife, "though he does, you say, refer to the endowments of children by the time they reach school age, he does not seem to give us much information how they are to be brought up till that age is reached; while, if we may infer from what you told us, my dear, he seems to consider that the whole business is finished at about fifteen or sixteen."

"I beg your pardon," I replied; "quite the contrary. He refers more than once to questions which had better be left for the more advanced period of training, questions which he says he hopes to treat at length on some other occasion. You must not suppose his subject is co-extensive with our present enquiry. And your first objection can be met by a similar argument; he has apparently meant to limit himself, though his title does not imply it, to education at school, not at home. As for Mrs. Hindley's point, which seems just, I think Professor Adler would defend himself by saying that the criticism is more verbal than real, and that, so far as real, the difficulty is unavoidable. It is a difficulty which faces every one who discusses life in the abstract—certainly in our present enquiry we shall meet it again and again. We are obliged to treat the separate parts of our subjects separately, and for clearness to make logical divisions; yet when we come to practice, we find the closest connection between those logically separated parts. And as for the special instance we are now considering, it must be remembered it is a branch of instruction, and there always comes a time in teaching any subject when a leap of some kind proves inevitable. It is never possible, with teaching in classes at any rate, so to graduate your subject that there shall never seem a clear line of demarcation. I would go further and say that even if it were possible, it by no means follows that it is always desirable. A boy often gets a great stimulus from being put on some distance ahead of the point he seemed to have last reached. Of course, it has to be done carefully, but human arrangements cannot equal the gradual subtlety and complexity of nature. I have little doubt, Mrs. Hindley, that in practice you and Dr. Adler would quite agree."

"May I venture on another criticism?" said the Doctor. "I think Professor Adler's view is not wide enough. He seems to limit himself entirely to an improvement in the practice of current morals, without considering their future evolution or ever setting up a true ideal. Now I hold that the most rapid advance in morals is likely to come from setting before people such different ideals from those now in vogue that the mere force of contrast will stimulate them to think, and thinking once begun I have no doubt of the result. It is to get people to think that is the supreme difficulty. But of this there seems nothing in Adler."

"That, I think, is true; he limits himself to an express improvement in the carrying into practice of current moral codes, and does not profess to start a new ideal. But no doubt he would have said that as his book was meant for a present practical purpose, and not as an attempt to sketch an ideal code with the best means of attaining it, such a procedure would be quite out of place. And I must confess, Doctor, that your method has great risks. You may propound such a scheme that people will only shrug their shoulders and scoff: 'Pooh!' they will say, 'he's a mere idle dreamer—nothing whatever to be learnt from him'; and then what good have you done?"

"You will have set some people thinking, at all events."

"Perhaps; but you may reach no one at all. I am by no means convinced that Adler is not wiser in setting to work at what lies just before him, instead of running after what I fear may prove the empty, delusive will-o'-the-wisps which you introduced to us earlier this evening as well as the other day."

"Now I do call that hard lines," said the Doctor. "Just when I thought I had made a convert, you throw cold water, ice-cold water, on the whole of my pet dream. I really did think I had got one supporter."

"Oh, you know, Doctor, I always criticise—it is my bent. And besides, you know I have expressly declared that I am merely investigating; it will be a long time before I give in my adhesion to any professedly complete theory, if indeed I ever do."

"Well," said Mrs. Hindley, "I propose that we get on. We certainly have yet a vast deal to do, and it is no good wasting time on idle recriminations."

"Hear, hear!" I said. "Let us commit ourselves to nothing, but make suggestions. I think it would be well, as we have now expounded the method of instruction to be used at school, and, *mutatis mutandis*, also at home, to go over the ground we have already traversed, and see what yet remains to be done. Who will undertake the job?"

"I think you had better," said Mrs. Hindley, "as your interest is the most direct. Moreover, you have been taking the place of prominence of late."

"Very well, I will try; but in the further exposition the Doctor will have to resume his place."

"No; I think by now we are more in your province: but we can settle that question by-and-bye. Meantime proceed."

"I need hardly go over the Doctor's conditions which we recapitulated at the beginning of the evening. Nor do I propose to state in detail the points which Professor Adler has emphasized, save to remind you that his procedure is a method of instruction based upon strict educational principles. One of these is very obvious—our advance must be from simple to complex. A second, to which the author himself constantly draws attention, is that we must go from the known to the unknown—a maxim which, in this particular case, shows that we must treat the different points of morality, not as arranged in a logical system, but as they appear in the life-history of the child. This is an important consideration to which we shall probably have to return, when devising our own complete scheme. Thirdly, we must make our instruction interesting and, above all, earnest. As for practice, we have so far only come to the conclusion that we can get the intellectual side of it developed by laying before the children cases of wrong action, and asking them to show wherein the wrongness lies, giving, as they grow older, reasons for their view. In this respect we rather diverge from Professor Adler, who would not have such tales of defective morality laid before children at all.

"Leaving now Professor Adler, whose very name I should think you must be tired of hearing, we will turn to the points we laid down for ourselves, which were in the main these. Dr. Hindley, with the keen-sightedness of a medical man, insists upon the paramount importance of attention to physical health first—the avoidance of what Mr. Herbert Spencer calls physical sins. Then we also had emphasized the importance of surroundings as shown alike in artistic and moral influences, in which connection we dealt with servants, and insisted above all things upon the duty of the mother towards her children. We laid it down, though not without some dissent, that the mother must sacrifice every part of her work rather than leave her children to others. We found that moral education begins at least as early as the cradle, and that one of the most valuable ways of promoting all kinds of development is to provide for the child companions of like age. For the most prominent characteristic of children is imitation, and therefore we say that however perfect a scheme of moral training we devise, what is of even more importance than the scheme itself is the character displayed by the trainer, and the necessity for the child always to see before him a lofty ideal loftily carried out. How much watchful attention and self-denial this provision requires from all educators, I need hardly say. We must, moreover, be constantly on the watch, and have all our commands obeyed without fail. Uncertainty of discipline is worse than none, for it encourages the spirit of gambling."

"That is an inserted remark," said Mr. Reynolds. "I am sure we never had it before."

"No, I do not know that we had; but I think it was hinted, and you must forgive me if occasionally I amplify what was said. If you object, we will postpone the point and discuss it later. But to proceed. The formation of habits is of the first importance, and it was in this connection that we learnt the imperative need of watchfulness. Further, we found that moral advance cannot go to the full without advance upon all lines at once—every circumstance produces influence upon a human being. We found, too, that in morals above all the wise proverb holds good, ' Prevention is better than cure.' We saw the importance of exact observation and of child study generally ; only by the collection of scientifically observed facts can we hope to improve on our present makeshift methods. Observation of children whose training has been defective is in this regard of especial value. We discussed at some length three of childhood's chief virtues—obedience, purity, and truth ; and in connection with the last in particular found that most people would say that the ideal standard is quite beyond any reformer's attainment in the present state of society."

" Oh ! " put in Mrs. Hindley. But I proceeded :—

" However, we are, I believe, sketching an ideal. Incidentally we realized that education in parental duties would be an indispensable part of all moral training. We laid down three points as of cardinal importance—the cultivation of a constant habit of cheerfulness ; the development of a sense of far-reaching responsibility, our least act often having an unending effect ; and closely connected with this responsibility the need of habitual self-negation. The last two considerations in particular are the two pointers of our whole system. We are to keep our eyes fixed on them throughout ; by them all else is to be directed. Finally, we touched upon the proper place of faith, which is needful at first, but must by degrees retire before reason ; the danger of provoking a spirit of casuistry, when we most of us agreed that if the guiding mind is healthy there is but little to be feared ; and lastly, the position and relative functions of reason and habit in moral training. Here, I think, we might put our position thus: Habit is essential, as being the only sure guide in sudden emergencies, when one has not time to think out the pros and cons, and, above all, as being the only clue for young children—apart from reverence and faith in their elders—before their reason is adequately developed ; but in the end reason must always be present, either justifying and supporting the habit, or else leading to a modification. Reason is the supreme judge, though the case may not always be laid before him. But morality in which reason has no part, where mere custom is the sole guide, is dead, dead, dead.

"I think that constitutes a very fair sketch of the main principles on which we are agreed. Do you admit thus much?"

As there was general assent, except for a reservation by Mr. Reynolds of the right to a separate view on some points, I went on:—

"We have often stated that our search is for an ideal. But I am not quite clear in my own mind what this search means. You, Doctor, I think, are mainly responsible for the statement; will you, before we go further, definitely explain your thought, so that we may understand the exact relation between our inquiries and actual practice? At present it seems to me we are trying to kill two birds with one stone, and run a serious risk of bringing down neither."

"My position," said the Doctor, "is simply this. We are trying to discover how best to devise a scheme of moral education. We have first of all to see what are the conditions under which such a scheme can be worked to any purpose, and then to plan adequate methods for carrying it out under those conditions. Further, we are bound to explain to ourselves what we mean by moral, whether we are to be content with the current morality so far as it admits of advance and improvement without seeming absolutely impossible of attainment, or whether we wish to sketch a project which shall lead to the cultivation of the highest form of morality that is ever likely, I do not say to be realized, but even proposed. Now these three heads we have been rather confusing; but they ought to be kept, at least in thought, entirely distinct. I started with the first point I have named—the conditions; we then went on to the second—the method; but the third, which ought surely in logic to have come first, we have only touched incidentally. Shall we then discuss this question, whether it is worth while setting up a standard of morality quite beyond the range of practical politics, or whether we had better confine ourselves to the improvement—such as we may reasonably hope to effect—of the actual opinion and, in morals, practice of the present day?"

"Oh, you know," said Mrs. Hindley, "I quite agree with your opinion. It is impossible to hope for a really great advance unless we can manage to startle into thinking. Mild revolutions are no good; dynamite attracts attention."

"Yes, and the policeman," said my wife. "I fear the only influence our hare-brained schemes will give us may be limited to the inside of a lunatic asylum."

"But it will surely in the end be possible," said Reynolds, "to make an allowance for present conditions, and so put in some practical suggestions without leaving out the enormous advantage which a lofty ideal necessarily brings."

"I am glad," the Doctor said, "that we have converted you at last. At first you were always raising the objection that my suggestions were quite hopeless for any practical effect."

"I did not at first see clearly whither you were tending, but when I did of course I fell in with your project. One who believes in Christianity is of necessity an idealist. But we must be prepared to suffer a certain loss from aiming too high."

"Don't you remember George Herbert's lines, my dear?" said Mrs. Reynolds,—

> "'Pitch thy behaviour low, thy projects high;
>   So shalt thou humble and magnanimous be;
> Sink not in spirit: who aimeth at the sky
>   Shoots higher far than he that means a tree.'"

"I am afraid I am in a minority," said my wife, "so I give up. We will not go into the question of the actual amount of gain or loss attending the two methods—the ideal and that which merely raises our current standard by a little. Let us take the ideal."

"Very well," said the Doctor, "let this then be henceforth understood, that we have our eyes on a moral ideal without of necessity hoping ever to attain it. At the same time we cannot reconstitute the world, and hence must have, at least as regards method, some reference to the constitution of modern society, or what seem possible developments of it. But on the score of feasibility no further objections can be raised.

"Bearing in mind then that we are erecting a very lofty, perhaps some may say, an unreal standard, we will go on to consider the other two points I raised. And first, for a moment, let us refer to the conditions under which we might hope for great success. Many a time you tried to upset me by objecting that my propositions were not feasible; but that objection we have agreed to debar. So the only question I have now to put is this: Does any one consider my proposals not desirable? If any one does, let him speak now, or for ever after hold his peace."

The Doctor paused a moment, and, as no one said anything, resumed:—

"Then I take it that you consider my sketch of conditions under which we might expect a healthy moral training as in themselves good, though I am not prepared to claim, nor would you assent if I did, that others may not suggest improvements. In no respect do I claim that my ideal is perfect; only that it sets in a clear light some neglected elements.

"We now come finally to the point I mentioned second—the methods of imparting a good moral training; and it is here that we have still a vast amount to do. We have seen what a good method can mean in the hands of a competent and trained teacher by the exposition which our host has given us of Professor Adler's suggestions; but I wish to repeat, what has already been noticed, that the method is confined solely to instruction, and instruction too of a formal type and at a given age."

"Doctor," I interposed, "you will remember that Professor Adler himself says that the training must be carried further than the subject he prescribed for himself allowed."

"Yes, I have not forgotten. I only wished to throw up clearly the task we have before us. That is twofold. First, to adapt the instructional methods already explained to home, the advanced years of school, and the University; for the discipline of life, which is the fourth period into which all training may be divided, can be left to take care of itself. Provided we have done well in the strictly educational years, the tone of life at large will rise and also its moral discipline. And, secondly, we have to consider the extent to which we can supplement instruction by experience, and review the various external conditions special to each period of training which can help or hinder, and that often materially, the growth of morality."

My wife here said,—

"The adaptation of Professor Adler's methods to the other periods in education ought to be a matter of no great difficulty; for certain rules of method for instruction always hold, no matter what the subject nor how advanced the pupil."

"Very well then," said the Doctor, "you being experienced in the matter of education both at school and at home, will perhaps, Mrs. Trelawney, relieve me of the duty of expounding method as regards young children."

With these words the Doctor rubbed his hands and looked delighted, while my wife began to protest that she had not thought out the subject, and could not be expected to do it justice. The Doctor, however, rejoined:—

"Now, Mrs. Trelawney, it is no good trying to make me believe that you are not able to deal with the matter effectively. I know you are thoroughly interested in education, well trained in it to boot; and that a thinking woman under such circumstances should not in the rearing of her own children have fitted method correctly to practice, I cannot believe."

Most of us expressed assent, but my wife still said:—

"There is a great difference between practice and the formulation of the rules which guide your practice. You can easily apply rules which you have long soaked in without being exactly conscious that you are doing so; but it requires not a little time and thought to arrange those rules and practice into a logical system."

"Mrs. Trelawney," the Doctor still went on, "I know that when the mind has been in the habit of living in familiar intercourse with an idea for a long time, and even applying it, however unconsciously, to practice, any one who, like yourself, has at all an analytical turn, and has had any training in exposition, will be able to express his ideas almost as well at a moment's notice as after long deliberation. Very often the heat of sudden exposition shapes the ideas into far better form than could ever be produced by the coolness of reflection, no matter how

I

prolonged, in the study beforehand. And even if you do not lay out your thoughts in perfect logical order, we will make all allowances; for, after all, we are but talking, not writing a philosophical treatise."

Here Mr. Reynolds interposed with the remark,—

"It seems to me that before we listen to Mrs. Trelawney we have a preliminary question of vast moment to settle; namely, what is to be our aim?"

"I thought that was settled long since," replied the Doctor: "the production of a perfectly moral man."

"An impossible attainment, I may remark in passing; but granted its possibility, still I would say your exposition is not sufficient. It is a vague generalization, and what we want, so to speak, are *media axiomata* within the reach of ordinary practice. We want some intermediate statements as to the questions we are going to discuss—definite declarations of the branches of morality we are specially proposing to treat."

"Oh, that is a more complicated matter."

"We shall have, I suppose," I said, "to take a leaf out of the philosophers' books, and arrange a classification of duties. Only by this means can we hope to avoid being lost in the dense wood of particular moral obligations."

"That is it," said Reynolds. "Now who will give us the classification?"

"I think," said Mrs. Hindley, "that either you or the schoolmaster ought to undertake the work. It is most nearly allied to your professions."

"Well," said Reynolds, "suppose you do it, Trelawney. If I remember rightly, you said Adler had a classification, and gave us a short summary of it. Let us start with that again, and, if we do not agree, modify it to suit our own purposes. What is his arrangement?"

"He says, first of all, that he wishes to keep clear of any implication of metaphysical or religious theories, such as are implied in most of the classifications propounded by the philosophers; and so he proposes to take for his 'guidance the objects to which duty relates, and disregard the sources from which it flows.' Here it would be well for us to follow him; for though it is true that we cannot be sure of being exhaustive unless our practice has a theory behind it, still practice is our aim rather than theory, and we must emphasize that side. Professor Adler points out that we owe duties to the following persons: (1) Ourselves; (2) Our fellow-men generally, on the common ground of their human nature; (3) Certain individuals among our fellow-men who stand to us in special relations. Into some of these relations we are born, from which fact spring, for instance, our duties to our parents, brothers, and sisters. Others we can voluntarily assume; but if we assume them, the duties they originate are as binding as those last mentioned. As a type may be taken the duties of husband or wife. Now to take the subdivisions. Class 1 comprises duties relating to our physical nature, to the intellect, and to the feelings; class 2, chiefly justice and charity; class 3, the family duties, natural or assumed; those originating in various professional relationships—*e.g.*, of employers and employed; our duties as citizens; and, finally, certain others of which Professor Adler says, ' The purely elective relationships of friendship and religious fellowship give rise to certain fine and lofty ethical conceptions, the discussion of which may fitly crown the whole course.' "

"I miss one point," said Mrs. Reynolds, "though I remember you said he introduced it. I mean our duties to the animals."

"There you will remember he takes a special position, and will only allow of duties as regards the animals, not duties towards them. He places them under the head of duties towards all men—rather an odd collocation of words."

"I should have thought they might better rank as a department by themselves," said Mrs. Reynolds, and I assented.

"But surely," said the Doctor, "his arrangement is not unnatural, though the wording may be odd. Are not our duties towards the animal creation merely an extension of some of the duties, sympathy, for instance, and charity, which we owe to all men?"

"Perhaps; but it will be only a small point of divergence if we part company in this way. Can anybody raise any other objection?"

"Most certainly," put in Mrs. Hindley. "It is utterly absurd to separate the family relationships from the duties to others. It may not lead to any practical harm, but I think it would be far more satisfactory to start by dichotomy, and divide thus: Duties must chiefly affect oneself, or they must chiefly affect others. Self-regarding duties again split into two—those which primarily affect the body, and those which primarily affect our other parts. These latter once more are twofold—on the one hand duties to the intellect, on the other duties to the emotions and the will, or, roughly speaking, to our moral side, our character. Other-regarding duties likewise branch into two—general and specific. Under the former come justice, generosity, and so on; under the latter our duties towards father and mother, brother and sister, husband or wife, and the members of our own profession, trade, guild, club, or whatever association it may be. Many of these might indeed be treated as but modifications of the duty of gratitude—one of our general duties to others. Civic duty too is little more than an enlargement of the same idea. So that I hold there are only two great main divisions of duty: the old ones of duties towards ourselves, and duties towards our neighbours."

"I suppose, then," Mrs. Reynolds added, "you also would class our duties towards animals under the head of our duties to others?"

"No; I forgot animals. I should make a separate class for them, as after all they do stand on a different footing from ourselves, and beginning my dichotomy higher up should start with the general group 'Duties to living things' and divide it into two branches—duties to animals and duties to men. For the vegetable creation, though I agreed with Mr. Trelawney's remarks some little time since, it is no use, I fear, to consider it now; but I am by no means sure our remote descendants will not think that we lived in outer darkness as we failed to admit there were duties in their case too."

"And what about the supreme duty of all," said Reynolds, "our duty towards God?"

"That," rejoined the Doctor, "does not at present come into consideration. It falls under religion, and you know we have expressly put religion on one side."

"I do not think," said my wife, "that our classification, whether Professor Adler's or Mrs. Hindley's, for our immediate purpose matters much: for after all what we shall have to consider is not the logical arrangement of duties, though that is a great help in avoiding omissions, but the proper educational order of treatment—an order which is and can only be the order of development, the order in which the various senses of the various duties begin to appear."

"That is practically," I said, "what Professor Adler aims at. He tries to group the various duties of each separate period of development round one predominant duty, so that there is a fixed centre to give a unity to the whole. The predominant duty varies at different ages and under different circumstances—at school, for instance, and at home."

"I am glad to hear that," my wife replied, "as it falls in exactly with what I have just said. But I wanted to add something more, viz. this, that the two classifications now proposed seem to embrace very much the same catalogue of duties, the only great difference, it appears to me, being the degree of importance attached to animals. This being so, we may, I think, conclude that we have before us the whole circle of duties. What then is its use? Not to give us the order of subjects to be treated, but only to help us to make quite certain that in the complete scheme we have omitted none. For my own part I do not hesitate to say that, if you insist on my giving an exposition, I shall certainly want some such corrective, as I shall have to take the duties in the order of their appearance, not in the order which logic may require."

"There is another point yet," said the Doctor. "We shall have to settle which of the duties are paramount— by which I do not mean what Professor Adler means by his 'predominant' duties, but which are, as it were, the final ones to which all others must tend. I have already for my own part emphasized the two which I consider more important than any others—the development of a sense of never-ending responsibility, and the necessity of complete self-abnegation."

"Surely both of these are merely general summaries of altruistic duties," said Reynolds.

"Of course they come under that heading, but it does not follow that it is unnecessary to specially name them.

For my own part I believe that the mere enunciation of them in a stringent form is one great step forward."

"I do not see," said Mrs. Hindley, "that much is to be gained by such generalizations. As Mr. Reynolds says, they are merely aspects of our duties to others, and should rather be regarded as separate duties than as a condition of all duties or a summary expression for all. Would it not be better to say that they are more important or more wide-reaching than other duties? But I hardly think they are entitled to override them."

"I disagree with you, my dear," replied the Doctor; "painful as it naturally is to me to have to adopt such a bold course, I am convinced that they can be taken as principles which will enlighten us as to our duty whenever we are in doubt."

"Well, to avoid what looks like a fruitless discussion," I said, "let us concede that these principles shall be expressly formulated and impressed upon our pupils. We shall still have the ground left open for further detail."

"I should say," said Reynolds, "that from one point of view no duty can be paramount. Every duty is a portion of the whole good, and so far can be neither better nor worse than its fellows. But granting the cases where duties clash, shall we not find their relative importance as we go along? For even if we do not actually treat of each virtue separately in our present discussion, I think our exposition ought to be such, I certainly hope it will, that we shall leave no doubt in the minds of our pupils as to the canons of reasoning to be applied whenever a conflict arises."

"Yes," I replied, "Reynolds, I think you have solved the difficulty. It only now remains to consider the necessary modifications of Professor Adler's methods, the special conditions and general rules which may be laid down for each stage of education, and, perhaps, at the end, the whole series of duties according to either his or Mrs. Hindley's catalogue. Either catalogue, we found, will prove tolerably exhaustive."

"Now, Mrs. Trelawney," Mrs. Hindley said, "we expect to be taught home-training by you. But I think, my dear," she added, turning to her husband, "it would be merciful not to press the matter now. It is already very late, and if we adjourn for a few days longer, we shall all of us have time to collect our thoughts, and Mrs. Trelawney in particular will not be able to plead that she has been set to a difficult task without adequate preparation. What do you say?"

The Doctor assented, as it was quite clear we could not finish our subject that night. So after a little discussion about the most convenient day for the continuation of our work—we finally decided on the following Tuesday week—our friends left us to find their respective ways home, while we retired to bed, thinking we had earned a good night's rest by no light mental work.

V

OUR next meeting was held at the Doctor's house, the appearance of which certainly bore out his wife's boast, that despite the time she bestowed on her children the household arrangements had not suffered much. Mrs. Hindley was indeed one of those women who seem never to touch a thing without improving it; full of refinement herself, she imparted to her surroundings that nameless charm which a woman of grace will often give without the least worry or even seeming to aim at it. She was bent, however, on the business we had in hand, and it was not long before she called upon my wife to begin her sketch of home education. We all turned to hear, and though I knew most of what was to be said, as my wife had often talked over points with me, I do not think I was the least interested hearer; for our discussions had been haphazard, and on some points we disagreed. However, I hope I listened attentively and have given an impartial reproduction of what actually passed.

My wife began by expressing her thankfulness that after all she had been forced to treat the subject; "for," she went on, "I did not know how much there was to consider till I came to arrange my thoughts in logical form. And further, my work has shown me how terribly deficient practice generally is, and not least my own. For this one result, if for no other, I have reason to be glad; for I trust that I shall not let my thoughts be barren, but that they will lead to better action, to the benefit of the suffering ones—my children. But I will not dwell more on personal matters, but will try what I can do to express clearly my views on the best way to teach and enforce morality in the home.

"And first, as to method. It seems to me quite clear that we cannot apply Professor Adler's method to any great extent in trying to train children from the age of nothing to the age of, say, six. Before the reasoning powers have shown themselves at all it is obviously impossible to attempt to train them. And this consideration leads me to lay down my first principle, which is that, as the aim of all moral education is to influence practice, we must teach the children to practise morality before we give them reasons for it. In short, we must do as we agreed long ago—develop a healthy habit first, and when that has struck its roots securely, then go on to explain the *rationale* of our action."

"Very true," said Mrs. Hindley; "but when would you begin the reasoning?"

"That depends: but it will be difficult before the child has learnt the meaning of words."

"But surely you would not deny that it is possible to train children to, at all events, elementary forms of reasoning long before they are able to speak? For instance, by the help of signs it would be easy to make a child understand the danger of playing with fire. We could put our fingers in the candle-flame and draw them out again very quickly with all the signs of being hurt. A child who knew that he might not touch fire would easily see the reason for the prohibition without going through the process himself."

"The experiment," I said, "would be far more effective if you let the child himself perform it."

"No doubt; but it is too dangerous, and if it were an act of the child's own, would not of necessity lead to reasoning."

"But," I went on, "is not this reasoning merely a process of the intellect?"

"All reasoning is."

"Well, if that is true, I do not think we are bound to discuss its methods when considering moral education. We must take our conditions from it ready made."

"I also," said my wife, "was going to object that in any case the reasoning could not be called ethical. It is reasoning about the sequence of physical events—about causes and effects."

"I beg your pardon," said Mrs. Hindley. "I adduced it as an argument on the necessity of obedience."

"Oh, I am sorry I did not quite see it in that light; but in that case of course my objection is void."

"Mine however," I interrupted, "is not. I still say that it would be better for the child to perform the experiment himself, and indeed I would say in any case this—that you must never try to teach the child anything till nature has shown indications of the need of it. That you know is one of Froebel's great principles. To go out of your way, as Mrs. Hindley suggests, to lay down a law about fire to be obeyed before the child has tried the experiment, I mean of course as long as you are by to watch, is a bad mistake in method. Such a case as you put, Mrs. Hindley, I therefore look upon as out of court."

"Well, perhaps," said Mrs. Hindley; "but it was only an illustration. I could replace it by another, were it worth while."

"I do not think that it is," said my wife. "I quite see your point and can imagine it might hold at times, though not, I think, often; though, as regards the actual instance you gave, I quite agree with my husband. Still, even though we grant that moral reasoning may begin in a crude form even before speech, it is impossible to lay down any rule in the abstract to be an infallible guide. We must in given cases use our own observation and check it by comparison with the detailed studies of infancy which have been published at different times. By such systematic scientific procedure we shall be led to notice the proofs of the budding of the different powers at the very first moment they appear, and further shall be able to interpret intelligently movements and indications of various kinds which to the unscientific seem quite without meaning. If every mother would keep a careful record of all the powers her child exhibits, with a statement of the date of their first appearance, we should in time have an invaluable record of——"

"Mother's nonsense," I interrupted.

"Mother's observation and scientific facts, sir!" my wife rejoined with an emphatic tone, which the Doctor supported by a look at me and the one word "Flippant!"

"It is true," my wife went on, "and that I suppose is what my incorrigible spouse there meant, that we should require to check one account by another, and should want some guarantee of the ability of the mother to scientifically observe at all. But if women were, as they should be, trained for the duties that will come on them as mothers, that point would be involved. Of course the finest accounts would live and the rest be discredited—the fate that overtakes every form of scientific investigation.

"But I must go on. In saying that we should aim at the establishment of habits, I should like to add that though we can scarcely reason at first, we can give that great reason which carries us so far,—which indeed is often taken as the final groundwork of morality, and which a child must for a time regard as sufficient,—that a thing is to be done because it is right, another thing not to be done because it is wrong. We are apt in discussing theories of morals to disregard the absolute nature of morality. Now I am not prepared to say that in the sphere of their investigations the moral philosophers are not justified in doing this; but for good education—our business at present—we are bound to at first treat morality as absolute. Hence I say, use this reason to a young child: 'The act is right because it is right, another is wrong because it is wrong.' As the child grows older other reasons can be given, leading him slowly, not perhaps consciously, to see that the rightness itself has a reason; but even to the days of leaving school, I think it would be well to still keep in sight the view of morality as absolute; if any choose at last to treat it as relative, that in its full extent is the duty of a man, not of one who is still being trained.

"But for reasoning itself with a young child, I may perhaps have rather overdone my point: I would only say that it takes time for formal reasoning to be appreciated, and the trainer must in every case avoid outrunning a child's capacity. This condition, thus explicitly stated, will not, I think, require repetition. It applies to education of every kind and at every stage, though the younger the children the more likely it is to be infringed. But habit even the youngest can begin to learn. Regularity can be enforced from the very first, regularity of food, bath, walks and the like. This leads unconsciously to the formation of habits which will never be broken save with pain, and so may become the sure foundation for more of morality than is supposed. Regularity leads to self-control, and the checking—almost automatic, one may say—of desires which for various reasons it may be undesirable to gratify. By automatic I mean that a check is applied before the mind has even realized the full knowledge of the evil desired. And how much of harm too is thus escaped by preventing the mind even dwelling for a moment on an undesirable course! Temptation is avoided and the right secured. Such regularity, of course, involves training in what has already been shown to be the child's chief virtue—obedience; for without obedience it would be impossible to attain. And thus training to obedience is the first training which a child can get in morality at all. And here I may perhaps say that the discussion about the proper time at which to introduce reasoning to a child will, I think, in experiment prove futile, for if properly trained the child will long accept as immutable the laws laid down, and will not probably think of questioning them till the idea is suggested by others. When he begins to question, however, then is the time for exposition—or when he begins to rebel.

"While aiming at the development in this way of the feeling of obedience and obligation, we shall be cultivating, more or less unconsciously, the primary spring of all moral action—the feeling of love. 'Obedience, gratitude, trust and love,' says Pestalozzi, 'are the beginnings of conscience,' and it is not the least of the debts that we owe to that extraordinary man that he first insisted on the importance of love as the chief factor in moulding children throughout their career. Certain it is that all sense of morality can be traced in the long run back to love—love of one's parents, love of mankind, love of God. And the cultivation of love has this particular advantage, that it can be relied upon as a guide, if properly trained, where all fear of punishment would be of no effect."

My wife pausing here for a moment, Dr. Hindley said with a sly glance:—

"I am glad, Mrs. Trelawney, to find that I have made at least one convert."

"What do you mean?" replied my wife.

"Why, when your husband first told you that I had

stipulated that love must be the guiding element in moral education, and, therefore, in education as a whole, you manifested not a little surprise."

"I was not aware that I made any comment."

"No; but you looked one, and that pretty forcibly," replied the Doctor; "though I admit that afterwards you seemed to indicate approval."

"Well, it was rather a startling proposition at first; but I have been considering it since, and having, moreover, in the last few days been looking at Pestalozzi again, I have come to the conclusion that he is right, though I should not like to fit his theory on to present conditions. But in any case you must remember that I am limited now to home education only."

"I think you made a bold statement, my dear," I said, "when you declared that all one's sense of morality can in the long run be traced back to love. The philosophers, I fear, would fall foul of you."

"I think, perhaps, I might put my view a little more clearly. I mean that every good action—action, that is, which involves compliance with a correct standard of morality—is originally induced by the desire to please some one—that is, it is ultimately based upon love."

"But what about the motive to which the old theologians were so fond of appealing—fear?" asked Mrs. Hindley.

"If an action is dictated by fear," was the reply, "I should not call it a perfectly moral action. It may have the outward semblance of one, and may be a step—I will not say unavoidable—in the right direction, but perfectly good it cannot be."

"I see now what your position is," said Mrs. Hindley, "and do not feel inclined to controvert it; will you go on?"

"There is another feeling," resumed my wife, "which shows itself very early, often even before speech, and which requires most careful handling, as it is the basis of much of our social life—I mean the sense of justice. Here, in particular, I think, we shall find the first call made upon us to give a reason for our actions and decisions. A child is apt to grow very jealous if it thinks it has suffered unfair treatment in comparison with another child; or if it thinks that it deserves a certain reward which is not given, it feels hurt, and is liable to have its confidence in those in charge shaken, perhaps for ever. Take, for instance, what is so common with quite young children, jealousy of the petting bestowed upon some one else—it may be merely the fact of the father or mother taking another child on to his or her knee. What is to be done? My own method of procedure is this. If the child is too young to understand language, I continue my demonstrations of affection to the other, but bestow some attention at the same time upon the one who feels aggrieved. I usually find that a very little notice is sufficient in such cases to kill the jealousy. But if it is still shown very vividly, then I disregard it altogether, as a lesson to the child that he cannot expect to have the whole of the world bowing down to him. But I make a favourable opportunity to divert the attention of the jealous child, and then, after a reasonable period has elapsed, abandon my petting of the other, without, however, bestowing marks of affection upon the one who has displayed the evil feeling. If, however, the child can speak, then I point out first of all that what is fair for one child is fair for the other, and that the one whom I do not happen to have taken has his turn at another time. Next, I appeal directly to the child's feelings, asking if he does not love his brother or sister, and if it is no pleasure to him to know that his brother or sister is happy. In some such way we can make advance upon two or three lines concurrently. But, above all, when jealousy has once been stirred, I do my utmost to avoid stirring it again, as I am convinced that with children of general healthiness of disposition it will die in course of time a natural death, if due care be taken never to expose them to circumstances where it may be aroused. There is no vice which lives so entirely by indulgence, and which can be so readily killed by neglect."

"But don't you think," said Mr. Reynolds, "that it is just as well to put a child in circumstances where it will have to make an effort to overcome its own evil bent? Otherwise, when will it learn self-control?"

"Ah," my wife said, "there you raise once more the most difficult of all questions in moral education—the question whether it is wise to deliberately practise the young in morality in cases where their failure to respond to our efforts is likely to do them moral harm. We have already touched briefly upon this question, but have never really settled it. For my own part I have no hesitation in saying that in the case supposed I would never intentionally put a child under conditions where his feelings of jealousy might be aroused, until I was practically sure from long watching that the victory would be on the right side. And who would say he was sure of that in dealing with the very young? Remember I am arguing for the present chiefly about children who cannot yet speak."

"I think there," said Mr. Reynolds, "I should certainly agree with you, but am not so sure with those of larger growth. When children can speak they are capable of understanding, at least to some extent, the grounds of action; we can point out to them the wrongness of their attitude, and easily exhort them to be good."

"Ah," said Mrs. Hindley, "exhorting is of course a clergyman's special work, and that, perhaps, Mr. Reynolds, is why you adopt that view; but to me it is absolutely loathsome. Habit is the point at which we must aim in the case of children as long as they are at home,—and afterwards also to a very large extent,—and every time you put temptation in a child's way you break the habit or run the risk of doing so."

"But you can form a habit of overcoming temptation."

"Also of falling into it. I say keep your children away from evil as long as ever you can. If temptation comes, then they must face it; but never deliberately put it in their way."

"I did not mean quite so much as that, only that you should not go out of your way to put them beyond the reach of temptations, lest by so doing you should bring them in the end not to strong and healthy habits, but only to the loss of all self-control."

"No, no, no, a thousand times no!" energetically exclaimed Mrs. Hindley. "It is like the doctrine Clough ridiculed:—

> 'Thou shalt not kill; but needst not strive
> Officiously to keep alive.'

'Lead us not into temptation' is the highest maxim, and I am surprised you should advocate anything else."

Mr. Reynolds looked thoughtful, and answered nothing, while Dr. Hindley said,—

"I think Mrs. Trelawney's distinction the correct one— probably the only one that will ever give satisfaction in considering this difficult point in the abstract—that we may expose to temptation where the failure to resist it will not lead to grave harm, but that where, as in the matter of jealousy, such exposure of necessity evokes an evil feeling which may easily grow very strong, then it is our imperative duty to keep the child from it as much as possible."

"It would make things clearer, Doctor," I said, "if you could give us an instance where grave moral harm would not be likely to be the result."

"Oh, that is easy enough. Take the case of giving from benevolence. There I consider we should all be justified in putting children in the way of exercising the virtue, as, even supposing they failed to respond,—and failure might not unfrequently come,—we could hardly be charged with having fostered a vice that is very malignant, save only in rare cases. And further, by means of appropriate teaching, opportunities of practice at the right moment, and example above all, it would probably be easy to get the child to act differently hereafter."

"Yes, I see. Certainly the matter is very grave," I said, "and I personally should be very chary of deliberately exposing a child to any temptation at all. Temptation will come of itself often enough; we shall then be able to watch how it is faced."

"But there is another point," said Reynolds once more. "Supposing you know a temptation is coming which you might remove, or you intentionally put a child in the way of one, would you not consider that you were acting justifiably, if you took the precaution of warning him explicitly, and set before him the principles by which he should be led?"

"In fact," said Mrs. Hindley, "the old practice of telling a child not to do a thing, and then leaving him just where he can do it. Bluebeard and his wives over again. No, certainly not."

"I do not think I should go quite as far as you, my dear," said the Doctor. "I think there is, perhaps, something to be said for Mr. Reynolds in this case. It is often useful to test a child's progress, and, under the same conditions as we laid down just now, I should say this method of exposing to temptation would be a very good and even salutary one."

"I am sorry to hear you say so," rejoined Mrs. Hindley. "I cannot but look upon it as distinctly immoral to deliberately expose a child to temptation under any circumstances whatever."

I saw Mrs. Hindley was getting warm, so said to smooth matters down :—

"Surely it all turns upon the actual case. Practice must be had somehow, and if we arrange the experiment, we can temper the wind to the shorn lamb. I think that, under circumstances not hard to imagine, even Mrs. Hindley would not object to expressly putting or leaving her children in the way of some temptations. On the general principle I agree with her, but logic must not be pressed too far in practical matters. The whole question is one of detail, and I should think in practice my wife's rule would be a sufficient safeguard. But will you continue your exposition, my dear? I am afraid we have rather run away from you."

"Oh, well, we have got some light on a very important matter, which we should have had to discuss sooner or later, and it is, perhaps, just as well that it has come now. Let me see, where did I leave off? Oh, yes, I was talking about children's sense of justice. This is of great moment, because it gives us the first opportunity of developing directly the altruistic feeling; for though primarily justice has reference to oneself, it is very easy to lead children's reason to see—though it may be long before their nature quite responds—that what applies to themselves applies equally well to others. In fact, to use a paradox, it is just their sense of justice which teaches them justice."

"Do you know Rousseau's treatment of the question?" I asked.

"Yes; and though he seems outrageous in trying to go back to first principles at once, there is much to be said for the line he takes. Undoubtedly the sense of justice is very closely connected with a sense of property, and if we can succeed in getting implanted clearly in a child's mind what constitutes property, and how it is connected with justice, we shall have gone a long way towards fixing in him a high standard of morality by which to guide himself in after-life."

"Certainly," said the Doctor, "excepting charity, I think there is no point in ordinary life where the standard of morality is so shockingly low as in the matter of justice. We are so much misled in our attitude towards it by our own prejudices and interests."

"Of course much of what I have said," resumed my wife, "reaches far beyond the years from which I first started. It seems to me that, if we watch carefully before a child can give clear utterance to his feelings and thoughts to see what his attitude is towards different moral questions, we shall have done most of what can be done in the very early days, and especially if we avoid exposure to temptation. But as the child grows and understands language, we must adopt something of Pestalozzi's method, which is practically what it seems Professor Adler did, and give the child instruction by object-lessons in morality. And this must be in two branches: for one thing, we must get at the child's own ideas on morality, his views on cases that actually occur; and for another we must illustrate by appropriate narratives, tales and poems, such as are within the child's comprehension. I am a very great believer in the power of poems and tales of noble deeds. Pestalozzi clearly thought much of it, as indeed he did of direct instruction in morality altogether. He even proposed to start in rather an odd way, by deducing moral facts from the use of language. But without going so far as that, I think we may safely affirm that the inductive method is the true one—to treat each question as it arises, and get the child's judgment upon it; then, if necessary, and if the point can be established to a child without confusing his sense of right and wrong, we must correct the judgment, but not necessarily, or perhaps for a long time, draw any general inferences."

"In fact," I said, "we must first gather our instances, then argue from particulars to particulars, and only reach the general propositions comparatively late."

"That seems to me nature's method of procedure, and I hardly think we can better it at present," my wife replied with a gentle smile. "But we must also encourage children to lay their difficulties before us, and instead of responding with a specific instruction lead them on to express, so far as may be, for themselves a general principle, which we must then see that they can apply. In this way we shall train not merely their moral judgment, but also their independence and power of decision.

"But you know I feel all this time as if I were talking the merest commonplace. Rousseau and Pestalozzi have well-nigh covered the field, if we make allowances for the former's extravagances and the want of system shown by the latter. It is simply the application of their principles that is needed, and how can we get that by sitting and talking here? More recently Froebel from one side, and Mr. Herbert Spencer from another have emphasized the factor, which had been too much neglected—the training given by the external world and circumstances; and beyond this all seems detail."

"But much still requires to be reduced to practice," the Doctor said; "for Professor Adler has only treated one department. Would you in home training do as he does in school, give set lessons?"

"In so far as one gives set lessons in anything, I think one should give set lessons in morality. Systematic treatment ensures comprehensiveness, and leads to appreciation of the importance of a subject. At the same time, of course, the set lessons to young children must always be very short, and need only be taken from time to time as occasion requires. Notes, however, must be kept of the subjects treated, and though the lessons may come at irregular intervals, they must be built on a logical connection—be parts of one complete whole. For the haphazard, spasmodic treatment of questions merely according as they arise is answerable for much of the present defectiveness of our ordinary moral training even in homes of high tone. To me it seems that a suitable occasion for giving instruction on these matters to children presents itself naturally at family prayers; and then, too, it can with advantage be combined with *simple* illustration from points of practice. I specially emphasize the word simple, because to introduce children to a mass of detail would be a fatal mistake. Still I admit that the main portion of the early training in morality must consist solely of checking tendencies to vice, supplemented where it is desirable and possible by an exposition of the wrongness of indulgence. I do not think we shall lose anything by always giving reasons where they are within the comprehension of the child; and where they are not, then a parent who had won the confidence of her child can always fall back upon the child's trust and love, thus exercising faith. There is another occasion, too, as Pestalozzi showed, where the parent can get hold of the child with advantage; when the child is giving vent to his love for his parents, we can appeal to him always to follow ways that will please, and show what those ways are.

"In the home it is probably better, as a rule, to deal with the children individually than to confine oneself to general talk addressed to them all together, as the greater part of moral progress during the early years depends so much on helping the young to resist, especially those temptations to which each in particular is prone. A child, too, then, is ready to open his heart and discuss difficulties, appealing for help. It may not be quite the same at school when he has grown older and more reticent, and is often able to apply his lesson without help from others."

"What do you think, Mrs. Trelawney," Mrs. Hindley asked, "of Froebel's insistence on the importance of keeping pets?"

"I think that though there is much to be said for it, there is also something against it. Undoubtedly there is in most children's minds natural sympathy with living things—they like watching and playing with cats and dogs and other pets; and undoubtedly this is a very good introduction to training in that sympathy for other creatures which in time will probably from animals spread to man. Interest, too, in things round us leads to care for their well-being. But, on the other hand, I never can quell the feeling that in many cases the keeping of pets means a certain amount of cruelty, not the less dangerous for being latent. In the case, for instance, of birds and rabbits, it involves confinement, and the consequent blunting of a child's perception of what is most conducive to the happiness of other creatures. The sin is perhaps more of omission than of commission, but it is a sin nevertheless. Still, if by pets we practically mean none but the domesticated animals, such as now without restraint naturally seek the companionship of man, then I quite agree that the training is invaluable.

"In this connection I should like to add one caution. Beware of cruelty. We are often told that children are naturally cruel. I do not believe it."

"Nor I," interposed Mrs. Hindley. "I call it a monstrous libel."

"But surely they do very cruel things?" said Reynolds.

"Yes," replied my wife; "but that is from ignorance. It is in most cases experimentation—a desire for knowledge; or, if you like, mere curiosity. It can easily be overcome by a clear explanation of the cruelty involved—a point which the child, at least the boy, will rarely think of for himself. But that was not what I meant so much, as that we should beware of ever letting children see cruel sights. It is sad to think how we ourselves have our sympathy with suffering often blunted merely by constant familiarity with it; how much more likely is this to be the case with a child who cannot reason."

"Yet here surely," said Mr. Reynolds, "I may repeat my point, that without actual experimentation we shall never be able to train in true sympathy and actual abhorrence of cruelty."

"On the contrary, I think we can train quite well by stories, where the feeling aroused will be one of pure sympathy, while the perceptions will not be blunted by familiarity. In fact, I rather think the child's horror at the sight of cruelty, when he does actually come across it, will be all the greater from his previous want of experience. Moral indignation ought to form a large part of our objection to evil in any shape, and this can certainly be aroused by narrative as well as by actual events. Don't you think so, Dr. Hindley?"

"Most assuredly I do; and in any case, Reynolds, don't you think the child will be likely soon enough to come across cases of cruelty,—the whole world reeks with it,—however much we may try to screen him from them?"

"Yes; but I still maintain that we can do much when we have the circumstances, as it were, under our control—

much more than if we wait for the circumstances to present themselves under complications. We are like an experimentalist in natural science; he can learn so much more, if he can arrange the conditions and form of his experiment, than if he has to wait for nature or chance to present the phenomenon he wishes to study."

"I grant that it would from some points of view be a more effective proceeding," said my wife; "but I cannot think that morals are parallel in all respects to natural science. We cannot treat them as subjects for experiment just as we should anything else. There is too much danger attached to the process. Just as the chemist treats chloride of nitrogen only at a distance and well-protected, so must we be cautious in experimenting on morals. Like that substance, morals are an explosive compound. The prevention of the formation of a bad leaning is better than its cure; it is wiser to wait for our experiments to present themselves than to run the risk of a dangerous result. But I must pass on.

"Truth is one of the virtues that earliest calls for training, and that the most careful. We have already discussed it at some length and with particular regard to home training, so I do not think I need cover the ground again, especially as, unfortunately, I differed from Mrs. Hindley on an important point of possible practice. I would only say this in rectification of any misunderstanding of my real position, that we must ourselves be most careful never to let even the youngest child see us do anything that he might interpret into an attempt to practice deception, whether in word or in act. For, after all, lying is not chiefly with the lips. Exaggeration has already been handled, and I do not think I need repeat what Mrs. Hindley urged. I will merely say that the tendency to lie shows itself extremely early, and a parent must be on a constant look out for it. But the virtue of truth has one valuable quality which many others have not—valuable, I mean, from the point of view of the educator of the very young; at that stage of life it practically conflicts with no other duty—it can be declared for the time to be absolute. I do not think, if our teaching has been sound, that as the child grows older and can draw distinctions, he will have any difficulty in deciding on the cases where truth is overridden by higher considerations. That is a point which will certainly come late. Now the reason why it is important to be able to train in a virtue which is at first absolute, is twofold: in the first place, the child will be confused if he is constantly coming across exceptions, and his moral perceptions will be blurred altogether; in the second place, at first the child is liable, as M. Perez well says, to think that right consists of what is not forbidden, while wrong is that which he has been told not to do. Hence he will rely entirely upon others, and when a case presents itself which has had no rule laid down for it, will probably be at sea. Under these circumstances truth will be his compass and will always point him straight until his own knowledge can correct it.

"In general, it seems to me that the training of quite young children must have these main aims—five in all—before it: the suppression of all evil manifestations, such as jealousy, temper, anger, greediness, to which the diversion of the thoughts is often a great help; the cultivation by this means of self-control; the development of love and reverence for one's parents, and through them of sympathy for all living beings; the direct practice of some of the easier and simpler virtues, self-denial, truth-speaking, generosity and the like; and, finally, the habit of observing and collating moral facts and passing judgment upon them—all, of course, in proportion to the child's development. Educators often make a great mistake in trying to force things on children's attention in which they are as yet unable to take interest. In moral matters this has most fatal results, and above all in religion."

Here Mrs. Reynolds interrupted with some energy.

"Mrs. Trelawney, I am surprised to hear you say that. Surely you do not mean to say it is possible to begin training a child in religion too early."

"I most certainly do mean to say it," was the reply, "and what is more, I think it is a very, very common mistake, and is answerable for a great deal of the hostility to religion, or at least indifference, which is so common nowadays."

"Would you explain?" said Mr. Reynolds.

"Certainly. You will grant, I suppose, to begin with,

that the religious sentiment is one of great complexity, and, at all events in its full power, beyond the grasp of the quite young?"

"Yes."

"Now all I say is this: If you begin to inculcate religion properly so-called when the child has not yet got its power of abstraction sufficiently developed to understand what is meant by God, you are talking to him mere words, and he will come at last to think that religion is nothing but empty talk; for by the time he is reaching an age when he is able more or less to grasp what it really means, and can feel an affection for an unknown person in virtue of his moral attributes, he will probably have grown tired of the whole business, owing to the sense of unreality he has so long attached to it."

"Surely it is a matter of ordinary common-sense and judgment," said Mr. Reynolds.

"No doubt; but my point is that in this matter most people are devoid of common-sense. The constant talking to young children is the main origin of the cant that is so often connected, I am grieved to say, with religious profession. Above all, I think a great mistake is made in taking children to church while they are still quite young. The service is too long and cannot be understood by them; and though they may like it for a change, in most cases, according to my observation, it merely becomes a weariness to the flesh. They may perhaps develop awe for a time, and so far a good result is produced; but we all know how changeable are children's feelings—how incapable they are of maintaining the same feeling for any length of time. Judging from what I have seen in school, I should say that no child ought to go habitually to church under the age of ten, and even then only to special services, which should be at once short and such as a child can understand."

"But," said Mr. Reynolds, "don't you overlook the value of a habit of church-going? What we are used to when young becomes to us a necessity when old; and hence I like children from the very first to associate their church with their higher feelings."

"I do not deny the value of the habit, if it is possible to form it; but in this particular case, when we know what are the seductions to which the child will be exposed later on, I am not sure that the mere habit will be of any great effect. Moreover, monotony, which is very likely to be felt while the child is not yet capable of proper religious emotion, is a danger that cannot be too carefully avoided; in religion it is, as in ordinary education, to use the words of Thring, the greatest enemy with which the teacher has to deal. Moreover, the matter of church-going is exposed to one peculiar difficulty which does not appear always in other matters connected with morality—people are apt to regard one as actually doing wrong, if one does not go at regular intervals. Now this attitude is especially fatal in dealing with the young. It should be our aim here, as in training to morality in general, to let the child lead himself. I am convinced that if we allowed children to go to church as they pleased and never pressed them to go when they did not want to do so, instead of getting tired of it and often abandoning it when they can, they would look upon it as a pleasure which would attract them always. I chose, indeed, this question of church-going, on which I do not expect general agreement, merely as the first illustration which occurred to me of the dangers of forcing emotion on a child before his powers are ripe; but I think the principle I have been trying to explain applies to all our dealings with the young. We must wait upon nature, not anticipate it; we must, as Froebel urges, let the child guide us, not ourselves guide it. Induction must rule; our arguments must be from the child's experiences; we must, as I have already said, have true Pestalozzian object-lessons in morality."

"Ah, my dear," I said, "I was wondering whether you would at last acknowledge the sources of your inspiration. All you have been laying down seems to me but an application to practice of Pestalozzi's theories."

"I am quite aware that it is, and thought I had already admitted my debts. I do not suppose that anything I am saying is of my own origination; but it is monotonous to be constantly stopping to say: This is from So-and-so; this from somebody else. Moreover, I thought that we were anxious here rather to get at some practicable scheme than to go into the history of education in its entirety."

"You will remember, Mrs. Trelawney," said the Doctor, "that I have expressly stipulated that my part of the discussion was not of necessity practical, but was to be regarded merely as an ideal which it would be worth while to keep before our eyes."

"Yes; but at the present point in our enquiry it seems to me that the ideal is consistent with the practical. But as to acknowledging my authorities, I will say here once for all that I do not claim anything as my own. I have read in such very different books and at such very different times, on moral education, without any thought of expounding the subject, that I have not taken the trouble to carry in my head the exact sources of all that I say. But I hope I do not appear ungrateful. Sometimes I know where I got an idea, but far more often not, even though I may be distinctly aware that the thought is not my own. Personally I consider that my main indebtedness is to five men—Rousseau, Pestalozzi, Rosmini, Froebel and Herbert Spencer."

"I should like to add another name for my own part," I said, "that of Plato."

"Ah, he is rather beyond my range, I grieve to say."

"But what of the Bible?" put in Mr. Reynolds. "I am amazed that you should make no mention of it."

"Oh, that was because I was thinking of systematic treatises on education. If I were to begin to enumerate works which are generally useful to education, I fear I should never end. But I think we ought to be getting on beyond the question of authorities. I do not, however, wish to go through all the virtues in detail; I think it will be sufficient to indicate method in the case of a few, and so far as possible to point out which are the first to develop. Progress will, to begin with, be slow, perhaps imperceptible, and we must not be discouraged by many falls; our aim must be so to train as ever to keep in mind that we have to develop a reasonable self-control, combined with love for others, the springs on which all the virtues move. 'Thou shalt love the Lord thy God with all thy heart, and with all thy soul, and with all thy strength, and with all thy mind, and thy neighbour as thyself.' These two precepts sum in brief the whole duty of man."

"Yet, Mrs. Trelawney," said Mr. Reynolds, "it was but a very short time since that you were arguing against the teaching of religion."

"I beg your pardon, Mr. Reynolds," my wife replied with some warmth, "but I was doing nothing of the kind. I was only arguing against the attempt to force the development of it prematurely. One often gains most by going to work indirectly. A wise loss of time is infinite gain."

"I am sorry if I misunderstood you," replied Reynolds, and my wife resumed:—

"All our efforts to train in morality will be but vain if we do not ourselves daily show that moral principles rule us, even as we would have them rule our children. Here is the chief reason why our moral training now is so defective. To take a simple instance, and a virtue which it is necessary to begin to train early—the virtue of punctuality. How many parents have I known who insist on their children being punctual at all meals, yet themselves never hesitate to be several minutes late when there is absolutely no reason why they should not have come earlier. They shelter themselves under that most dangerous of snares, the fact that there is no one in a position to reprove them."

"Yes," I put in, "and I am sorry to say it is a very common failing with head masters, who would be most angry if one of their assistants did the same thing."

"For my part, I consider such procedure not merely foolish, but absolutely immoral. How can a mother who behaves thus expect her child to understand the importance of punctuality, or not to try to secure for himself what he considers to be the privileges of his parents? No. The first duty of every trainer is to submit to the laws he lays down for the trained, save in those cases where it is clear even to a child that a distinction can be drawn between what a man is allowed to do and a child. But such cases are not many."

"I am very glad to hear you say that," put in Mrs. Hindley; "you know I hold truth-speaking to be not one of those cases."

My wife laughed, and merely saying, "I do not wish to re-open old discussions," went on:—

"There are many other conditions which conduce to easy development of a high moral tone without being themselves actual points in the systematic training to morality. They seem to me supports rather than parts of morality. Such are the influences of clean and beautiful surroundings, and of music. I am a very great believer in the moral influence of art."

"There I certainly cannot agree with you," said Mrs. Reynolds. "It seems to me it is mere indulgence in the pride of the eye."

"Do you mean to include music in your condemnation?" Dr. Hindley asked.

"No; I was thinking of painting in especial. It seems to me, even where not actually vicious, to be mere self-indulgence; if not immoral, to be completely non-moral. I am a great believer in the high ethical value of asceticism."

"But surely, Mrs. Reynolds," said the Doctor, "you would not deny that fine architecture, for instance, has an elevating effect—that it is inspiring to worship in a grand cathedral rather than in an ordinary, it may be an ugly, church!"

"Some people, I know, find architecture a hindrance to the free flow of religious feeling. Personally I am not sure that I should object to it, though certainly I cannot say that I have ever been conscious of having my religious emotions stirred by the sight of a grand cathedral."

"Do you mean to say that you do not feel elevated by the sight of a noble building?"

"Pardon me, Doctor, I did not say that. What I said was that I have not been conscious of having my religious emotions stirred. I said nothing about being elevated."

"But surely they are much the same thing."

"Not to my thinking. I draw a strong line of distinction between being elevated and having my religious feelings stirred."

"Ah, I have often heard that there are people who draw that distinction; but for my own part it seems to me a distinction without a difference."

"It is clear, Doctor, that we must be very differently constituted," went on Mrs. Reynolds. "To me religion is a thing quite apart from the exultation or feeling of joy produced in the mind by a grand sight. I am aware that many nowadays treat the two emotions as the same, if indeed they do not try to make the latter entirely take the place of the former. To me it would be as rational to say that delight in the open air and the power to do hard mental work are just the same thing, as to say that elevated feelings and the emotions of religion are identical or nearly so."

"Well, you would perhaps admit this much," the Doctor urged, "that when the feelings are roused in this way, one is more open to religious influences."

"No, I would not admit even that. Religious feelings seem to me so absolutely unique that in most cases exaltation of the other emotions prevents me fixing my mind on heavenly things."

Here Mr. Reynolds interposed, saying:—

"I could not go so far as that, but I must confess I have great sympathy with my wife's position in general, that art and religion are things apart."

"Well," said my wife, "I did not expect so strong an opposition. I thought I was laying down a proposition which would meet with universal assent. But I find I am mistaken."

"Very much so, my dear," I put in, "for you may add me to the number of your opponents, as regards religion at all events. With me art often gives the death-blow to religion. I well remember the first time I heard a choral service in a cathedral:—I had been brought up, as you know, as a strict Evangelical:—the effect upon me of the elaborate music and ritual was to make me boil over with anger, which, do what I would, I could not master. So far from having a religious effect the artistic surroundings had quite the reverse. I hope I should not be affected in the same way now; but still it is necessary to remember that such temperaments do exist."

"Well, my dear, I am surprised. I know that you are not fond of elaborate ritual, but I had no idea your feelings had ever been so strong. However, we have rather run away from my point, which was the effect of artistic surroundings upon morality, not upon religion. Oh, yes, Mrs. Reynolds, I know what you will say, that what applies to the one applies equally to the other; but I do not think that of necessity follows. I am not prepared personally to admit without argument that religious feelings are so far unique, so far distinct in character, I should say, from moral ones, as you seem inclined to maintain; but I will admit that there is a difference, and I can quite understand people who emphasize the distinction asserting that while art may have a good effect upon morality, it may have none at all, or a bad one, upon religion. However, it is clear that this point is one on which there is a vital divergence among us likely to be overcome by no amount of argument—a type of the divergence in the outside world. Hence in my other remarks on art and morals, I must be understood to be expressing my own personal opinion, not speaking for us all. I am sorry that it is so; but I was quite prepared to find that the whole of our subject—so little worked out as yet—might well disclose great differences of thought. I am only too glad to know that so far we seem to be pretty well agreed, and must not complain of one schism, even on a point so near to my heart.

"I was going to maintain, and for my own part maintain still, that artistic surroundings have a really direct effect in fostering good morality. Few people surely would now deny that the sight of fine pictures, statues or buildings elevates our feelings and raises us for the time beyond our common selves, just as does a lovely landscape or the wonderful glow of a rich sunset. Now this feeling of elevation—purification I should prefer to call it—puts the mind into such a state that it is directly susceptible to the finer emotions, of which assuredly the moral are the chief. Hence it seems to me that if we habitually surround the child from the cradle onwards with lovely sights and sounds, we are likely to keep him in a more receptive state for our moral lessons than if we leave him exposed, I will not say to what is ugly, but to what is merely commonplace. The effect seems to me precisely analogous to the effect which the narration of heroic deeds, whether historical or fictitious, and the recitation of stirring poetry and other appeals from literature—an indispensable portion of all moral training—exercise upon the heart, opening it, as they do, to an appreciation of what is great or noble, and suggesting, by natural working, imitation. The effects of art may not be so directly related to practice, but the general result seems to me undistinguishable. And though the fact hardly bears upon the training of quite young children, the same may be said of dramatic art."

"Ah! that reminds me," I said, "of a well-known saying of Aristotle, who, if I understand him rightly, represents tragedy as a direct moral influence, purifying, as he says, by means of pity and fear, the passions which fall into the same classes as those two."

"It sounds rather a complicated remark. I have not heard it before, I am ashamed to say, and must admit I hardly understand it."

"Oh, well, you are no worse off than our friends the critics then, for no one as yet seems to have thoroughly comprehended it; so you need not worry yourself on that score. The remark only seemed to me to bear a general resemblance to what you had been saying. But I think you might proceed."

"I had just mentioned dramatic art. The last important, I may perhaps call it from our present point of view the most important, branch of art remaining is music, about the moral effect of which till a few minutes ago I should have thought no one would have disputed. We know that the ancient Greeks thought it one of the most direct of all ethical agencies——"

"Forgive me interrupting you, Mrs. Trelawney," said Mr. Reynolds; "but has any one here ever heard an attempt at a reproduction of Greek music?"

No one seemed to have done so, and Reynolds proceeded:—

"Well, I have; and I remember thinking when I was listening to it that I could quite understand how it was that the Greeks, and Plato most explicitly, attributed to it so great a moral power. It is so very unlike ours that we can form no opinion by merely inferring from modern music. Greek music seems to have been much simpler and rather monotonous, and, perhaps for that reason, it appeals more directly to our moral feelings. I am, unfortunately, not musical, and cannot lay out the difference in musical terminology. Still, the fact remains that, to me at least, it seemed a standing proof of the correct observation on which Plato based his theories, difficult though a modern finds it at first to accept all he says on this curious subject."

"I am glad to hear you say this, Mr. Reynolds," said my wife, "for it helps me in my present point. I should not like to be asked to expound in detail the exact effect of different kinds of music, but of its soothing and often inspiring power no one even among the ordinary public can have much doubt. We need only consider hymns and marching music, to say nothing of national airs, to see that some of the different kinds may excite emotion very strongly."

"I do not call that the same as being moral in their effects."

"Ah, Mrs. Reynolds, you are subtle in your objections. It is a point which I should like to discuss later on, but meanwhile, will you allow me to assume it for the purpose of developing my position? Here, if I may, I will just quote one example as an absolute proof of the moral influence which music, I do not say always, but at all events often, exerts upon the hearers. Do you know the overture of Tannhäuser? You do not, Mrs. Reynolds? Well, you have a pleasure in store. But what I was going to say was this, that when I first heard that overture after I knew the opera, the whole of it seemed to me a representation of a moral struggle—a most terrible moral struggle—between the powers of evil and the powers of purity and goodness; and so vivid was the reality of it to me—I could follow every movement through having already heard the opera as a whole—that I was quite exhausted with the protracted agony of the conflict; I began almost to gasp for breath, and was within an ace of falling from my seat. I have heard the overture more than once since, and it always affects me in the same way, though not quite to the same extent, for it has not always been Richter conducting. I look upon the intensity of my emotions then as a proof of the moral nature of music, for the moral feeling was present to my consciousness throughout, and it was much more that than the mere music which exhausted me so completely."

"You must be unusually sensitive," said the Doctor;

while Mrs. Hindley, who was very musical, and who had, while my wife was speaking, been half nodding to herself with a pleased look upon her face, now said:—

"I am delighted to hear what you say, Mrs. Trelawney. I always quote the overture to Tannhäuser as my crucial test of the power of music to represent and appeal to the moral emotions. It is grand beyond measure, grand because full of the awful struggle between right and wrong."

"Now I think it is of the first importance," my wife resumed, "to apply music to the moral purification of the young. After all music is a language invented to express emotions beyond the ordinary range of speech, and who, when his heart is stirred by moral beauty, does not constantly feel the need of such a mode of expression? And just as music can express these feelings, so it can stir them into activity; and knowing as we do the delight which it is to most young children, I say that it is our duty never to neglect the chance of rousing or stirring emotions by music, or of using it to bring the child into a proper frame of mind when we are proposing to appeal to his moral nature.

"There are still one or two points I should like to touch upon, and you must forgive me if my remarks are rather disjointed. First, I would utter a warning against a very common fault—showing children off. I am convinced that serious moral harm often results from this practice. And what is the origin of it? Merely a foolish pride in ourselves. It leads to the development of vanity and conceit with no counterbalancing gain. The only cases in which I can conceive it to be at all justifiable are when a child is unduly diffident—cases which I think are not very common. And often the admiration expressed is directed to quite wrong objects, especially smart remarks which the child has not meant to be smart at all, so that he cannot understand our admiration or amusement. Laughing at things said in this way is apt to make a child self-conscious and unnatural, and to lead it to talk merely for impression's sake without any regard to truth or the exigencies of the conversation. Then again there is the very grievous mistake of praising a child in public. Praise is one of the most valuable weapons which a trainer

L

possesses at home or at school; but it should only be wielded in public under the most exceptional circumstances. And how often at home is the praise administered to unworthy things—good looks, cleverness, beautiful clothes —for which the child can claim no credit at all. Here it is in especial that servants are dangerous. I never let my children express any admiration for their own or other people's dress, contenting myself with getting them to feel that duty requires them to be neat and tidy, but that great display is no matter for pride. And here I may remark in passing that such neatness and tidiness is a great help to a child morally. It is the only justification that I can see for the rather snobbish attitude of many of our public schools, which insist upon boys wearing particular coats and hats; were it not for my sense of this possibility of moral gain, I should condemn the practice without reserve. As it is, I think it is overdone; the appeal to a gentleman's appearance is snobbish in essence, and often leads a child to think that any manual work which is apt to stain the fingers or soil the clothes is of necessity degrading."

"I must say I rather differ from you there," said Mr. Reynolds. "I think the practice is of very great value."

"That I admit, if carried out in the right spirit; but with many of our masters I fear it springs simply from a desire to separate their charges from those whom we with such terrible arrogance call, if you please, the lower classes."

"Thank you for that remark," said Mrs. Hindley. "Our attitude on that question is beneath contempt."

"It is curious," I said, "how vital such prejudices are. It seems to me the chief defect of the moral thinkers, not excepting even the greatest, among the Greeks, that they condemned all trade and manual labour as unworthy of a free man. And yet many historians hold up the Greeks to us as models of true democracy! Now true democracy must be based upon an admiration of worth wherever found, and the man who does his work nobly, even if it be but scavenging the streets, deserves far more honour and has a far nobler character than the man who folds his hands in idleness and says : ' I am a gentleman—I am entitled to do nothing.' "

"Yes," said Dr. Hindley, "it is surely one of the greatest advances we moderns have made, that we have come to recognise the nobility of work *per se*, of all work, no matter how unpleasant its surroundings. We do not always act up to our nobler feelings, especially in the matter of trade; but that all work deserves to be honoured it should be one of the primary objects of the educator to impress: the young should be taught that to despise another because his work is more unpleasant than their own is a mark of uncharitableness—of the meanest of vices. In fact I would go so far as to say, the more degrading the work, the more should be the honour."

"I do not think," my wife continued, "that it is possible to develop this feeling better than by making children work themselves. You know manual work is at this moment causing great revolutions in the educational world. Sloyd—to take one single instance—is a typical agent of great power, not merely in destroying a view of labour so degrading and unchristian as that you have described, but also in directly expounding the value of many a virtue,—neatness, precision, cleanness, perseverance,—which is in itself of vital importance and yet is touched so effectively by no other training. Rousseau and Pestalozzi never tire of preaching the need of doing things for oneself; the latter even made it a cardinal principle. From him we can learn that manual labour is not merely not in antagonism to, but that it furthers, and that distinctly, both intellectual and moral advance; and it is, to my thinking, in this direction that we should look for the next great advance in education.

"Let me now turn to another point, where moral education rests mainly with the home—I refer to the proper use of money. My own children are young as yet, so that I have not experienced the full difficulty; but I know one wealthy lady, whose children are now grown, who once said to me that in bringing up her children her greatest difficulty had been to teach them how to use money aright."

"I too have found the same thing," said Mrs. Reynolds; "even still I am at sea how best to treat the question."

"There are such great diversities of disposition," said Mrs. Hindley; "I do not think it possible to lay down one rule. A child tending to meanness requires different treatment from one who is extravagant, and these divergencies you find in even the same family, though all the members, so far as one can see, have had practically the same bringing-up."

"Yes," said my wife, "that increases the difficulty; and here again, I think, individual handling is more effective than general treatment. My husband and I have adopted the principle of making our children a certain allowance, even when they are but five or six years old; of making them keep accounts——"

"How on earth do you manage that?" interrupted the Doctor.

"Oh, by getting them a small account-book, making them tell us what they have spent, and entering it before them so that they can see. We then balance accounts in correct style, and so get the children into methodical habits from a very tender age. Of course it is but a little at first, and takes time even to reach the formidable sum of one shilling."

At this there was a laugh, and my wife went on :—

"Then we have a money-box, and encourage the little ones to put something by for use at emergencies, birthdays, holidays, treats and the like, and above all to spend partly in charity, especially at the charitable season—Christmas; but giving to beggars in the street we will not allow. Children can soon be brought to understand that such people are mostly impostors, though at first, from their keen sense of pity, they are inclined to give all they have. But we select some philanthropic society, the objects of which the children can understand, and when we send our own contributions, ask for help from them. But it is important that the objects should appeal to their sympathies; children's hospitals are a case in point, and the children's country holiday fund. Further, from time to time we take them, where possible, to see the places to which they have sent some contribution, and, giving notice a good time beforehand, encourage them to buy some little gift, flowers, fruit or toys, to leave behind them when they go. In this way they see how much may be done by money, and I really think it is a valuable lesson in the best means of dispensing charity.

"As the children begin to get older we make them pay out of an increased allowance for some portions of their personal expenses, small articles of dress perhaps, or, it may be, short railway journeys or the like. It teaches them economy and the care of their possessions. Moreover they have to make good any damage, unless it is so serious as to be quite beyond their reach."

"Aren't you rather likely to make them worry too much?" asked Mrs. Hindley.

"I admit there is a danger; but we try to get over it by abstaining for a time from making suggestions for rather out-of-the-way objects, or for any charitable expenditure. If the danger becomes pressing, we increase the allowance at times, though never on request; at times we make presents of such things as the children may otherwise have to buy for themselves. Of course we are careful that our reasons are not known—the act seems quite spontaneous. And, further, we always beg our friends on no account to give money without telling us first; to a small present occasionally we do not object, but a large sum we do our utmost to prevent. The practice develops as the years go on, and so far I have found it most valuable and effective. It is a practice which, I think, in the matter of pocket-money, schools might follow with advantage."

"Don't you find, Mrs. Trelawney," Mr. Reynolds asked, "that the children are reluctant to let you know what it is they have spent their money on? I sometimes feel that in trifles of this kind children like to have little secrets."

"I must enter a protest against the word trifles; but for the main point it seems to me a question of confidence. I have not yet found that any one of my children has refrained from spending when he wished, because he knew the matter at last would be sure to come under my supervision. But one rule I observe most punctually: when the money is spent I never criticise, unless the object is clearly bad. Extravagance practically corrects itself. Further, when the child is about eight or nine we take another step—we open a savings-bank account for the youngster. We do not, however, as some parents do, promise to add in due proportion; for our aim is not to encourage saving, but rather to show that, when properly handled, money can serve many different purposes.

Lessons in thrift should be taken later, roughly about the school age; in many cases indeed, if the children are well managed, they ought to be found quite superfluous, since after all life will of itself, save in the most exceptional cases, soon teach the requisite lessons. Ah, Doctor, I know what you would say, and I grant that it is these exceptional cases that perhaps require the training most; but I venture to think that on our system, before extravagance and want of thought had had the time to take deep root, the lesson would be already learnt. But to allow children to handle money freely without giving guidance or suggesting objects on which to spend it, makes me think of the reply the Irishman gave to the man who, on tumbling into the water, exclaimed piteously that he could not swim—'Then ye'll have a mighty iligant chance of learning now!' The allowance ought to be sufficient to give a little indulgence, and yet to leave enough for benevolent purposes."

"All I should be afraid of," said the Doctor, "is that the cares of this world would enter too early into the little soul. Such a result could not be desirable."

"I can only say I have not found it. But the possibility I do admit; yet it seems to me not hard to overcome. And, after all, it is a choice of evils, and I would rather face the risk than allow my children to grow to manhood in dangerous ignorance alike of the value and of the management of money, and without having received any practical lessons in the true charitable disposition of it."

"What do you think," Mr. Reynolds asked, "of Rousseau's theory that we ought to teach children to appreciate charity by being ready to give ourselves, but carefully excluding them from all participation in a matter which should be kept for full-grown men? In this way he says a child will treat charity as a privilege to be enjoyed in his maturer years; he will, as he grows older, become more and more anxious to assert his right to a proper share—his appetite, in short, will be whetted by refusal, and form at last the foundation of a life-long habit."

"Oh, that I regard as an extravagant paradox, though I admit I have sometimes been taken by it myself. It is, of course, a theory which might equally be maintained in respect to a large portion of moral education. But still, on the whole, it seems merely a paradox. True that desire is often whetted by refusal, but against that we have to set the opposite fact that experience of a pleasure makes one desire it again—a point especially to be weighed in connection with charity.

"I should like to lay down one general maxim which is of cardinal importance, not merely in dealing with children at home but throughout all education—leave them as large an amount of liberty as you can. Trust them and they can be trusted. Command little, and forbid not at all. Children are often overburdened with injunctions, on points, too, which are of no practical value in their effect on moral development. Remove, as far as possible, all means of doing harm, and then leave them to themselves. Herbert Spencer's theory of natural punishments I strongly support, extreme though the point is to which he pushes it. True and healthy the principle seems to me in the main, and its general application would work a much-needed reform, at home and school alike. Though I have just expressed dissent from Rousseau's doctrine, yet the thought which I imagine underlay his injunction represents a real fact; it is often the mere knowledge that an act is forbidden that makes a child, and, alas! not only a child, long to do it. If the law were not there, there would often be no desire."

"That," said Mr. Reynolds, "is like St. Paul's well-known sayings: 'Without the law sin was dead,' 'by the law is the knowledge of sin,' and 'the strength of sin is the law.'"

"Is that his meaning? The facts seem to me just as represented, and we have to bear them constantly in mind in all our dealings with children. But if we should have to forbid at all, there is one point made by Rousseau I should like to emphasize: it is of no use to argue that a certain act is not for the child's own good. Unless the harm is such as will come directly, and such as the child's mind will then and there appreciate, we are simply appealing to a vague abstraction which never reaches his feelings. Rather than use that argument I would say: 'Do not do it, because I should not like it;' or would leave the command absolute, without interpretation. And again I would say, be very chary about appealing to the sense of shame. I do not, of course, mean that you may never point out how a feeling of shame ought to arise, but what I mean is that the deliberate exposure of a child to scorn because of some fault committed is a direct and deadly wrong. Shame is a very double-edged weapon, tending to harden as much as to cure."

"Have you read," asked Mrs. Hindley, "the wonderful account which Tolstoi gives of his own village school, and the remarks he there makes upon the working of shame?"

"No; I am sorry to say I have never even heard of it."

"Well, let me recommend it. He takes just the line that you do. Indeed I would advise any one who is interested in education to study the whole work; it is quite revolutionary. I know it is much scoffed at by practical schoolmasters, but such a fate is not uncommon with great reformers. To me it seems more like Pestalozzi's mode of action, if I may trust mere reports of that man's work, than anything else that I have ever heard of."

"You have whetted my appetite, Mrs. Hindley," said my wife. "I shall certainly see what he has to say.

"Another point I should like to emphasize—it would perhaps have better come in connection with art—is the importance of the study of nature. Froebel, as no doubt you know, made this a cardinal point in his system; it should certainly be adopted in all homes. In towns there are, no doubt, difficulties in the way; but they can often be got over by pictures and models, and by excursions into the country. The value I am now urging is not the intellectual but the moral. Can the beauty of nature fail to work a softening effect upon any child, while the wonderful complexity and yet clear tendency of all arrangements to one great end, will this not rouse—we may be sure it will—his loving and admiring wonder and reverence? So we shall play upon two of the great chords of ethical sentiment, for, if I may rest on a poet's authority,—

'We live by admiration, hope, and love.'

Such intercourse with nature is also a ready way of teaching the child that everything is individual, and that it is his duty under all circumstances never to destroy that individuality.

"There is one habit on which Dr. Abbott dwells strongly in his suggestive little book, *Hints on Home Teaching*,—the habit of attention. So far does he go as even to say that of all habits it is both intellectually and morally the most valuable."

"That surely is exaggerated," said Mrs. Hindley.

"I think so; but you should read his own words on the matter. Of its very great importance under both these aspects I have no doubt whatever; but I referred in especial to that view just now in order to bring into high relief one excellent point he makes—the intensity of moral harm done to quite a young infant when friends will persist in diverting its attention, for no good reason at all, to some newly-presented object or plaything. Attention and will are too closely allied to allow us to play with the former with impunity. And yet Dr. Abbott's charges, I fear, come home not merely to the generality of nurses and relatives, but even to the parents themselves. Deeply engrossed in the study of one object, why should a child be diverted to another? Here, again, if we follow Dame Nature's guidance we shall not go far wrong. Let the child itself show when its interest is exhausted.

"I do not know that I have more to say, except to add that throughout life moral training should find its centre always in the home. Whatever work the school may do, it can only be subsidiary and supplementary to this. Some points, I grant, in particular those relating to our duties towards the State, the school can attack with more effect than can the home, above all when our aim is to stir enthusiasm, for which numbers are a great help; but, whatever the school may try to do, painful experience in teaching days has shown me that if home-influence runs counter, but little result will be produced."

There was a few moments' pause, when Mr. Reynolds said that there was one point he would like to raise, which it seemed to him had been quite overlooked, a point suggested by the last remarks—the effect, that is, of numbers. "Mrs. Trelawney," he went on, "has, it seems to me, fallen into the trap which has caught so many of our great authorities; she seems to have taken a solitary child instead of treating of children in groups. I know her procedure is not singular, but the method leads to defective results. Locke's treatise and Rousseau's seem to me especially to suffer in this way: they assume arbitrary or rare, if not impossible conditions, and then expect the result to apply to all mankind. Now, I grant that this mode of reasoning is natural,—it makes the argument so much easier,—still the defect seems to me radical. Man has been defined as a social animal, and surely it is important to treat him first of all from the point of view of this leading characteristic. And the younger the children the more marked is their sociality. Yet, Mrs. Trelawney, here you are laying down a scheme of moral training in the home, yet leaving on one side, as it seems to me, this prominent factor in a child's composition!"

"A very good and effective criticism, Mr. Reynolds," said Mrs. Hindley. "I shall be curious to hear what Mrs. Trelawney has to say."

We all looked at my wife with some curiosity, but she, after a moment's thought, said quite unconcernedly:—

"I admit I exposed myself in some way to the attack, but rather, I hope, from carelessness of expression than from a want of perception of the fact. In the first place, I think it is not quite true that I overlooked, even in the main, the social factor in the child's composition. I referred more than once to regard for others and, as the mainspring of action, dwelt prominently upon love. Surely this is to admit the social element."

"It is not the same thing," said Mr. Reynolds. "My thought was rather of the effect upon training of dealing with several children together, their influence upon each other, and the modifications of teaching which will result from association. Those questions I do not think you touched."

"That is true; but how, in the abstract, is it possible to treat them adequately at all? The variations will be endless, as endless as the characters, and it would be a hopeless task to enumerate the resulting modifications. I would only say this, that I do not think either the method of treatment or the subjects treated will differ in any material way, whether we deal with a child individually or with several children together. As in training of intellect, so with morals, the question turns largely on economy of labour. It is true the mixture of children will lead to peculiar difficulties and to extra work on the trainer's part, but it will also lead to compensating gains. The difficulties will be twofold: one, the difficulty of adjusting the teaching and practice so nicely to every one's peculiar disposition; the other and more serious, the difficulty which arises from possible bad influence exerted by one child over another. But to balance the latter risk there is a possible gain—we may light upon a child who is a distinct help, an elevating influence upon all his mates. And in any case to handle the subject thus in public will certainly produce a development of interest with, probably, discussion among the children themselves. But apart from these points I do not see that there is much else to be said; the actual appreciation of the consequent difficulties, and the proper way to meet them, must be left to the judgment of individual teachers. I would only say that if there is one child whose influence is distinctly and permanently bad, it will be wise to separate him from the rest and try a special course of treatment. But such a case is more likely to occur at the school stage of life, say from seven or eight onwards, than in that earlier period, infancy I may call it, which we are now especially considering. But great difference of method, or perhaps even of result, between individual treatment and corporate at this stage, there will, I think, be practically none."

"But, Mrs. Trelawney," said Mrs. Hindley again, "there is still one case you have passed over where the sociality of the child shows itself very strongly and where potent causes work to modify our efforts—the influence of companions out of actual instruction hours and especially the influence of children's games."

"Ah, now I do plead guilty to a very grave omission; but at the same time the question you have so suddenly sprung upon us is one of extreme difficulty. I do not so much mean the limited one of games as the other and broader branch, which is practically nothing but the wide question, a question that to me seems well-nigh unanswerable, of the advantages and disadvantages of home and school respectively. Whatever I may say on this vital question, I should put forward only as tentative; but on the question of games I do not suppose we are likely to differ very much."

"You will admit, no doubt, their value as training in self-denial and self-control?"

"Nay, I should go a great deal further and say that, especially with the very young, I have found no means equally easy for reaching their dispositions. Not merely are the qualities you have mentioned well brought out, but perseverance is necessary, co-ordination of means to attain, it may be, a distant end, the feeling of delight in not merely one's own but also others' activity, the development of a spirit of cheerfulness—in itself one of the most valuable of influences that can forward the development of a healthy morality—and beyond perhaps everything else, the appreciation of the efforts of others, especially when the elders know well how to join, and gratitude brought home to the children's hearts in the most direct way. I am dwelling of course solely upon the moral advantages; of the intellectual it is not my place now to treat. And it is here that I find the Kindergarten system to be of such immense value, even with allowance made for the occasionally rather unnatural handling of children's games, the attempt to draw lessons from them too directly and the removal from the children of all initiative. But these defects, where they occur, are but a slight set-off against the cardinal merit of the system. The stimulus imparted in all ways by association with those of like age is a boon that cannot be over-estimated; all that is needful is to watch the children to prevent indulgence in evil feelings, of which games are often provocative. But it is precisely games which often give the trainer his best opportunities of experimentation and of winning an insight into children's characters; for their energies are then keen-set, and under the stimulus of a desire to gain a given end they will probably give free play to their strongest inclinations. Of rivalry I do not propose to say anything, for it is a weapon of very keen double-edge, too dangerous, in fact, in most cases to employ."

"I am afraid, then," said Dr. Hindley, "you cannot much approve of the system in vogue at most of our schools, where the main stimulus seems to be drawn from the desire to win either prizes or marks."

"No; that method, I think, is morally bad, and does not produce half the result supposed. But girls' schools are freer from the iniquity than boys'; you had better ask my husband what his opinion is."

"It is one of the points on which I feel most strongly," I said. "I was keeping it in reserve till we reached the general consideration of school morality; but as it has turned up now, we may as well say what we have to say. I have abolished marks in my own school, save as a very passing record; nor do I find any diminution in interest. The boys work quite as well without them, and their absence involves one great advantage—poor ability is not discouraged. Jealousy, moreover, meets with no encouragement; each boy is judged, not with reference to other boys, but with reference to himself, and allowance is made for natural powers. Hence, too, there is no food on which to batten the self-conceit which cleverness so often shows, albeit cleverness is no merit of one's own."

"Yes," said Mr. Reynolds, "I can understand those advantages; but I think the evils you speak of are comparatively rare. Surely it is a good training for a boy to learn not to let his feelings of jealousy master him because he has been beaten by another boy, and the same with cleverness and self-conceit."

"There again it is the question between the avoidance of temptation and the exposure to it in the fervent hope that the tempted will succeed in winning the victory. No, it is surely better to avoid the temptation altogether."

"But don't you think," went on Mr. Reynolds, "that a little rivalry is good?"

"If we can be sure of not stirring evil feelings, yes; but can we be sure? In any case, the chief aim in fostering such rivalry is to furnish a stimulus; now I say that in any proper school such a stimulus ought to be unnecessary. If the children do not do their work from love of it or from a sense of duty, there is something radically wrong, and the wrongest thing of all is to have recourse to an anti-social feeling by way of stimulus. Duty should be done for duty's sake and not for the sake of reward."

"Bravo, Mr. Trelawney!" said Mrs. Hindley; "I am glad to hear you speak so strongly on the subject. I quite hold with you and your wife that rivalry is too dangerous a weapon to be used systematically in the education of the young. Of one thing we may be quite sure, that the exigencies of after-life will develop the anti-social feelings quite strongly enough without our fostering them in cases where they can have so dangerous an influence. How often do we find a spiritless person who has no desire at all to surpass his neighbours? And if we do, may he not be all the better for it?"

"But, Mrs. Hindley, there is such a thing as trying to excel in good; surely you would not condemn that?"

"Now, Mr. Reynolds, let us be quite candid. Can you tell me of any case that you know where ambition or rivalry is limited to that?"

Reynolds laughed and confessed that he could not, and Mrs. Hindley went on with some vehemence:—

"Then you must forgive me if I use a strong word about such an argument when I say that it is the merest cant. Now to discuss morals adequately we must first of all rid our minds of cant. Your argument, Mr. Reynolds, was but a logical subtlety without practical reality, and, pardon me if I say, unworthy of you. But I hope and believe that you only used it from a dialectical necessity. I repeat, then, that rivalry is usually, if not always, a rivalry in selfishness, and as such to be crushed with a heel of iron."

When Mrs. Hindley had laid down the law in this emphatic way, none of us felt bold enough to attempt to answer her. I merely thanked her for coming so valiantly to my assistance, and asked my wife to resume her argument where she left off.

"Let me see, where was that?" she replied. "Oh, I remember. Just before I introduced that unfortunate word rivalry. I had been running through the moral advantages of games. I do not think it is necessary for me to say any more, as the point is very clear, and I willingly admit that children in general intercourse and in games in particular develop each others' morals, though, perhaps, in a very haphazard way, just as they develop each others' intellects and physical powers in a way that is more effective, at least within certain limits, than our own efforts at more systematic training. Hence I feel that I was guilty of a really unpardonable oversight in not touching on the question at first."

Here my wife stopped and looked as if she had nothing more to say, whereupon the Doctor said:—

"But, Mrs. Trelawney, the rest of your work, if you please. You must be aware that you postponed a most important discussion, and yet you now look as if you thought you had done the whole of your duty. Come, we cannot let you off."

My wife laughed and replied:—

"Well, I really did hope you had forgotten the other point. I was most anxious to escape it, as I feel I am utterly incapable of dealing with it. Do let us leave it alone and pass on to something else."

"Mrs. Trelawney!" exclaimed Mrs. Hindley with a look of horror, lifting up her hands in well-feigned surprise; "can it be you who have made that remark? Here we are discussing the principles of morality as they are to be enforced upon children, and when you come to a point of vital importance you actually show yourself so utterly deficient in a primary sense of duty, despite the admirable lecture you have just been giving us, as to propose running away! Fie, fie! I should never have expected it. What will your husband say?"

"Oh, I say it is the wisest thing," was my reply; at which the whole company started in horror, save only my wife, who said, laughing:—

"There, Mrs. Hindley, you see I have a good champion. Now I am no longer ashamed of my cowardice. But suppose *you* tackle the question, as you seem to consider it so necessary; pray, which do you consider preferable, to bring up a child at home or to send him to school?"

"Oh, I have no hesitation—send him to school."

"And her also?"

"And her also."

"On what ground?"

"On the ground of wider experience and the rubbing off of corners. 'Home-keeping youths have ever homely wits.'"

"But we are considering morals, not wits, at present."

"It makes little difference. Morals will be improved as well as wits."

"Always?"

"Not always perhaps, but generally."

"And what about the other cases? Would you deliberately expose them to harm?"

"I do not think the harm outweighs the good to the generality. A child of exceptionally weak will I would keep at home."

"But what special advantage do you consider school confers that cannot be had at home?"

"It teaches self-reliance and consideration for others."

"But surely that can be taught at home if there are more children than one and if the parents go the right way to work."

"If, if. But there is another point. At school there is more certainty of regular discipline without regard to favour."

"That is again a question of an if. If the parents are suited for their work, home will be as good as school, besides being more under the influence of love; and you remember we are supposing that our conditions are ideal, in which case parents will be well fitted for their work."

"But we are also supposing that schools will be ideal, and on that supposition love will reign supreme. So that point balances the other."

"It seems to me," I said, "you ladies are chopping logic to no purpose."

"Thank you," put in Mrs. Hindley—a remark I disregarded.

"If the conditions are ideal both courses will be perfect, and there is nothing more to be said. It would surely be more correct to say, not that the conditions are ideal, but that we are aiming at an ideal training. However, I should like to put Mrs. Hindley one question. Do you mean by school a day-school or a boarding-school?"

"Oh, a day-school certainly."

"Then in that case," said my wife, "I should not disagree. The moral dangers connected with a day-school ought to be easily counteracted by the home; the point I really dreaded and to which I hoped to force you at last, was the entire loss of women's influence. It did not seem to me that that would be outweighed by the gain from companions of all sorts and kinds."

"Ah, but," said Mrs. Hindley, "you remember we agreed earlier on mixed schools and mixed teachers."

"True; I am afraid I was arguing from modern conditions. But now that we are agreed that it is desirable to get a variety of companions for the young and yet to retain them under the sheltering influence of home, I would only say that there is something to be said for the position which, for instance, Canon Isaac Taylor takes up, that a large class formed at home, but only of such numbers as would be within the reach of home discipline and admit of similar supervision, would adequately meet the case. I am not myself quite convinced of the wisdom of the solution, but I think it would be worth consideration."

"Yes, possibly," replied Mrs. Hindley, "though it can hardly differ much from a small school. But as we have escaped the terrible battle which seemed imminent owing to an agreement in essentials, it hardly seems worth while for us to go into that question. I move that we pass on. Now, ladies and gentlemen, speak up if you please. Has any one anything further to say on the question of home education as laid before us by Mrs. Trelawney before we dismiss this branch of our subject and tackle another? If he has, let him speak now."

VI

MRS. HINDLEY paused and looked round us all, when Mrs. Reynolds said quietly:—

"I was waiting and waiting all the time Mrs. Trelawney was talking to hear what she had to say on a very important question—the question of punishment. But she said just nothing at all."

"No," said my wife, "there is nothing to say."

"Mrs. Trelawney! what do you mean?" said Mrs. Reynolds with unfeigned surprise.

"I mean that there is, or should be, no such thing as punishment."

At this Mrs. Reynolds visibly started, and we all looked surprised, which my wife noticing went on:—

"Under ideal circumstances no punishment would be necessary, and even now in a well-regulated home it seems to me to be easy to dispense with it—punishment, that is, in the strict sense of the word. In education, I take it, the only aim of punishment can be reformation, and we have all this time been trying to discover such a means of moral education as shall dispense with the necessity of reformation altogether. It strikes me as a curious request to make, that after drawing up such an elaborate scheme we should revert, as it were, to weaker conditions and confess the breakdown of our machinery by considering punishment as if it were the driving wheel at length."

"I am afraid, my dear," I said, "even your favourite Pestalozzi would not bear you out there. He admits the necessity of punishment at times, even of corporal punishment."

"But you forget he had not the management of children from their birth. I am now regarding the case of children under our proposed regime from the moment of their birth.

You know I believe strongly in Herbert Spencer's doctrine of natural punishments."

"Then you do believe in punishments after all," said Mrs. Reynolds.

"Ah, but those punishments are not what is usually meant by the term. Hence it was that I said there is no such thing in my scheme. Natural punishments are the natural results of actions produced by the laws of nature working without interference from us."

"Would you not then allow us to express our displeasure when children do wrong?"

"Most certainly. To a child well brought up that is at once the most natural and the most dreaded of the results of evil-doing. Have you not read Herbert Spencer's book? Then I would advise you to do so; the whole point is put so lucidly and so convincingly that I can conceive no thinking person, at least, if he felt he had the strength to carry it through, not taking it as his cardinal principle in the management of children."

"Then I'm afraid, Mrs. Trelawney, I am not a thinking person," said Dr. Hindley.

"Well, Doctor, I never accused you of being so. But surely you do not mean to say you disagree."

"Indeed I do. Take the case of wanton and deliberate cruelty to a dumb animal. What natural punishment is there resulting from it to prevent its recurrence?"

"First, the displeasure of the more sympathetic elders; secondly, to prevent the child repeating the act, never allowing him to have anything to do with animals; thirdly, the explanation of the horrible nature of the offence and appeal to the doctrine of *quid pro quo*."

"Do you think that enough?"

"For children properly trained, yes. And further I would remind you that I have laid down the principle not in isolation, but as a part of a carefully reasoned out whole. Granted the conditions I have already explained, it seems to me the doctrine fits in to admiration."

"Well, I am not sure that I do not withdraw my objection. I was never opposed to the doctrine in the abstract —I thought it proceeded upon the right lines; my great objection was that I could not always see how the natural penalty was to ensue,—but on that you have enlightened me,—or how a principle of such great difficulty was to be always carried out."

"Difficulties are incentives to encourage us to fight. Surely, Doctor, you would not resign like a coward. I am sure your nobler self would recall that last remark. If we succumb because of the difficulties, how are we to produce a reform at all?"

"I deserve the rebuke," said the Doctor mildly. "But may I put a further question? Would you pursue the same course at school?"

"Certainly I would, though the question is really rather beyond my province. The mass of punishments are merely the results of vicious systems. I know one school for girls where the only punishment is—now what do you think? —Taking the offender's name off what is called a silver list—a list of the class written out and kept posted for that express purpose. I have not been able to discover that the discipline of the school has suffered at all from the mildness of the punishment. Why should not every school act similarly? It is an appeal to a right motive, and acts just as forcibly as an appeal to a wrong one. True, it is not the natural result; but granting the infirmity of our nature at present, and the imperfection of current arrangements, I do not consider it a serious infringement of the principle I have been upholding."

"It reminds me," I said, "of a case Locke mentions, where children were kept good merely through the fear of having their shoes taken off."

"And again," my wife went on, "we all know that in a school that is properly conducted, the punishment most dreaded is being reported to the Head, though nothing else follows than what boys, I hear, call expressively 'a jaw.'"

"There too I can bear you out," I said. "Many a boy has confessed to me, in the days when I was an assistant, that he would far rather do any number of other punishments, or even be caned, than have a lecture from the head master. I am certain that in this case there is no danger in working upon a boy's sense of shame."

"Well, I can see," said Mrs. Reynolds, "that there is a great deal to be said in your favour, Mrs. Trelawney; but I should be half afraid to try the experiment myself."

"But you must allow for the corruption produced by the other system. After all few faults of children are deliberately intended; they are mostly due to thoughtlessness or weakness of the flesh; by encouragement and forbearance I have seen children improve in a way which no amount of punishment would ever have produced. For that too is another disadvantage of our ordinary method, that it tends to provoke resentment and defiance—two of the worst qualities it is possible to engender."

"I have often tried," I said, "and sometimes with marvellous success, the principle of inducing the child to give me a promise that he will try to refrain from certain acts in future. Of course I am careful to point out that it is difficult always to carry out the promise, and that to make the promise and break it is a very serious matter; but on the whole I think the system works well."

"It seems to me," said the Doctor, "liable to very grave objections; though after all I fear that the same holds of almost every proposal one can make in moral matters: our whole discussion has been little more than a balancing of pros and cons. But your method seems to me dangerously like exposing a boy to gratuitous temptation. And it is really a serious matter to put a child in the way of breaking a promise; if he comes to regard a promise with levity, then all I can say is—God help him hereafter."

"I have thought over the danger, but in practice have not found it great. Children have for the most part a full realization of the important nature of a promise, even when given to a master; and if that master has treated them rightly, they will try to keep their word. But I never ask for more than a promise to try, and I sometimes think it well to put on a definite limit of time."

"Yes, it would be well to safeguard it, and though I am not prepared to say I quite agree, yet I feel that your practical experience in the matter is a factor of no slight weight. But I think we need hardly enter into the question more. We seem to have gone well over the ground of the moral training to be aimed at in the home, and the question of punishment has led us by an easy transition to the next branch of our subject—the training to be given by the school; the only question is—who shall handle it? who is to be the skittle set up to be knocked down?"

There was a general chorus of "Mr. Trelawney! Mr. Trelawney!" while Mrs. Hindley added: "You remember he put himself forward before, and undertook the work which he said my husband should have done. I think it only right that for a punishment—a natural punishment, mark you—he should now be compelled to continue the exposition, the more so, as he is the only working schoolmaster present."

"Well, Mrs. Hindley," I replied, "I really did hope that by this time you would have forgotten what passed more than a week ago."

"You are very complimentary," Mrs. Hindley retorted. "What a lot of interest you must suppose I took in the discussion."

"I never flattered myself you took so much interest in me. However, I suppose it is natural, though not a punishment, that I should be your leader in this branch of our subject. I have indeed been trying to arrange my thoughts on the point, and will make an effort to be short. But first, I should like to say that much of what my wife has said applies equally well to training at school. You will easily, I think, yourselves see what statements are universal and what specific, so that I need hardly go over them all. The general, indeed, should form the majority, for morals are not limited by time or place; conditions may vary for applying the rules, or there may be differences in the surroundings, which require us to emphasize by way of warning, or give us peculiar chances of impressing certain points; but in the main moral training must be one and indivisible, an organic growth, suited to the regular organic development of the steadily and gradually growing mind. Hence, though we have parted our subject into branches, I hope we shall all remember this is but a logical not a real separation; the fact is important to emphasize, as much evil results from putting away different parts of life, as it were, into separate water-tight compartments. Further, you will remember that the pure question of method in the matter of instruction we have been over at length, and I should be only wasting time to touch it again; please then assume the results of our dissection of Professor Adler's book as already established, when I go on to consider the points yet unhandled. These points, I think, will be found to be mainly a series of cautions—what to touch and what not to touch—moral influence brought to bear, not in systematic class-teaching, as expounded by Dr. Adler, on the value of which we are now agreed, but in the every-day surroundings of school work, and the special occasions or emergencies which may arise of themselves, or may be made by the master. Hence, I may be disjointed, as it is hardly possible to gather such *disjecta membra* into a logical sequence. I shall, however, be glad if others will fill any gaps I may leave.

"On the importance of love as a ruling factor throughout, enough has been said; we must, however, remember that in school this quality is more likely to appear in the form of happiness than in the shape of that more direct and keen emotion which we naturally look for in the home. If the spirit is there, all will do well; if it is wanting, our efforts at moral training will turn to dust and ashes. I remember being told of an incident in a school which occurred at the coming of a new head master. The boys of course were on the *qui vive*, eager to pick holes and, with their keen perceptions, to label their new ruler at once. He showed himself one morning and opened proceedings by an address to the boys, and this is the report which one of them gave to his people at home: 'When we saw him, we thought we should like him; but when we heard his voice, we knew it.' They had managed to divine, I suppose, that the man was really fond of boys, and likely to do his best to make them happy. It is the primary condition, useful in every branch of education, but indispensable in moral. And it naturally leads me to emphasize the point, to which I am not quite sure we have yet given its due importance, that the tone of the trainer is of the first moment; he may be very defective in method, but if his will is right and he can make it felt, his work will be a great one. We commonly are told that example is all-important, and we have, indeed, ourselves already said so; but I should like to correct the statement, or rather make clearer what we should mean precisely by example. I grant the imperativeness of it, but inasmuch as many of the virtues to which we have to lead our children are such as we have already made an essential part of our own character, so that we act up to them without an effort and quite unconsciously to ourselves, I think we are likely to lose part of our influence if we rely too much on the hope of the children merely copying us. The mere copying is of value, but it may be copying what seems a dead thing —a law of nature, the difficulty of observing which the children will not realize, because they do not see the struggle which has secured its observance among ourselves; if this is their attitude, as I think it well may be, there is danger that when the temptation comes, they will fall from mere misreckoning of the danger, and of their own strength to meet it. But if we fix our attention—and what I say now I do not mean to limit merely to school life —not on the force of example, but on the tone of character which all our actions display, so as to make our tone, as it were, the very sunlight by which the moral character of our charges is to live and grow, then I think there is more hope that we shall reach our end with greater surety than if we are merely correct in our conduct without the spark of enthusiasm and kindliness which makes children feel that morality is a living thing with a vital effect upon our whole being. I hope you understand me; the difference seems to me important, but I find it very difficult to put clearly what I exactly mean."

"I think I understand," said Mrs. Hindley. "Example, you would say, is but an object in nature, like a plant or a stone, which may excite admiration for its beauty, but which may not lead us any further; but the force of character, illumined by the desire to encourage others, is not an object but a power, like electricity or heat, doing a work of its own—in this case stimulating others to copy us, a result which inevitably follows, but which admiration for an unliving thing may or may not produce according to circumstances."

"Yes, I think that hits off pretty clearly what I mean, though it is an analogy, and I am always afraid of analogy in argument. The idea of power is, however, a good one to introduce; it is the guiding and stimulating force of character, which is after all the leading factor to consider. Hence it follows at once that in choosing our schoolmasters we must find out those who are born leaders of men; a man may have himself an excellent character, and yet for all his effect upon his pupils, may leave them cold. This proviso interprets to some extent, I think, what we meant when we agreed at the beginning of our discussion that the schoolmaster must be the exceptional man."

"I am afraid," put in my wife, "it leaves the poor parents whose case I have been defending, rather in the lurch; they cannot alter their natural endowments, whereas we can pick our schoolmasters and additional trainers."

"No doubt that is true, but it is a misfortune which I do not see how we are ever to get over, unless you are prepared to accept a Plato-like resolution that only given people shall be allowed to marry."

At this there was a smile, and Dr. Hindley said: "No, I am afraid that is too much even for me at present, advanced though I am, and readily as I admit that some such course is desirable in the case of those tainted with hereditary disease."

"Well, then, I fear we must leave the matter to stand. But this fact, to which we have come indirectly, furnishes surely an additional argument, and to my thinking a strong one, for insisting that every one should be sent to school, and not kept at home for the whole course of his training. It may not be true now, though I will not say it is not, but it certainly should be true in a proper state of the public mind on the question of education, that the average schoolmaster has a higher moral tone than the average parent in any given class of society. Otherwise what is he there for? A pumping-in machine, I suppose."

Here Dr. Hindley interrupted me with a smile, saying :—

"Ah, yes, Trelawney, we know from of old your rooted objection to the parent; it has not appeared for some time, but we had it in force at the opening of our discussion."

"Well, but wouldn't you agree to what I have just said?"

Dr. Hindley shook his head, and replied, laughing :—

"Oh, I'm not going to be such a fool as to give myself away by expressing an opinion on a subject which only vast evidence could settle, and which then would probably be settled after all merely by personal prejudice. No, thank you."

"Well, I shall take it then that silence shows consent.

But to proceed. There is an important error into which I fear we are likely to fall, if we do not put it before ourselves in explicit terms. We have been talking so much of moral education and emphasizing its importance for so long a time, that I am afraid when it comes to actual practice, we may conclude it is our duty to be constantly on the subject. There could not be a greater mistake. The conclusion is natural after ardent pleading, but here, at least, I am convinced it would be the mother of vast harm. It is on a par with the main fault of our present education in England,—to my thinking a grievous fault, likely to result in serious damage to the whole national character,—that of over-help, guiding the child too much and never leaving him a moment to develop of himself. You, Doctor, have already dwelt upon the danger, and I need not go over the ground again. I only refer to it here, as we might be led astray from our consideration of the subject in the abstract. For moral development especially the child must be left alone; if as a child he does not learn to fight temptation unassisted, when, pray, will he do so? He will grow up flabby and boneless, the sport of every wind that blows. And here, I think, we may perhaps content you, Mr. Reynolds, who have been pleading strongly for the necessity of battle. I quite concede its importance, and would say further that if we can so arrange circumstances as to leave the child to face only those moral dangers which are suited to his strength, then so much the better. But it is seldom we shall be able to do that, I think, and still more seldom that we shall be able to bring the temptations ourselves ; hence my objection to the theory you propounded, for it will be difficult to be sure, even when circumstances seem most advantageous, that the temptation will not be far harder than we think. But if we can experiment, as we suppose, with safety, whether the experiment be arranged by ourselves or by circumstances, then let us do so; only caution is necessary, the very utmost caution.

"But to return to the point of which I was treating, it will be well not always to go out of our way to shield a child from temptation, and it will be one of our first principles not to be for ever dwelling upon morality. We shall have set lessons at certain fixed times ; we shall have irregular talks as urgent occasions arise; we shall secure, so far as may be, that the whole tone around is one of encouragement, and then we shall have done our best; in the intervals, which will be many, the child must stand alone. The watched pot never boils, and if we are constantly leading the child to think about his motives and teaching him self-introspection before his reasoning faculties are well developed, we shall ruin his will—for no power can be his to balance reasons fairly; and as for the growth of a spontaneous habit, fresh, cheerful, and natural, we absolutely kill it. Don't overdo it, don't overdo it—that must be our danger signal; better leave without direct instruction than develop the morbid and self-conscious morality which makes, I fear, either a hypocrite or a prig.

"That is a caution I have thought it well to lay down clearly, as it applies to all stages of moral instruction, and really sums up the one great argument against formal instruction on the subject at all. I now propose to go at some length into various matters which may help or hinder the actual formal instruction which we should give on the lines laid down by Professor Adler. You will remember his book is limited to a consideration of instruction. I do not hope, and after what you have already heard you will hardly expect me, to be able to give you definite information as to practice. I can only suggest certain plans of action or arrangements which, helping morality, may perhaps be slightly more direct in their practical bearing than the lessons suggested by Professor Adler.

"And first I would say this, that a crucial test of the value of the home training comes as soon as the child enters school. The alteration of atmosphere is a severe trial to one who has not learnt to stand on his own legs; if he can face the novelty of his surroundings without being overthrown, he may be trusted to progress. I am supposing now, what is the commonest case, at least among children of our own class, that the child, never having been at a kindergarten, enters a small school about the age of eight. The larger the school, the greater as a rule the temptation, and the more bewildering to a young child; hence I would recommend that a small school be chosen, a day-school, and that, if possible, the child should not enter it till about ten years of age, unless indeed he has elder brothers or sisters who can to some extent encourage him in his new sphere. It would be well indeed if all children first passed through the kindergarten, not merely because of its excellence both morally and intellectually, but because they are then from very early years accustomed to mix with large numbers of others, and have learnt as they grow older, to lean upon themselves almost without knowing it. But this we cannot expect at present, and I do not conceal from myself that even the kindergarten is not perfect. But whether this be so or not, the fact remains that our home education ought to have so prepared the child that the temptations of school life, coinciding as they do with the withdrawal of that closer care which watches him at almost every turn, shall find him ready to fight them boldly, plunged though he be for the first time into the bracing experience of real life.

"Now one of the primary conditions of good moral arrangements at school must be the classification of children—I was going to say according to their years; but inasmuch as at the same period there may often be almost as great a divergence between the moral as between the intellectual development of different children, I would rather say according to their advancement in moral perception. It is not an object very easy to attain, but we must at least try. We frequently see great harm done from the habitual intercourse of children who are at very different stages of moral culture. One boy will have arrived at such a stage that he can discern when a given rule will admit of exception, while other children who are allowed to constantly be his associates, receive a shock every time such a case occurs. I do not quite see how the evil is to be remedied as long as schools are regarded chiefly as intellectual workshops, and perhaps it occurs more often with children of larger growth than those whom I have just specified; but it is well to bear it in mind."

"But surely, Mr. Trelawney," said Mrs. Hindley, "that collision of moral insight is one of the means by which we secure moral development."

"No doubt it has its value, but I think it would be

better if we could ensure that such shocks did not occur save just where we thought best."

"Ah, Trelawney," said Reynolds, "I fear you want too much. Surely nature, that is God, may be trusted to do something. After all, however much we may theorize and try, we are liable to overlook essential points and make havoc of the fairest-looking scheme. I would not go too far; some risks we must run, and only hope that our precautions have prevented serious evil. You seem to me to be wanting too much in faith."

"Yes, Reynolds, I think your rebuke is deserved. But it is always my tendency to think more can be done by what I may call mere machinery than experience ever shows to be really practicable. I fancy I have overstepped the mark, and am willing to recall what last I said. Let nature then, in this respect at least, have her way—or rather perhaps our social arrangements. All I would still maintain is, that we should take care to avoid the more flagrant evils, the mixing of children of great diversity of years. Most educators are alive to the danger, but, unfortunately, with the prevalent idea that the aim of school life is to develop the intellect—whereas surely the proper aim is the training in morality, all else being subsidiary to that—I fear we are not always as strict as we might be, but too frequently let the intellect decide. The difficulty is great, especially in view of what parents expect.

"I have already insisted on the necessity of cheerfulness in the whole of school business, and as I turn over in my thoughts what actually passes in the every-day routine of school, the first thing that occurs to me is the need of a definite aim, and regularity in its pursuit. The former point at least is often overlooked. The aim of school life—what should it be? I just now declared that in the first place it should be morality; but without going over all the various details which naturally enter into our conception of its final end, I should like to treat specifically of one or two facts which it is necessary always to have in view. The aim must be determined by what is to follow, as it must be with every part of education, if our education is to be a really organic whole.

"To say that education is a 'preparation for life you

will probably condemn as a mere truism. But truisms are useful when from them we can deduce some practical maxim to guide our conduct. And that, I think, we can do here. It follows, in the first place, that school moral education should aim at fitting children to guide themselves well—no matter the period at which they leave—amid those special circumstances into which they find themselves thrown. Now these vary greatly, from the case of the child who has completed his standards and enters at once upon the work of his life, to the case of the young man who only leaves school to pass to a higher school—the University. Hence difficulties, as the teaching must be adapted to such very different ends. In the case of the child of working parents, our aim must be to give it a firm grasp of those principles which are likely to be of most service during the rest of his life. Little more can be done than to implant moral principles, showing how they apply, and warning him to beware of such conflicts of principles as may arise hereafter. It will hardly be possible, however, to give him concrete examples in any large number, though a few may be given, and some may occur even among the cases that turn up at school. If so, the most must be made of them."

"Pardon me interrupting you," said Mrs. Reynolds, "but I should like to ask why you think it necessary in the case of children so young, whose reasoning powers in very few cases will have reached a high development, to dwell so much upon cases where reasoning comes in? Why not leave the child to settle for himself when the difficulty arises in his later life?"

"Because I am afraid, if he is not already warned, he may say to himself when crises come that none of the rules given him can possibly apply—they conflict with each other, and therefore nothing can be right. That is likely to be the result on such a mind as we suppose—a mind which cannot look for much direct moral help among its surroundings. Will not the young boy or girl at once say that all he learnt at school was mere schoolmaster's talk—that all the great praise and importance attached to proper conduct was merely to suit the special conditions of school—that as duties conflict, there is no law at all, he may simply please himself? Such an attitude would be fatal, and yet I believe it is the common attitude of many who have been carefully trained in categorical morality, but, not having been shown the ultimate foundation, when difficulties come, throw everything overboard. Here, indeed, is the cardinal point of all; most can recognise a simple duty, and most will fulfil it; but the foundations of morality are sapped when simple rules no longer hold, and the unhappy victim has never been shown any clue by which to find the true path. Most wrong-doing, I believe, at least of the lesser kind, comes from ignorance rather than wrong intent:—

'For evil is wrought by want of thought
More than by want of heart.'

To this end all our enlightenment should be directed—the furnishing of a clue which shall always show the right. I do not, of course, pretend we can give such a clue in all its completeness to a mere child who leaves our hands at the age of twelve or thirteen; but if we have shown him that such a clue is necessary and taught him to use it upon simple occasions, when, in after-life, with his greater reasoning powers, he comes across a difficulty, then he will, we may trust, have a chance of finding his way, which he never would have had if our teaching had been purely formal.

"With those children who leave school at a later period, at, it may be, fifteen or sixteen, we shall alter our training if we are wise, so far at least as to give them an insight into the true rules upon which morality rests, and to make the idea of the conflict of duties not merely an idea which they are to develop by after-experience under the rough handling of the outer world, but a living idea, a living principle by which they will have learnt to guide themselves, and whose value they will know from actual experience. We shall, in fact, have more time to arrive at the result we have to prematurely force in the case of the younger ones, with the hope in the latter instance, though hardly, I fear, the certainty, that the plant which has been forced may eventually prove as hardy as the one that has been allowed to develop according to the gentler course of nature. With these older children there will have been time to let our lessons sink in far more thoroughly; much, indeed, which we shall have taught by twelve to the more hapless class we can safely leave here till perhaps two years later. Moreover, we shall now be able to go into a larger list of virtues, and to show their bearings more thoroughly than we have been able to do with the first class named; our foundations thus will be broadened as well as deepened, and we ought to find later a more solid super-structure. In the first case we may hope, in the latter case we should be sure, that some of our teaching will cling for ever."

"But," said the Doctor, "if your principle is to hold, it seems to me we shall be landed in a very strange paradox. If school is to be the preparation for life in the most effective way, and if after-life involves, as it surely does, the chance, nay, the obligation, to manage oneself with the very least of help from others, does it not follow that we ought to give children while still at school the means of managing themselves, and that the earlier they are to leave the more freedom they ought to have?"

Every one was clearly rather startled by this remark, and for my part I really did not know what to say. I thought for a few moments, and then replied :—

"No, Doctor, I really must give it up. I confess your objection has quite overthrown me. I cannot believe it would be a good thing to do, and yet I cannot believe that my principle is wrong, or that either of the inferences we have respectively drawn from it is faulty. I am completely nonplussed."

We looked at each other a little while in silence, till my wife, who had been going on with her work, said :—

"Why, surely, after all the answer is not very far to seek. Does it not lie in the point you were last discussing—the conflict of duties?"

"In what way?" I asked.

"Why, we see that we ought to allow children more liberty in proportion as they are likely the sooner to have to stand entirely on their own legs. On the other hand we see that it is a dangerous thing to do, and moreover ridiculous, if a child, and that too a child whose moral training is presumably inferior to that of others, is to be allowed more liberty than those very others, liberty which he will not in all probability know how to use so well. But it is a question of balancing the one end against the other, and it seems to me that if we grant the greater liberty, but qualify it by remembering the force of the other consideration, so that what we allow is not perhaps actually more liberty than we shall allow to other children at a more advanced period of their moral proficiency, but simply greater freedom relatively, which after all may be freedom under strict supervision, we shall have reached our end. Freedom in this connection where those whom we are considering are of necessity *in statu pupillari*, differing from grown men, surely only means a relative freedom at the best."

" True," I replied; " but it does not seem to me to much lessen the paradox. Still, you have suggested to me the real solution; at least I venture to hope it is so. It is this—that in view of the early emancipation of certain children from all moral control, our discipline over them should be lighter from the first, and we must relax it more speedily and with greater leaps than we should do with children who will be with us longer."

"But that remains a paradox still," said the Doctor. "Why not say the earlier the emancipation, the more stringent the control?"

"Because I am afraid of the sudden rebound. So I am afraid the paradox still is there. Really the question seems likely to reduce itself to a question of practical efficiency in the trainer. We shall have, I fancy, to proceed on the lines of giving a greater freedom—and yet I do not say necessarily great; it may be only a relatively great freedom in proportion to the tender years of our flocks. To those who are to leave us early, the course will bring great difficulties in its train; but if we aim at it throughout, no doubt we shall be able to conquer most of them. And moreover, it seems to me that this very difficulty proves the correctness of a principle which the Doctor has made the fundamental one in the whole of our training—the principle of rule by love. Now if we rule by love, we ought to have no fear of our teaching being dropped because we were not able to prolong it as we wished. On the contrary I think that the younger the children the more are they likely to retain their affection for us and to guide their after-conduct by what we should like. And moreover, it is undoubtedly true that children who come from those classes where love is comparatively little bestowed upon them value it more and are more readily influenced by it than children of a more fortunate position. So that it seems to me that here we have reached a most unexpected corroboration of the truth of a principle which was most likely to be called in question—the principle that in all we should be guided by love.

"The same general thought must be kept before our minds in training those who will be with us till eighteen or nineteen. As we can advance more slowly and with a greater wealth of illustration and practical experiment with the second class of children than with the first, so when we have those who are passing from boyhood altogether, we shall do well to lead them on to the more complex problems of morality and get them to express their views in set treatises or essays. Throughout our aim must be to be gradually removing the leading-strings and props which support the feeble younglings, till, with the case of the oldest, who will soon be their own masters, we should be able to throw off the restraint altogether and say: 'You nowknow what is the path of right—walk in it rightly and prove yourself a man.' That is, I well know, the aim of our schools now; but I cannot admit they altogether do well: we have but to consider how wild are the youths just emancipated from school, how childish, as I have heard it said by the Head of one of our great public schools, are the mass of undergraduates, to recognise that there must be something fatally wrong. What that wrong is, it is not easy to see. You will say that with the responsibility of monitorship and the larger freedom allowed to the Sixth Form boy, you have gone as far as possible consistently with the welfare of the school as a whole: how is it then you do not succeed better? For certainly it is true that the average Sixth Form boy is far less childish than the average undergraduate a year or two his senior."

"But," said Mr. Reynolds, "you will always get a little outbreak of uproariousness when the last checks are removed and the young man feels for the first time that he is really free."

"No doubt; but I think it is excessive with undergraduates, and is often far worse than mere uproariousness Where does the fault lie, and how are we to cure it?"

"I should ascribe it to three distinct causes," said the Doctor: "first, that at school with the sense of responsibility his monitorship brings, a boy has, as it were, an outer check upon him, taking the place of the old control; secondly, that it is impossible at a boarding-school to give him that absolute freedom which is the sole guarantee of power to manage oneself—the freedom conferred is not a real freedom, but only the removal of two or three of the chains; thirdly, he has seldom been really instructed in morality; he has done right because he must, either from fear of his master or from a sense of shame, and not because he would."

"I suppose then, Doctor, your cure would be to have no boarding-schools,—a point on which we agreed before,—to give proper instruction, and to give real freedom in everything to the oldest boys at a school?"

"Not necessarily to the oldest, but to those whom we now take to be most suited for monitors."

"I see; but how far would you extend this freedom? Would you let them, for instance, stay away from school when they liked?"

"Certainly, if their moral development is such that you think they can be trusted in other matters."

"Really, Doctor, when shall we reach the end of your revolutions?"

"When the world is perfect according to my ideas, not before."

I laughed, and said:—

"Well, I am so far in sympathy with you, that if my elder boys do not work, I merely expostulate and say that if they do not by then know the value of work, they ought to, and I am not going to bother about teaching them any more. I seldom find the method fail. And, after all, if we do otherwise, what does it amount to? We keep the boy at work for a year or two longer, get him entered safely at the University, with, it may be, a scholarship to the credit of the school, and then leave him with calm conscience exposed to manifold temptations we know he has not the strength to resist: whereas it would be far better for his parents to have discovered of what material he was made at first, and turned him out to work at some employment or other which would at least keep him from mischief and not lead him to think he came into the world merely to be lazy and possibly corrupt others."

"Dear me!" said Mrs. Hindley; "I wonder, Mr. Trelawney, how long you have been preparing that little explosion?"

"Oh, it's a pet theory of mine, and you must excuse my warmth. But I do seriously think that less moral harm would be done—to take this point of view alone—if schoolmasters were not so anxious to drive their boys into getting scholarships without any regard to their moral character. Better let a boy know less and rely on himself more, than know vastly more and be weak as a reed. And in this point, at all events, we have such an easy chance of really insisting on the moral point of view. It is no good to retain the whip and spur till the very end of a boy's career at school. The fall we may be sure will come, unless our foundations have been laid extraordinarily deep. But if we are to go as far as the Doctor suggests, I fear we shall scare parents out of their wits. If you can get their consent, well and good; but if not, such a scheme is a mere chimera."

"You forget, Trelawney, I have over and over again claimed that I am not legislating for the world as it is. We have already admitted that to secure good morality, the world must advance along all lines at once. Given a time when it was likely we could carry out such a scheme we should also have parents prepared to accept it."

"Ah, that simplifies matters considerably," I said; "and I agree with you in thinking that the plan would be desirable. Desirable, indeed, I admit it to be now; but I can hardly say I think it anywhere within reach of present-day politics."

"Nor I," said the Doctor; "but that is neither here nor there. Will you please resume the thread of your argument?"

Thus appealed to, I went on:—

VII

"WE have now, I trust, explained sufficiently in detail the bearing of the first maxim I deduced from the truism that school education must aim at life—a maxim, I would repeat, which is equally applicable to the moral training of home. I now invite your attention to a second, which is that we must warn children not to expect to find their own moral code as yet in general acceptance; the world, we must tell them, is not as advanced as they."

"But why not leave them to find that out for themselves, which they will do soon enough?" said the Doctor.

"For the same reason that I gave in answer to Mrs. Reynolds—the fear lest in discovering that their own views were not the same as those of the world at large and that they could not always get the world to bow, they should hastily conclude they were themselves wrong and all they had learnt an enthusiast's dream. Everything might then go, and all love's labour be lost. But if they are warned, two good results may ensue: first, they may go out with the intention of reformers, keenly set on proving the superiority of their code; secondly, they will believe, when they see how far the world is below the beautiful dream of moral perfection which they have indulged, that it is all the more desirable to make every effort to reach the consummation so devoutly to be wished. For this, I think, at least is universally true, that one who has been once inspired with the love of true moral beauty, though he may fall from his ideal to even a large extent, yet never wholly shakes himself free from its power, and will make efforts at times to show its beauty to others. And with all our young men and women turned out with heads and hearts full of noble dreams of moral beauty, I think that but a few generations might see the world vastly changed.

"Next, I would bring home to the minds of the children that a different code applies in many things to children from what applies in the case of grown men and women. Of course this is one of the greatest difficulties in our way, but it must be faced and exemplified whereever possible. Arguments from analogy may here be of use, as, for instance, that it is harmful for a child to sit up late, whereas to a man it would often be injurious to spend as many hours in bed as are necessary for a child. But moral examples can also be used: a good one to take would be obedience. A child must be prepared to accept the bidding of another, because it cannot yet see all the bearings of a question; but for a full-grown man to do exactly as he was told, where his own interests were concerned as much as those of the other, and where he had himself as good powers and opportunities of forming a judgment—a frequent case in politics—is nothing short of either criminal laziness or cowardice. It seems to me very desirable to make this point very clear, as one of the commonest objections which children raise is: 'Why may not I do it? So-and-so does it'; and it is but a discontenting answer to reply that what is good for grown people is not necessarily good for little boys and girls. It is emphatically a case where reason should be used as soon as ever it is possible.

"Another point I would mention, but in this I shall be passing from injunctions to warnings—that is, injunctions reversed. Avoid moral precocity. A child may be led by constant talking of morality to think that its conduct is all that can be desired. Should you see traces of such belief, you may be sure you are doing harm. The danger is, of course, only too closely akin to the other danger which accompanies all teaching of morality by set discussion—the danger of thinking that talk about morality and moral action are one and the same thing. The type of character meant is not uncommon, I grieve to say, in the religious world,—we have indeed already referred to it,— and unhappily not so rare as to be altogether unknown even amongst young school children. I, at least, have met with more than one instance of it. It is the outgrowth of unwise probing into a child's sentiments and undue fostering of self-introspection. The harm is often done at home, but may be produced or certainly increased at school. But we must beware of confounding or letting the child confound intellectual knowledge of morality with morality itself. And, on the other hand, I would say this—never make a child do what he thinks to be wrong. Cases of conscience of this kind do arise, and however foolish we may think the child's opinion to be, if we cannot persuade him otherwise, we must let our point go. To force a child to act against the bidding of his conscience is to sap the very foundation of all morality. It is our duty, then, to bring reason to bear, and if we fail, well, we fail, though we have done our best. But here, too, I would add yet another caution—we must not argue too much. If we spend too long a time or too much effort in trying to persuade a child to see as we know to be best, we are likely to develop both vanity and obstinacy. The proverb here applies: 'Answer a fool according to his folly and he shall be wise in his own conceit.' No; we must allow the matter to pass if driven too hard, but bear the point in mind and attack it from time to time, though indirectly and so that the child will not see our aim. And similarly I would say: never force an apology, never even suggest one. It is not an uncommon method of making a child escape punishment, but I would rather let him go scot free than suggest to him a mode of conduct which, from the circumstances under which it occurs, often ends in nothing else than telling a public lie. If the offender's own conscience suggests this mode of reparation, well and good; but I think it will be found that it seldom does. Repentance with children, according to my observation, usually takes the form of leading to increased affection and a greater and more persistent effort to please, rather than to the performance of what is perhaps the hardest of all tasks to a self-respecting being—the open confession of one's own fault. I am aware that such confession is a wonderful moral discipline; but how many of us would willingly undergo it? And, after all, I think that in the case where an apology is practically forced from the child, it is as much a desire—perhaps not expressed to oneself—to gratify our pride that leads us to recommend that particular course as any real concern about the child's moral welfare.

"In many of the points I have lately been discussing, you will easily see that I have trespassed beyond my province: for much of what I have said applies equally to home as to school; in fact, we may say they are general principles of morality. But now I should like to pass on to other matters which do really concern schools in chief and above all, though even here I will not say but what you may discover germs of thought which are of use in every branch of ethical training; for, after all, as we have said, such training must be one and continuous from first to last; it will, therefore, be only one proof the more that our principles are right, if we find that those we lay down for one branch of the training are really in essence applicable to them all. But I do not propose to stop any more to dwell upon this feature; the stretching of our maxims as far as they will go is a task that may safely be left to ourselves.

"Let us first treat our subject by considering in what point lies the essential difference between home and school. The most obvious difference is suggested by the grouping into classes which occurs as soon as a child enters school. Here, first, he gets his initiation explicitly into life, where each individual as an individual is unimportant, where each is merely a part of one great whole. It is the bringing-out and emphasizing of this vital point—a point of the first magnitude in regard to morality—that seems to me to constitute one of the leading features of school life and at the same time its claim to occupy a very high place in any system of moral training. For, after all, does not a really living morality turn more upon the fact that one grasps one's own insignificance in comparison with others than upon any other single fact whatever? We are each single cells together helping to make up the whole mass of connective social tissue. School is the real initiation into social claims and social life. The family, it seems to me, may be and too often is, at least from some points of view, an anti-social centre, a circle for the sake of any members of which we are often willing to disregard the claims of society at large. I see you do not quite grasp what I mean."

"No, I certainly do not," said the Doctor. "I always look upon the family as the centre from which spread our altruistic feelings; they take their origin in the love which is naturally engendered in any family which is properly conducted, and from there, as we grow older, we extend feelings similar, though not perhaps so strong, to the larger family of humanity around us."

"I am aware that is the ordinary view," I replied; "but it seems to me there is something to be said for the other point of view too. What I mean is this: I should not, of course, deny that as you, Doctor, have just said, in the ultimate analysis our social feelings can probably be traced back to our regard for the various members of our own family; but, on the other hand, it often happens that the members of a family, who may be completely social in their dealings one with another, may be so locked up in one narrow sphere, as it were, as to care nothing for the claims of the outside world when they come into conflict with the interests of their relatives. And is not this essentially an anti-social feeling? It is simply a large extension of selfishness. Take an instance where a relative or friend has done wrong and it is in one's power to protect him from suffering the consequences, if we choose to adopt a line of conduct which, while it will save him, will not inflict any harm that is apparent at the first glance on any special individual. To make a strong comparison, such conduct seems to me little better than honour among thieves. In fact, to my thinking, the proper argument to adopt is that in proportion as the wrong is a wrong to society at large, and is, as it were, diffused generally, the more it behoves us to protect society even at the expense of our own near friends. If the wrong is a wrong to a single individual, he may usually be trusted to protect his own interests from a mere feeling of self-regard; but if the wrong does not come home specially to any one, then, as good citizens, it is our duty even to go out of our way to denounce the offender, though at much suffering to ourselves. The case is by no means of infrequent occurrence. Take the administration of public offices for instance. How often do we wink at what may be perhaps mere slackness in the discharge of duty, though often, I fear, it is far more than that, simply because the offender is a friend of our own or a member of our party! Sometimes our error may be comparatively venial, as when we help the offender to re-election; sometimes it takes the form of actually suppressing evidence we can give or indirectly conniving at his offence. Smuggling is a common form of transgression in this respect; many people who would not defraud the customs themselves yet say nothing when they know their friends do it. Now I maintain that such a course is absolutely wrong, and the principle I lay down is in brief this: that private feelings of affection must be utterly disregarded in all cases of wrong-doing, and the more petty the wrong and the less directly it is an offence against any one in particular, the more it behoves us to put society first. What is every man's business is no man's business, and were there not those very devoted people who make it a point to show up a wrong wherever they come across it,—the action which is exemplified by the proceedings of societies for prevention of cruelty of various kinds,—then, I say, the world would be very far from progressing even as well as it now does. A development of this sense of public duty, of the importance of public claims as against private feelings, seems to me one of the main directions in which we should try to work to secure an improvement in public morality, and especially by teaching children the correct view."

"Your theory is a noble one, Trelawney," said Reynolds; "but I fear there is little chance of its being carried out. And, after all, does not this strict feeling of justice lead you to a too complete disregard of the counterbalancing principle—the great one of mercy? Forgiveness of wrongs is often the most effective punishment."

"True. That is a principle I often apply at school; but I think it is more effective with children than with grown men; and certainly I feel very strongly indeed that it is our business as educators to try to raise public tone in the respect I have named, even though in considering the theory in the abstract we may lay too much stress on that one principle which is too often disregarded. Society stands paramount; from society the individual gets his entire meaning. And this brings me back to the point from which I fear I have rather digressed—the fact that school is the opening of really social life. From this one fact seems to me to follow a chief principle by which we must guide our instruction always — at home we shall cultivate in especial those virtues which are self-regarding or which result from deep sympathy and love for our fellows; at school we shall cultivate chiefly the social virtues, extending the feelings of love and sympathy, which the child brings with him from home limited to a comparatively narrow set of persons, to the wider circle of humanity and indeed of all living things. I do not mean to say that the two spheres can be kept apart either at school or at home in their entirety; I only draw attention to the main distinctions and leanings. What is separate in discussion may not be separate in practice. And this consideration of our social duties will naturally culminate in the consideration of that special form of them to which so much attention has been recently drawn—one's duties as a citizen. But it is a great mistake to cut that off from other moral training, as if it were a branch apart; one's whole duty as a citizen embraces everything, and therefore all our moral training should be working to that end, and if it has been conducted in the right method, we shall, when we come to treat specifically of civic duty, find that little remains to be done save putting in a new light duties already quite within our grasp, already practised.

"And the grouping of children into forms and associations enables us to teach them some other valuable lessons, which I think I need do no more than mention. They are such as these: the balancing of claims of conflicting societies, of the duty perhaps towards a class or a house as compared with our duty to the school as a whole, or of the claims of the school as compared with the claims of home—a point which takes sometimes, though in a good school but rarely, the extreme and difficult form of a conflict between the commands of a parent and of a master, in regard, it may be, to such a matter as night-work; the necessity of submitting to greater order and method than is always necessary or desirable at home, in order to further the general school life; development of patriotism or *esprit de corps*, by which I do not mean that blind unreasoning form of it, which ends simply in saying that all we do is good, and if ever others differ, they must be necessarily bad; but a thinking admiration and love of one's fellows, due to a real regard for them, and not separated from the willingness to boldly rebuke their faults whenever one discovers them; in short, doing the best for the welfare of the school from the highest attainable point of view; and, above all, the leading children to feel that we have duties even towards our enemies; and that because our love for our schoolfellows is weaker than our love for our own near kin, it does not therefore follow that we are right in treating them worse. Here, in fact, I think we shall find the great difficulty, in leading the child to extend his sympathies to those with whom he comes in contact, not because, as at home, he loves them and they do him good, but because it is his duty as a human being. Of the more manly virtues which are developed by removing the child from what I may call, without disparaging intent, the nursery atmosphere to school, I hardly think it needful to speak. They result very largely from the natural conditions of things without special interference from us, whereas what we are considering now is rather those points in which morality wants guidance from the trainers of youth.

"But I should like here to insert a caution. It seems to me that boys—I do not think the case holds in the same way with girls—pass through a stage that I may call non-moral, when their moral perceptions indeed appear to remain the same, but their moral feelings are asleep. In the rough I should say the age is usually from about twelve to fifteen. Up to twelve or thereabouts the child is amenable to the softening influence of sympathy and love; but then comes a time when the boy is apt to speak of the tenderer emotions as, in his expressive language, 'bosh' or 'rot.' Appeals to his heart, to use popular phraseology, seem useless, or less useful, at all events, than before; while that motive power has not been replaced by the perception of duty as a right in itself. The stage is a critical one, and here, if anywhere, I think the opponents of our system may reasonably urge that love breaks down. It does not altogether, but as a conscious motive to the boy it seems for the time dead. At this stage, then, we may have to resort to command more than at other periods;

but my own experience shows me that it is precisely now that reasoning begins to be useful and produce great effects. The boy is, of course, still guided by affection, if he is rightly handled; but it now requires to be reinforced by direct teaching, showing that he is in such a position that he cannot do merely what he likes. It is a curious phase, but happily only passing. In many ways it is the most critical stage of a boy's moral development. Cruelty is a very frequent accompaniment, especially manifesting itself in that abominable boyish vice—bullying. A calm disregard of the feelings of others is prominent throughout. When such conditions prevail, we must not be surprised if for a time our pupil make no moral progress, or even seem to retrogress. But we need not therefore despair. We can use the time well for gathering moral percepts and working them up into generalised forms; for the intellect now is often peculiarly active, and begins to take an interest in all that goes on; and though the moral judgment, which we can now be training, may not bear fruit in immediate action, the conclusions reached will not be forgotten, but will be stored up in memory, and in most cases be applied when the conscience begins at last to develop in full vigour, about the age, roughly speaking, of sixteen. It is well during this transition time to make comparatively few calls upon the boy for moral action in unusual directions, rather give him opening for his animal spirits; for if they are allowed a healthy development, we shall find him later charged with a fund of energy which will influence his moral conduct in unexpected ways. After all, morality depends, in a more vital way than we often recognise, upon the condition of the animal organism; and if during this period of moral lassitude we can work upon some of those parts of a boy's constitution which will affect him afterwards, then I think our time will by no means be wasted.

"It would be impossible, and indeed undesirable, for me to attempt to lay down a complete, or nearly complete, list of the methods in which we may help the moral growth of the children put under our charge at school. In many points now all good schools are agreed. It will only be necessary to dissent here and there; and I can best perhaps attain the end we have in view by taking some points in detail which it seems to me can be improved, or where we are at present altogether defective. Of course I am speaking now of handling subjects quite apart from the set intellectual instruction in ethics on which we have already dwelt. I shall probably find occasion to add a few warnings, and my omissions will, I trust, be supplemented by suggestions from each and all of you.

"To begin with, I cannot insist too strongly upon the value of always opening and closing school with prayers."

Here Dr. Hindley at once exclaimed:—

"But you forget, Trelawney, we are trying to consider moral education apart from religious influences altogether."

"If you go as far as that," I replied, "I fear you are attempting an impossibility. It is impossible to drive out religion from the air, as impossible as it is to exhaust the oxygen."

"But you yourself agreed earlier to this course of proceeding."

"Pardon me," I said; "what I agreed to was trying to devise a system of moral as apart from religious instruction and education. To expect to do so apart from religious influences altogether seems to me beating the air."

"Yes," said the Doctor, "I admit the correctness of your statement. I certainly exaggerated. But still, you are now going further than your own position, and directly introducing religious training."

"Not necessarily, I think," was my rejoinder; "for even apart from directly religious emotions, attendance at divine service has a sobering and solemnising effect, which the educator is quite at liberty to use without committing himself to religious training."

"I fear," said Mrs. Hindley, "you are getting too subtle for us. I admit the solemnising influences of a religious service under certain circumstances; but I should find it hard to believe that those influences were not religious in themselves. However, let us hear what you have to say; we are not bound to admit it as a good part of purely moral education."

"Well, then," I resumed, "it seems to me that school

prayers at the beginning and end of school, by the sobering effect which they have, lead boys to realize that school life is an earnest life, and that it is important to approach it in the most serious way. But to attain this end fully the prayers must not be a mere formal business, hurried over without any attempt to bring out the noblest side of them. The reader, who, of course, will be the head master and never a chaplain, will give much time and thought to reading them in the most impressive way, so as to bring home to the boys' minds the idea that it is not a mere piece of routine which has to be finished as quickly as possible, but is, a type of the way in which everything in life should be done. To this end it is well that the prayers should be varied; with the young, at all events, I think the constant repetition of the same prayers is apt to seem monotonous, and does not lead to the desired effect. At the same time, I would rarely have extemporaneous prayers. My own feeling in regard to them, though I am aware that on this point there is a large divergence of opinion, is that they are seldom, if ever, impressive, if only for the reason that you cannot expect people to be able at given moments to express the deep emotions which a state of prayer should naturally arouse."

"Really, Trelawney, I do not think now," said the Doctor, "you can deny that you are treating the subject from a purely religious point of view."

"Perhaps I am going rather far," I answered; "but still I am not sure that a state of prayer is in every case necessarily the same as what is usually recognised as a religious state. It seems to me that in moments of serious thought one naturally falls into the state which is identical with a state of prayer, as far at least as the mere emotions go, though I do not deny that the feeling of devotion to a personal God may make a difference. But that difference, I should say, does not constitute a difference in the actual state of prayer *quâ* prayer. However, the distinction is a subtle one, and I may not carry you all with me, so I will not labour it any more. Of course, if you cannot accept my position, and it might be controverted from two opposite points of view, you must drop from your recollections what I have just been saying.

"But to proceed. Because of the desire to make services impressive, I should avoid the use of prayers—of which many have been composed—which do not breathe a real spirit of deep earnestness throughout. It often seems to me that the collections of what are called family prayers are wanting in precisely that element which would make them most valuable. They seem merely a collection of every possible petition which is likely to be often made, but without the life which is of the real essence of true prayer. A long prayer often strikes me as being unprayerlike exactly in proportion to its length. Of course there are divergencies of feeling on this important matter; but for my own part I think there are but few prayers in English which are worthy to be put on a level with those in the Book of Common Prayer. But, no doubt, I am not an impartial judge, as I was brought up as a member of the Church of England; and it is very hard to sever the emotions awakened by a thing itself from those awakened by its associations. However, I give it as my own opinion without wishing to force it upon you. Indeed, for my own part I regard the literary beauty of those prayers as no small item in their influence. The perception of beauty has always a moral influence—you may deny that the influence of this particular beauty is religious; I do not think you can deny that it is moral.

"For the sake of the impressiveness of the services, I would not have a boy read the lessons. It is a rare thing if he can bring out the meaning as well as the head master, with his greater width of experience, ought to be able to do. In any case the whole service will be short, occupying scarcely at most ten minutes; and a lesson from the Bible need not perhaps occur at the end of school. I would have, too, a special selection of lessons made, consisting of those parts which are most likely to appeal to the young, whether from their literary or their moral beauty. A great many parts of the Bible are quite beyond the comprehension of boys and girls at school; these parts I would have omitted entirely. Moreover, the head master should on special occasions choose such parts as are likely to show their own bearing upon recent incidents, whether in the life of the school or in the history of the world. I do not think we can possibly go too far in bringing our services into vital connection with the every-day affairs of our life. I am convinced that religion has lost much of its influence because we keep our churches open only on Sunday, and observe Sunday in such a way as to lead people to think that religion is to be followed most duteously then, but during the rest of the week we may do as we please. We want a more vital connection between every-day life and religious and moral feelings, and some of the rules I am laying down would, I think, go far towards supplying the defect. And further, it seems to me we should gain in this union if we sometimes chose our lessons not from the Bible but from other authors who have left us valuable thoughts on morality. Or we might make collections of such passages, and read one or two of them occasionally as a supplement to the passages from the Bible. Whatever we can do to bring the young to feel that the Bible is a book for everyday guidance, and for treating in the same way as we should treat other books, is a clear gain to the cause of progressive morality.

"Further, I would have the head master just occasionally give a short address on some of the leading points in morality. I do not like to speak of a sermon, because it is apt to call up too stilted and lifeless ideas—I beg your pardon, Reynolds—and, moreover, seems to cut one off from all possibility of indulging in the lighter vein of address with humour intermixed. I am a great believer in the light style of treatment, especially with children. Hence I recommend addresses and not sermons. Let them be of the most familiar style, just as a friend talking to friends. If the master is in earnest, the earnestness will appear, and will lose none of its effect from its surroundings. Boys, I know, like this kind of address; it might even occasionally be intermingled with questions to some of those present. And, above all, let it be practical. I have myself found it valuable to take a single virtue, point out its importance both for the present and for the future; give illustrations of it, especially drawn from what has happened in school to oneself; and put it all, not in grandiloquent language, but just as one would tell a story to a friend. Boys see the point so much more easily if one takes incidents in their own career, and can quote the excuses they give in their own words. Hosts of such illustrations present themselves to one who is on the look-out; and by this means we can bring home to the boys' minds the fact that morality is an affair of every-day life, not a treasure to be kept under lock and key and brought out for display now and then.

"But these addresses must be short and of infrequent occurrence. I would never give more than two per term, and usually only one. I have two reasons for this course: first, the desire to prevent them being monotonous; secondly, the fact that they will require very careful preparation; and we cannot expect a master who is constantly preaching to be able to produce much that is new on each occasion. If our sermons in churches were rare treats, instead of occurring with regularity every Sunday, I think, Mr. Reynolds, you and your fellows would rejoice, and at the same time would produce ten times the effect you do."

"I quite agree with you," said Reynolds, "but I fear we should often have empty churches; for, though I am sorry to have to confess it, I believe it to be true that the mass of people come very little for the service, but chiefly, if not entirely, for the sake of the sermon."

"Well, in a school, where the head master can do as he pleases, I should advise him to adopt my plan. Nor would I readily allow any one except the head master ever to preach to the school as a whole—I mean any one on the staff. In boarding-schools where there are houses the house-master could, if he pleased, make similar addresses to his own boys; but I believe the addresses to the whole school would gain in weight if it were distinctly understood that the head master was the representative of the school as a whole, that he was speaking as the mouthpiece of the tone of the whole school, and that it was a privilege he could not delegate without to some extent weakening his influence or neglecting his duty. He is in the school the source of all honour and all law; instruction will come from his lips with far more effect if this principle be understood than from any other. And, moreover, I would say something more, that he is probably at a disadvantage if he is in orders. Boys are apt to treat the addresses of a clergyman merely as a part of his professional duty, and accordingly to think that while such laws as he expounds may be good for the clergy, they do not much matter to the rest of mankind. With a layman preaching there can be no such suspicion. I would not, of course, say that a clergyman may not produce quite as much effect as his lay brother; all I mean is that he starts at a disadvantage. Character is the foundation of a man's influence in every case, and in time the clergyman may prove himself to have as powerful a character as the layman; but I think the layman may, with a rather weaker character, produce at once an effect which a clergyman will take a little time to reach.

"Sunday observances hardly come within our sphere, as we agreed at the outset that our ideal schools would be day-schools; but as a concession to the exigencies of the world as it is, I should like to say here just one word or two on what I consider are its opportunities, and the best way of making use of them. I mean, of course, apart from religion. To begin with, I should say that the formal moral instruction can effectively be given to boys on a Sunday, without in any way trenching upon the religious aspects of the day. But services I would make very short indeed, with a sermon as a great rarity. Nor would I ever compel a boy to attend——"

Here Mrs. Reynolds exclaimed in a horrified tone, "Mr. Trelawney!"

"No, I would not; but I should take care that he was well looked after if he did not choose to come, and not allowed to spend his time just as he pleased. Moreover I would have an abundance of music, sacred, and the higher kinds of secular music, interspersed with the service, so that the purely and directly devotional part would be small. Boys, as a rule, are not capable of deep devotion, or of a prolonged strain on the devotional feelings; and in those cases where a boy is so capable I should say, as a rule, it would be better to try and control the tendency, as there is a great danger that such people will become morbid as they grow older. You need have no fear that you will kill the religious instinct altogether. I would also have some services almost entirely of music and readings from some of the great writers, with quite informal lectures occasionally combined — lectures under no very stringent regulations as to the subject that might be treated. I would do anything possible to influence moral tone without considering religion at all. And, throughout the day, I should see that there was plenty of occupation so as to kill that ennui which is so common among boys when they are insufficiently occupied; for it is out of the question to make Sunday as other days. Debating societies and science work I would also encourage, and the exploration of the surrounding country, not in top-hats and Eton jackets like so many unnaturally stunted men, but in such attire that they would be able to look for plants, insects, and stones, without a feeling of incongruity. I am afraid my proposals would not be very acceptable; but in this case I think the end justifies the means, and the more we break down the barrier of separation between ordinary days and Sunday, the better I am sure it will be for the world.

"Let me now turn to matters where the question of religion cannot even be raised. Herbart, the great reformer, whose ideas are at present so influential in Germany, has advocated strongly the necessity of co-ordinating the whole of school education with a view to forwarding one main end, and that a moral one. The proposal strikes me as one of the greatest advances that have ever been made in the theory of education. It is a truism to say that everything we do has some effect or other, whether for good or for evil, upon our character, and if it is possible to choose our subjects of instruction in such a way as to maintain a moral ideal, we shall be availing ourselves to the utmost of the opportunities which are now too often neglected. My own view is always that everything must give way to moral considerations. To dwell upon the moral side of steady intellectual work, to insist upon the fact that accuracy in work is a moral virtue, and to be emphasized as such, to draw out the more obvious bearings upon character of the routine of school, both in work and in play, can hardly be necessary here; I think we may take it for granted. But the acceptance of this point of view leads to one or two corollaries which are often disregarded, and which I should like to accentuate in full. The first of them is this, that if all our arrangements at school have a moral aim, one of the prime factors in which is the insistence upon punctuality and regular procedure, then it follows that we must adhere with the utmost possible strictness to whatever time-table we have laid down; if we expect our charges to be regular, we must be regular ourselves, and not encroach, as is so often done, upon the breaks for relaxation which the scheme has taught children to expect as their right. We must leave off our work to a minute, just as we begin it to a minute. And I should like especially to condemn a practice I have often observed, not least I am sorry to say among head masters, of postponing their entrance into a class-room till such times as suit their own personal convenience. I am not speaking now of those occasions on which a Head may be detained quite unavoidably, though even then, as I shall explain in one minute, I think it better he should go to his class-room at once and set his boys to work, returning afterwards if necessary, but of those occasions when, as I have known for a fact, he has merely stayed talking or finishing a piece of work about which there was no urgency whatever. Such conduct is a direct lesson in immorality. Accidents there will be, no matter how strict our general rule; but if boys know that one is particular upon the point, they will see that any divergence from rule is an unavoidable necessity. Such excuses can but rarely affect an assistant-master, and in his case such absences are the more to be condemned. I fear that many will say that a head master will have a hard time if he cannot take things a little more easily than when he was a subordinate. To that I should reply that the greater the trust the greater the responsibility; the master is the servant, and the more exalted his mastership, the more complete his servitude, servitude to his office and servitude to his conscience. If he wants an easier time, he should take a less responsible post. It is no answer to urge that he is the fountain of law, and that the sovereign source of law can unmake as well as make. True that he can, but unmaking is different from disregarding a law in force, and if the sovereign himself will not obey the laws laid down for the community, he cannot expect others to do the same. The best stimulus to law-abiding is to abide by the law oneself.

Irregularity of observance is fatal, especially in dealing with those whose sense of law is as yet none too firmly fixed."

" I will now take another point which springs from the principle of regularity and accuracy which we agreed was a truism a short time ago."

Here the Doctor interrupted me, saying: "What did you mean, Trelawney, when you said just now that you were going to explain another reason why it is better for a Head, even if he is detained, to go to his class-room as soon as a lesson begins, and then return to finish whatever business he may have that is absolutely urgent? I do not see that very much is to be gained."

"Oh, yes, I forgot that point, and am glad that you reminded me. Surely, however, you can see that one point at least is gained—he has some security that his boys are at work, and not merely wasting their time. If he goes up and sets them writing of some sort, he can easily check them on his return, and see whether they have been merely idling. In the case of a good school, however, despite the natural frailty of boys, I do not think he will find it essential to actually check them : my own experience has been that boys like being occupied when properly handled, and if set to work in school, even without supervision, will start it with zeal when they have once passed the stage of quite young boys. And even with these last I have often found that industry is the predominant characteristic. A few good boys in a class will, in this respect, influence the whole. But that was not the special point I had in my mind. It falls to the lot of a head master, in the case of offences being committed, to investigate very closely the sources of the mischief. Now when boys are pressed, I have found the source of evil to lie—especially in that matter which is so urgent, and I fear very common among boys, evil-talking—in the few odd moments when they are left to themselves during the absence of a master from a room. This point, I think, I have mentioned before. Large intervals of time are not half so productive of evil as the fragments when a boy has nothing to occupy him, and does not think it worth while to set about anything serious. It is idleness which is the mother of most evils at school; by occupying idle moments we may starve out great sins. Hence, if a master who has to be absent from some unavoidable cause, will take care that his boys have something to do, he will be aiding moral training in a very material way, a way of which he probably will have no suspicion till the matter is pointed out to him.

"But now I will pass on to the point of which I was going to treat when Dr. Hindley called me back. When once it is fully recognised that accuracy and regularity of work are moral virtues, I think we shall have done away with the necessity of all artificial spurs, such as place-taking and prize-giving, and, even from that point of view, of that great impediment in the way of a rapid advance in intellectual education—examinations. So far as these practices are matters of stimulus, they are an open confession of failure to teach practical morality. For my own part I object to marking and prizes altogether. I remember in my own case, how, when a boy, I calculated what were the most paying subjects, and threw all my energies into them, caring little what happened to other parts of my studies."

Here my friends laughed, and I was obliged to join, while Mrs. Hindley said: "Well, really, Mr. Trelawney, that is a confession to make. Are you not ashamed of yourself showing such a mercenary spirit?"

"Oh," I replied, "I can see the harm of it now on looking back; but I do not consider the responsibility rests with me, but with defective school arrangements. I was fourteen at the time when, as I remember, I first worked out the principle, and at that time I do not think I could be altogether expected to realize the meanness involved. Now a system which will lend itself to such a proceeding I say is fatally defective. No doubt it would be possible to arrange marks better, so that every subject should be more on an equality than was the case at the time of which I am speaking; but it requires an immense amount of labour—labour to my thinking quite lost. It is well-nigh impossible to allot the same number of marks to a subject which has but one hour as to one which has two. Yet that ought to be the case to avoid leading to an evil like that I have mentioned. But further, there is another very grave error too. It is commonly urged that marks are a stimulus. It is true they are a stimulus to one or two boys, especially those who are near the top, but the mass of boys they leave quite unaffected, and I have known cases where they have been to the dull a very pronounced and bitter discouragement. I have in my thoughts at this moment one boy of exceptional dullness, who yet was a fairly steady worker, but rarely, if ever, got above the bottom place. One day he said to me in a tone of complete despair, not unmixed with bitterness: 'Whatever I do, sir, I shall never get any higher.' And what could I say? I knew the facts to be as he stated, and here he was in danger of losing all self-confidence and becoming cynical besides simply because of defective school arrangements. The harm done to that boy no amount of gain to the better boys could outweigh; and the more so when we remember that it is usually those boys who are most stimulated by marks, who really require no extra stimulus at all. The result of the system is, I fear, that we do not exert ourselves as much as we might to stimulate boys by nobler methods. And we encourage by the system immorality in two ways. In the first place we teach boys that they ought to measure their own worth and that of others by comparing themselves with those who have been more or less highly gifted by nature, basing comparison of personal merit on endowments in which there is no merit at all. For I should like to ask any schoolmaster how often he finds that the top place in a class, in a small school especially, is due to sheer hard work, and not in the main to superiority of natural gifts. Yet surely the only way to judge of moral worth, which should be the aim of such classification of boys, is to compare a boy not with others, when the terms of the comparison are not equal to begin with, but with himself in the past and himself only. For at school our desire is not to fix moral worth as it will be judged at the end of a man's life, but to elicit whatever power of effort there may be, in the hope that moral growth may be great and lasting. And, as for urging that marks are chiefly for intellectual ends, what does it matter whether we arrange boys according to their intellectual powers or not? School is but a transition period, and to stamp a boy as better than others, because his intellectual powers are greater, is of a piece with that absurd worship of the intellect which has led to our awful sacrifices at the shrine of examinations and the inculcation in the popular mind, through the deadly system of our elementary schools, of the belief that the power to pass examinations makes a man. And this very consideration brings me to the second way in which the system encourages immorality. Not merely does it set up a false standard of what constitutes merit, but it is a direct incentive to vanity, and is thus likely to materially harm many a boy in his after-life. Who does not know the unfortunate boy, who being exceptionally gifted with intellectual ability, finds that he can retain the headship of his class without effort, and so never falls under the ennobling influence of hard work? And what will such a boy be likely to do when he goes out into the world, where the prizes are more to the hard-workers, and where pure intellectual powers, as regards getting on, are almost at a discount? Power that is practical and hard work are the ruling factors in what is called success in life; the intellect counts for but little, at least the intellect as we consider it at school; hence, many a hard knock and bitter disappointment awaits the youth who thinks that, because he has carried everything before him at school owing to his greater intellectual endowments, he is therefore to be worshipped by every one hereafter. No, it is character that tells in life, not brain, save in special pursuits; it should, therefore, be character we should consider first of all, even in our excessively intellectual system. Our prizes should be given, if they are to be given at all, not necessarily to the head boy of a class, but to that one who has shown most devotion to his work, and who has made the best of whatever powers, no matter how poor, he may have received at his birth. The impossibility of ever carrying out such a system would soon prove the absurdity of prizes altogether, even if the English public, with its rooted mistrust of any one who cannot show that he can account for the trust imposed in him by a practical reckoning of its outcome in £ s. d., once allowed us the chance of disposing of the prizes on what we might consider the fairest method. You can imagine the outcry of the British parent when told that his Tommy, who was top of the class, had not received the prize, but that it had gone to his neighbour's Willie, who, though bottom, had worked harder than any one else! But till your parent is willing to trust his schoolmasters, you will never have a system of education which shall aim more at moral than at purely intellectual ends."

"My dear," said my wife, "I knew you were strong on the system of marks, but I did not know you were also bitter. Don't you wish you had been a woman?"

"Well, in the presence of so many ladies, and especially in answer to you, my dear, I am afraid it might be rude to say just what I feel on that question; so I will content myself with saying I have not yet seen the advantage—though, of course, I am open to conviction. But why did you ask?"

"Because, had you been a schoolmistress, you would have found the system you condemn far less prevalent; girls' schools are largely free from the evil thing."

"Yes, I know; it is another point in which you can teach us so much. But I fear there is no one so unteachable at present as your average British schoolmaster."

"Ah," said the Doctor, "I remember your saying something like that before, when I put in a claim for the doctors."

"I think," said Reynolds, "I might also claim for the clergy at least a right of consideration in any competition for this great distinction"—a remark at which we all laughed, while the Doctor went on:—

"Well, I don't think we will dispute on the question. It reminds me of a remark I once heard that everybody is a radical in his own profession. I'm afraid it is not true; the world would progress faster if it were. But what I was going to say was this, that the mark system has always been a puzzle to me, and I am glad to hear a strong attack upon it. I can understand that there are certain arguments in its favour, but they seem to me an illustration of the fact of which history furnishes so many examples, that the superficial arguments are by no means always good. I know from my own observation that in the German schools, for instance, marks are practically non-existent, to say nothing of prizes and place-taking. I fear our practice is but another illustration of the terribly mercenary spirit which pervades everything we English do."

"Yes, I feel that too, but you must remember," I went on, "that the Germans have behind them the great stimulus of the conscription. Still, I am convinced our system is wrong in itself, and, further, that if we could but carry out our proposed reforms, and base the whole of education more effectively upon love, and develop a liking for the subjects taught by teaching more rational things, and in a more rational way, we should find it not merely wrong, but absolutely superfluous.

"A third corollary which follows from our principle of regularity is, that we must have one definite aim running throughout the whole of our lessons, which should, during all of a child's course at school, be a continuous development from a comparatively simple beginning to an elaborate whole. Each class must denote one step in advance, and each lesson, too, a step in organic connection with what has preceded it. We must have what the Germans call a definite *Lehrplan*, and not merely a piece of tesselated pavement, such as we usually mean when we speak of a time-table. It is obvious that to get at such a plan we must have a thorough knowledge, both theoretical and practical, of psychology. I am not sure that we have made it clear enough, hitherto, that no effective training, in the best sense, can be given, on the side of ethics as well as on the side of the intellectual and physical development of the child, without a systematic study of the theory of education on the part of the trainer. And I say this, not at all overlooking the fact that one of the most valuable incentives to a high moral tone on the part of the young is the character of their trainers, and the love and admiration which they may feel for those who are trying to guide them aright. Even the noblest of characters is liable to err, but his liability to error will be far less if he knows thoroughly from the abstract side the kind of material with which he has to deal. He will be able to correct his mistakes, and only under such conditions will he be able to make scientific experiments, and verify them, seeing truly their bearing upon practice. Theoretical knowledge, too, will keep him on the alert, and prevent him becoming hidebound with empirical rules, which may help for a time, but which, not being founded upon scientific induction, are always liable to break down in the presence of an exception. And when we consider the complicated character of the material with which the educator has to deal, who will be so bold as to say that those exceptions will be rare? Surely education is the only science in the world in which the professional exponents would be so bold as to declare—and surely England is the only country in the forefront of civilization where such an assertion would be possible—that practice is everything, and theory worthless. But the point I wish to make in especial, at present, is that this abstract knowledge is of as much value in the sphere of morals as in the sphere of the intellect. And I do not now mean by abstract knowledge a knowledge so much of ethical theory as a knowledge of psychology, physiological and otherwise. What we have to get at is the power of noting instances and drawing from them strict scientific generalizations, together with that freshness and elasticity of mind which permits one to be constantly throwing away false inductions for the sake of truer ones, and modifying one's practice in the light of greater knowledge. In the schoolmaster's profession, above all, is such elasticity desirable, and to be fostered by every means in our power, inasmuch as, owing to the conditions under which he works, the schoolmaster is liable to become more the slave of routine than probably any other man who occupies so responsible a position. The harm done by error and mistakes in practice is often so subtle, and the outcome of it often so long delayed, that it may either be not apparent at all save to a very minute examination, or it may show itself at a time when the child has passed away entirely from our control, when the schoolmaster has altogether lost sight of him, so that he has no opportunity of reflecting on what are the real losses he has caused the child to suffer. And how can we hope to get over this difficulty save by studying our profession in theory, and making minute and systematic observations?

"But enough now on the value of scientific training for the teacher in the theory of his profession. I return once more to the question of a *Lehrplan*. How many head masters, when constructing their time-table, think of anything else than fitting in the number of subjects which their scheme, or the public for whom they cater, demands, or so arranging it as to give the maximum of time to those particular subjects which will pay best in some examination for which they enter the unfortunate children? And here is another evil of examinations: a schoolmaster has to sacrifice his own ideas of what is best in the abstract in education—supposing indeed he has such ideas at all—in order to comply with the requirements of a syllabus drawn up in many cases by those who have no theoretical knowledge of what true education demands, and even if they have that, have no practical experience of what are the real mental powers of children at the age when they present themselves. It is a question of subjects, subjects, subjects, not as it should be of mind, mind, mind. In any case such examinations cannot adapt themselves to the conditions of particular schools: they introduce a cast-iron system which it becomes almost impossible to amend, and which suffers not merely from that very great disadvantage in itself, but from another not less grave—the tendency to absolutely kill all consideration for individuality. Now if there is one point on which the teacher should consider he is under a law of the most imperative character, it is in regard to individuality. The whole tendency of civilization at present is to grind down every one into one mould; but it is a relic of savagery which cannot stand divergence from the common type, and the real hope for advance lies in the difference of individuals: as John Stuart Mill says somewhere, I think, 'Variety is the soul of life.' The fostering of individuality in both morals and intellect should be the great aim of the teacher: who knows but that it may lead to the production of a genius? I do not think I need go over the points I could enumerate in which we sin against psychology in our ordinary education. Even when we grant that in certain subjects a more or less co-ordinated system of study is pursued, still it is rarely even there that it follows the natural order of development, as, to take one glaring instance, is seen in the habit of beginning a language by teaching the grammar first. A more pestilential heresy I think I do not know, yet its power in England is almost universal. But I will not go into the matter in full, as the details belong rather to intellectual education. I will only add one other point, which is that even where a subject in isolation has had a careful scheme of treatment devised for it, its organic connection with the other branches of study pursued has often never been considered, still less have we aimed at so arranging matters that the mental development fostered shall be a direct help to morality."

VIII

HERE Reynolds stopped me and remarked:—

"I was going to say, Trelawney, but your last observation has almost cut the ground from under my feet, that much of what you have now been saying seems to have little or nothing to do with what is our special subject of enquiry—moral education. You appear to have run off to the intellectual. Now I know you will say that every branch of education affects every other——"

"No," I said, "I was not going to take that line."

"But," went on Reynolds, "while I grant that, it seems to me there are limits. And if you were not going to take your stand on that ground, I should like to hear what your answer will be."

"This," I said. "During my last remarks I have been thinking of Herbart who insists most strongly upon the fact that what he calls the whole body of thought, including in the term all individual experience and the summed experience of the race as a whole,—I hope I am expressing his views rightly: it is always a ticklish matter to put in our own words the thoughts of a subtle and careful thinker,—that this whole body of thought is the main element in forming the good will on which the production of a moral character really depends. He binds up together in the closest union intellectual and moral education, and it seems to me that he is right in so doing. Hence I say it is of vital importance that your intellectual education be an organized whole, and organized not merely in such a way as to secure the natural and regular development of the intellectual powers, but also so as to secure the development of morality as its final end. If our intellectual instruction be haphazard, we are thrownig away a great support to morality. The view is a subtle one, and though I think it would be easy to press it too far, still its great importance in the history of recent education must be my excuse for thus dwelling upon it now. I may have gone rather more fully than was necessary into the purely intellectual matters raised by the theory, but I think it is desirable to emphasize too much rather than not enough those points which are most readily overlooked. For further details and applications I would refer you to Herbart's own writings, especially the *Allgemeine Paedagogik*. Herbart is very strong on the point which I should think we should all concede, that in the long run moral advance must be the pupil's own work: the teacher's business is to make the conditions most favourable for securing that advance without interruption.

"But there is one point which this argument has suggested to me that I should like specifically to name and it is this: we must be most careful what books we allow the young to read in literature, in science what experiments we allow them to perform. Nothing must be admitted which has a bad moral tendency, and in the case of literature I would go further and say that our choice should be such works as will directly tend to foster a sense of duty, a love of right, and, above all, a liking and consideration for the rest of mankind, particularly those in a more unfavourable position than ourselves. A vast deal more than is usual might be done in this direction. Mere literary beauty will go far to purifying the mind, but when we can combine with that, as we can in numberless instances, the inculcation of virtues of different kinds, especially those which at any given stage the child is most capable of appreciating, why should we not do so? Tales of cruelty and wrong should, above all, be avoided, unless the moral at the end is so clear that the child will come away with a feeling of hatred for the wrong-doer. And in history especially I would have the teacher point out the utterly indefensible nature on any moral ground of a great number of the acts there related and passed without a comment, especially in the matter of wars and the seizure of other people's territory: even though his judgment may in some cases be wrong, it is better occasionally to condemn unjustly than to let the child go away with the idea that a different code of morality should prevail among States from that which obtains among private individuals.

"Yet another corollary follows from our principle of regularity. Every lesson itself must be an organized whole and further must lie in organic connection with what has preceded and with what is to follow it. Here again you may say I am treating a purely intellectual matter, but I do not think so. Granted that our intellectual training is one step to morality, it is important that every step should mark a steady advance. Now if each lesson is a flabby unorganized mass of facts, we cannot expect that the child's mind will feel itself advantaged or that it will go away profited as regards the ultimate end: we shall produce a feeling of chaos, which is even worse for morals than for the intellect. Doubtless this treatment of a lesson is not an easy matter, and it requires elaborate preparation on the part of the teacher; but here, I think we shall find of use the principle laid down by the Doctor at the beginning, that the teacher must have an abundance of leisure. Certain I am that due preparation and regular co-ordination of work in this way, both in the larger groups and in individual lessons, will do much towards impressing upon a child's mind the value of order and system and a hatred of anything like work scamped: and how large a constituent of a high morality these two feelings are, I hardly think I need declare.

"There is yet another point which the desire for regularity has suggested to me, though here I should not like to be dogmatic: the question as to the desirability or otherwise of one master in the main always having under his control the same set of boys. I am not thinking now of the system of form-masters as opposed to masters of subjects, but rather of the system, common I believe in Scotland, of a master travelling up the school with his form. The gain, of course, lies in the fact that by this means the boys are kept almost entirely under the control of one man who will therefore be able to exert a constantly developing influence upon their character. He has more chance of training them on a reasoned system than if they are handed over from time to time to quite fresh masters.

On the other hand, two considerations may be urged. The first is that it is good for every one to have experience of characters of different sorts, and if our schoolmasters are to be, as we agreed at first, the picked men, then the divergencies of character will not affect the fundamental points of morality: all the men will in essentials act up to the same standard of morality, and all of them will be gifted with great moral earnestness. Secondly, if the school be organized on a real moral system, so that the ethical training is as regular and systematic and based upon psychological laws as much as the intellectual, then the system may be carried on from year to year, even though the children are passing through different hands. The infirmity of human nature may come in our way, but that is a difficulty we shall always be liable to encounter: apart from that it seems to me that, compliance with our conditions being granted, we have not so much to gain from keeping boys always under the management of one man. And further I would say that we are all of us liable, even with the most accurate system, to be guilty of unintentional oversights: these can be corrected, and would probably be so quite spontaneously, by transferring the children to fresh hands.

"In boarding-schools, if I may touch again on present arrangements, the difficulty is no doubt met by the system of house-masters. Their special business is to follow a boy throughout the whole of his school course, and thus an opportunity is presented for systematic watching and careful training of the moral character. It would be good if the system were more generally extended to day-schools as well. It is easy there also to group boys into houses, each in charge of a master; and though I do not altogether approve of the fostering of great rivalry between these different organizations, I cannot shut my eyes to the fact that an immense gain attends upon the development of a corporate influence and feeling and the entrusting of each boy to the special supervision of one master, who thus has opportunities for advice and help which might not present themselves spontaneously. But on the other question of masters going up with their forms, I am not quite so certain, though one may perhaps regard it as merely a variation upon the system of houses. I am, however, inclined to think that the variation and change will give interest; but I say it merely as a personal view, and am quite open to conviction the other way.

"Before I pass entirely from the question of regularity and the points it suggests, I would refer to another practice which seems to me to border on dishonesty—the practice of throwing over time-table arrangements when examinations press, in order, as it is called, to cram up for the last. If it is not actual dishonesty, it certainly tempts boys to think that they can make up for earlier laziness by hard work then, and also fosters the noxious idea, noxious both mentally and morally, that the aim of education is to make a show. From every point of view the practice deserves the severest condemnation: it teaches that law is a matter of convenience instead of something absolutely unswerving. I cannot say too strongly how vast an influence for evil such a practice may have, but with this final condemnation I think we may now leave our great doctrine of regularity to take care of itself.

"There still remain many points to which I should like to advert, and many which I shall be obliged not to mention at all. I have sought rather to lay down general maxims with certain illustrations, than to go thoroughly over the whole ground, partly because it would be impossible to avoid letting some points escape me, partly because those who have been properly trained will, when once they have the principle, be able to trace out its many ramifications, partly also because I am anxious that we should always bear in mind that every branch of education is one continuous whole, and that, though much that I have been saying applies primarily, as I have put it, to education at school, yet the vast mass of it is simply the application of principles which can be used equally well for every stage. It was from my desire to have this fact kept in mind that I made the precepts as general as might be. For the rest I will try to be brief, and if I sometimes lay down a rule categorically, I do so because I am sure you will be able to see its reason and bearing without further enlightenment.

"The first point I would make is one drawn from Professor Adler. Explain clearly what is the influence upon moral development of all the studies and school arrangements through which the children are made to pass. I quite feel that this point is far too much neglected, though it would assist materially both in fostering readiness to work, and also in developing faith in the foresight and goodness of the masters. It is a simple lesson in moral ratiocination, where no harm is likely to accrue. Further we must, above all things, be careful ourselves never to lose temper for one moment, never to show scorn or contempt, no matter what a child may have done, and never under any provocation whatsoever to indulge in satire. I am not sure whether in dealing with children I would even admit what is known as righteous indignation. The weakness of children's wills has always to be remembered, and moral indignation seems to me a weapon it is only right to use when dealing with those whose wills are well set. It may be right in dealing with boys of seventeen or eighteen sometimes, but with children under fifteen I should say never. And this weakness of their wills suggests to me another point—that it is very easy to misinterpret their acts and to be severe upon what is but a childish outbreak. We often make into faults what are really none and embitter the child by so doing, as he thinks himself unjustly treated. I would always allow children all possible liberty, and for this reason would not lay down such ridiculous rules as that they must not in playtime run up and down stairs or make a noise in the building, if others are at work and it causes inconvenience. I would point it out and appeal rather than command, and though the child may forget again a few minutes afterwards, yet this training in self-control by a voluntary act is far more valuable than a passive obedience to a command, and if we are really devoted to the children and not merely to our own convenience, it is surely worth the extra trouble and annoyance to ourselves. As for the fault itself, if fault it can be called, it will be dropped in the course of natural development; and, as I think we have already said, it is an egregious waste of energy, to say nothing of unnecessary friction and chafing of nervous power, if we are going to try and correct at an early and unnatural age those faults which will soon outgrow themselves. One thing is certain, a child's life may be made miserable by constant correction of trifling faults which in themselves are not morally wrong at all, only thoughtless and inconvenient to us."

"But don't you think," said Mrs. Reynolds, "that it is our duty to put a check on such outbursts of animal spirits and similar proceedings in order to teach consideration for others?"

"I certainly think they present an admirable opportunity of teaching consideration for others, but I hold the best way to secure that consideration is not by punishing for mere thoughtlessness, but by explaining to a child the annoyance caused, and, if I know children at all, the mass of them will at once try to carry out the suggestions put before them. And if they do not, we can take advantage later of some opportunity when the child wants quiet, to go on our own way despite his remonstrances, carefully pointing out that we are treating him as he treated us. That would be once more in accordance with Herbert Spencer's theory of natural punishments. Despite a certain appearance of cruelty and selfishness, I think that educationally the practice is sound.

"Another case where advice is morally better than compulsion is in the matter of taking notes. Never compel boys to do so, only advise them and point out the advantages that accrue. Devise means also to prove hereafter that your estimate of the value of taking notes is a true one. By constant exposition of the reasons for our actions on such lines as these we shall be enforcing that principle to which the Doctor long since assigned such cardinal importance,—the necessity of teaching the young to realize the doctrine of far-reaching, may we not say unending, responsibility? In everything that is done the effects should be clearly pointed out: the near effects first, and then the trains of reasoning brought into prominence whereby the remote effects, which so often decide the real value of an action, may be clearly perceived. Thus we may hope to lead to a habit of never acting without careful thought, and if we have given this habit at school, I think school will have conferred the greatest gift upon its inmates that lies within its power.

"Take care that everything be done really well. So we accentuate the sacredness of work. I remember being struck when reading Pestalozzi's life by an anecdote about his training of his son. In his diary appears an entry something to this effect: 'My boy held his pen rightly to-day: by God's help I will never allow him to hold it wrongly again.' That is the true spirit, the spirit which sees even in trifles a high moral discipline. Always let there be plenty of activity, and always maintain a cheerful tone; activity and cheerfulness are the two great protectors from evil dispositions and evil acts. By activity, however, I do not necessarily mean that you are to prescribe tasks; only put the boy where something can be done, often, perhaps most often, of his own choosing, and you are doing right. He will not resent suggestions from you. And after all much of what we usually call mischief is, from the boy's point of view, activity and really healthy activity. Froebel dwells in most explicit terms upon the value of an activity that produces some definite external result: such work has a moral influence of the highest value, and should be enjoined upon all from prince to peasant. The modern development of Sloyd is an important move in this direction.

"Let children of all classes be trained together. Not merely shall we thus get rid of snobbery, but we shall have direct opportunities of insisting on that virtue to which I attach as much importance as to any— a feeling of real communion with others, no matter how different in surroundings from ourselves, a power to put ourselves in their place, a genuine fellow-feeling, the only true basis of real charity. To attain this feeling thoroughly, it is necessary to train also the conceptive faculties and the imagination; but with that aspect at present I am not concerned. I will only say that this feeling of real charity is, to my thinking, the crown of all social life.

"Arnold, I remember, has a caution somewhere against a kind of action which is very natural and common, and which yet, as he shows, may lead to grave harm. He says that we should never force a boy to do an act which, though right in itself, would be done by him from a wrong motive. Were that caution the only fact we knew about Arnold, it would sufficiently establish his lofty position as a moral trainer. It shows a depth of insight not often found among us, content as we are to enforce the right act without any regard to the spirit behind it. And yet surely morally the spirit is everything: with a wrong spirit even an externally good act becomes evil. The difficulty arises from our not always realizing the principle which every educator should always have in mind, that the code which applies to men requires modifications with children: we have to feed them first on milk, before they can swallow our strong meat. And I think under the same head would naturally come the two principles before mentioned—that of never forcing a child to an act which he considers wrong, though it may be perfectly right in itself; and secondly, of never forcing an apology for a misdeed: it will come spontaneously from a child of high moral principle, but if suggested its value is entirely gone; while if offered as an alternative to some other punishment,—on a system which admits of punishments at all,—not merely has it lost its moral value, but it has become distinctly harmful—a virtue converted into a bribe.

"Remember that mere ignorance of evil has itself dangers, and when considering how far it is wise to keep children away from contact with it, adopt as a rule the middle course, opening their eyes to make them see under such conditions as are sure to lead to a right choice. It is wrong to spring upon a child suddenly a mass of evil of which before he has had no conception. Hence if ever it is necessary to send children away to school, I hold it to be one of the father's most imperative duties to utter a word of warning as to the evils he may find, of which he previously had no knowledge. Virtue is not innocence due to ignorance of wrong, but innocence due to rejection of it. And the choice we may thus put before a child has suggested to me another matter, in which we may offer a choice and so avail ourselves of small openings for the exercise of will. There are numberless cases where the will comes into play where morality is not directly involved; but so far as they carry an appeal to volition, so far they are of help in moral training. I mean such cases as those where a child is offered a choice between two seats, or between a red pencil and a black one, or between two kinds of nibs, or between copying a poem or a piece of prose, and the like. There are plenty of boys who will say they do not mind, but such an attitude should never be allowed to pass; tell them they must choose and at last they do so, and thus take a forward step in making up their minds. Let the children, in short, decide as many things as possible. And again we can give them a number of small offices to discharge—monitorships, setting up the blackboard, and the like; such offices are good training in thoughtfulness and neatness, and, to a certain extent, also in self-sacrifice. De Quincey, I remember, has in one of his essays—let me see; I think it is in the first volume of the works collected after his death by Hogg; it is just at your elbow Doctor, I see; do you mind giving it me?—Ah, yes, here it is, in the essay called 'Education.' It is a review of a book giving a curious and interesting account of an experiment made by some one who leaves himself unknown, of throwing the vast mass of the discipline of a school into the hands of the boys themselves. There were magistrates, judges, juries, and the laws were laid down by a committee of boys and enforced by themselves acting as courts of law. There was a recognised series of punishments, and, from another point of view, of rewards also. The narrator, if De Quincey may be trusted, speaks in the highest terms of the results of the system, and, above all, of its moral effect. Those who have read the account will, I am sure, agree with him, despite the great difficulties there would be in starting such a system. The plan would be but a natural, though most valuable, extension of our present half-hearted attempts to make boys responsible for the discipline by giving them monitorial powers. We have already discussed the great disadvantages attaching to our present monitorial system; the plan of governing as a country is governed seems to me to get over the difficulty, as public opinion in the school is at the back of the rulers, and every boy may be connected more or less directly with the system of administration. Moreover, an appeal being allowed shows that the chance of a wrongful conviction is likely to be small. As a practical example of what may be done towards reducing absolute to self government, I do not think the value of the essay can be overrated. Whether the original work is procurable, I do not know; I have never seen it.

"A variation on the monitorial system is the practice which Dr. Arnold adopted of putting a boy in charge, as it were, of another—making him a kind of elder brother, specially interested in that boy's well-being. Such a system when carefully worked and with a full knowledge of the characters of the two boys involved, can hardly be productive of anything but good, both to the elder and to the younger, especially as regards its steadying influence upon the former. The great objection to the monitorial system —its likelihood to develop a kind of priggishness and to lead, unless the monitor is very judicious, to a certain amount of resentment on the part of other boys, besides the great strain it imposes on one's force of will—entirely disappears in this other case. Here the younger boy has a guide to whom he can go, especially in those difficulties for which it should be our main aim to provide, cases where there is doubt as to the right course, or where the temptation to evil is so strong that it can hardly be overcome without encouragement from outside. Masters cannot always mark such cases for themselves; yet it is here, above all, that most good will be effected, if only we can discover the difficulty, or if the boy has such confidence in us that he will of himself solicit our help. However this is a case comparatively rare; we have in most cases ourselves to lead the boy on. But full confidence is common between boy and boy; so that in this respect our deficiencies may be supplied by such a kind of monitor-friend. No doubt consultation will be most often adopted in those cases of moral action which fall under the comparatively subordinate head of prudential actions, but not so always; circumstances will arise where deliberation is required even in grave moral matters. By adopting this line of procedure, too, we shall have a chance of cultivating the noble sense of chivalry, particularly when a small and feeble boy is put under the wing of one who is strong and able to hold his own. Of course, the character of the strong boy must also include those finer elements to which the sense of chivalry will appeal; but this is a matter of observation and insight for the master. Frequently those feelings are latent, and can only be effectively stirred by a method such as that I have adopted from Dr. Arnold.

"There is one other matter which to me always presents great difficulty, and I am afraid I shall horrify you by the view to which I incline—the matter which boys expressively call 'sneaking.' It is perhaps the case where the boyish code of morality comes most directly into conflict with our views as men. A boy's idea of sneaking is very comprehensive, and covers everything from the telling of a trifling fault to the answering of questions put by a master, or the reporting of serious moral delinquencies. It is curious that the feeling does not seem to exist among children in the elementary schools at all. Is it a right feeling to encourage or not? I shall run counter, I am afraid, to the general set of opinion, when I say that a master ought to try and upset the code which boys ordinarily observe on this matter. I do so on the ground that it is impossible for a school to be healthily organized when the aim of a boy's conscience is to protect those who are known to have broken the law. And by analogy I would say that in ordinary life it is our duty to take far more active measures to secure the punishment of evil-doers than is generally the case. Until we have in public a higher sentiment on this question, I can quite understand the strong feeling that the boy's attitude towards sneaking is the correct one. But surely that attitude implies mistrust of the masters—it is a fostering of the old, most deadly idea that the master is the natural enemy of his boys. No doubt the monitorial system may obviate some of the difficulty, and so far it is a gain; but I think we want to go much further. The ideal thing would of course be that an offender should be willing to give up his own name when challenged, or better still, in grave cases, without challenge; but, until our moral nature is much nearer to perfection than at present, I fear such a consummation is more to be wished than attained. It is reached, I am glad to say, that is the former alternative, not unfrequently; yet by no means always. Now in such cases I say that it is the duty of every boy to disregard the claims of an individual schoolfellow and have regard solely to the welfare of the school as one corporate body. Of course, distinctions must be drawn. To have boys reporting every little offence, such perhaps as climbing a forbidden tree, would, of course, be undesirable; the public tone of the school should be a sufficient check in such matters; but in the case of offences of a really grave nature, where the mere occurrence of the offence is a proof sufficient that the tone of the school has not prevented a boy disgracing himself and his fellows, and where the act as an example may have serious results for evil, then I say a boy of truly high tone will report the matter of his own accord, if he cannot induce the offender to voluntarily confess. And in such cases I would have the master explain clearly to the school that the reporter was discharging a most unpleasant and difficult duty, but that it was a duty which he owed to every one, and that each individual boy, not excluding the offender himself, would have had just cause of complaint had he allowed the tone of the school to be lowered by winking at such a grave offence, and so becoming himself an indirect accomplice. If attention is drawn to the corresponding point of view of statute law, the boys, I think, will be easily convinced, or at least the riper-minded from whom the influence will spread. After all as in the case of so much else with boys, their views upon sneaking are largely an unthinking tradition, and my own observation has led me to conclude that it is easy to modify boys' sentiments on almost every moral point, if only we will go the right way to work and explain to them why our view differs from theirs. No doubt the change of attitude will constitute a difficulty in a school where the common sentiment is already existing; but it can be brought about by constant watchfulness and always insisting upon the point, and would be an immense gain to every one concerned. The mere knowledge that other boys were likely to report grave cases would itself be a powerful deterrent from any serious misdemeanour."

"I am indeed, Trelawney," said the Doctor, "surprised at the attitude you adopt, and though I can recognise some force in what you say, yet as an old public school man it goes against the grain, and I cannot believe you would readily get any set of boys to adopt your view."

"Going against the grain seems to me a poor argument, however natural it may be; it is a survival from the days of our less civilized forefathers, a kind of atavism, which

I am surprised you should show. Whatever has been must be, would adequately sum the argument."

"I grant that your scorn is to some extent well-deserved, but I feel that there is much to be gained by leaving boys to hold that they are capable themselves of managing their own affairs. And it seems to me your system would lead to an evil which I have been expecting you to dwell upon, the danger of interfering too much, of constantly prying and so never leaving the boys a chance of standing on their own legs. If you keep them under tutelage for ever, you will never grow strong men."

"Yes, I admit the great danger of that result, and I think we have already sufficiently dwelt upon it. But I do not think it is likely to be much fostered by the reform I have just advocated. Of course on De Quincey's scheme I described above, the difficulty entirely disappears; but taking the world as one finds it at present, I think it a mistake to pry too closely; in fact I constantly repeat to myself that one of a schoolmaster's first duties is to shut his eyes wherever he can. If, for instance, I am compelled to leave boys alone in a room for a little time, I make it a point to set them some work and then never to enquire whether there has been talking or any more serious disorder, unless it has reached such a pitch that I could not fail to be made, to the boys' own knowledge, conscious of it. Moreover I never tell them not to talk, merely to get on with their work while I am out of the room. That trust begets trust is a principle I rarely find fail. But in the case we have been discussing, that of serious moral offences,—offences against discipline are, as a rule, on a different footing,—I do not think we can be too particular, nor do I really feel that we are weakening a boy's power to stand alone. I do not wish to upset altogether at present a boy's feeling about sneaking being bad form, but I do wish to modify it, as it seems to me to savour rather too much of the old adage about honour among thieves. But I quite appreciate your strong dissent; and so with your permission will leave the matter as it stands, with the simple remark that it is one of those cases where the decision on the right course of action may lead to disagreement.

"But this question of telling tales has suggested to me

another point which I think it is the duty both of parents and of schoolmasters to take vigorously in hand, checking not merely others but above all themselves—I mean the telling of stories to the discredit of others. Often such tales are told for the mere fun of the story; even so it is a practice which is most undesirable; but often there is a spice of malice interspersed, which is the source of much harm and the ruin of all charity. The habit of discussing the characters of others, even when nothing uncharitable is meant, is productive of great evil and should always be checked sternly and decisively. In this connection I do not think we need do more than take the Epistle of St. James for our text; what we find there will bear deep meditation, and is likely if digested to improve our practice. Idle talk is the source of many an evil deed: with children, in particular, we cannot be too careful. It is a bitter and humiliating thing to confess, but I fear it is only too true, that when we begin to discuss the characters of others, for every good point we dwell upon three bad. So much more ready are we to pick out the evil than appreciate at its true worth the good. And even when stories are told with a merely humorous intent, I am afraid they are rather like caricatures,—which, by the bye, should be rigorously kept away from children,—they are amusing but at the same time appeal to a low feeling. At least there is a very great danger of their doing so, if we introduce them before a character is well set. For my own part I would try and avoid them altogether. But before I finally quit this topic, I should just like to say, having already mentioned St. James, that his epistle strikes me as being a perfect compendium of the principles on which we should found our moral training. I should describe the book as the epistle for children, beautiful in language, simple in expression and deep in thought, full of the richest instruction which it requires but few words to expand. Many of its sayings might be hung up as decorations on the school walls: and though it is easy to exaggerate the good done by the constant presence around us of golden maxims, still I think that in many cases if they are at hand in beautiful designs so that the teacher can turn the children's attention to them whenever he is inculcating any moral precept, there is a very considerable gain. And so rich a source in brief of so much moral instruction I do not know as we find in St. James.

"I am afraid I must have wearied you by my long enumeration of special points on which I think help can be given in moral training. But my excuse must be that being a schoolmaster myself, I have naturally had the subject constantly before my thoughts; and being most anxious for the continual development of our moral standards, I have not liked to pass over any single thought that has at any time occurred to me, even where I am not quite certain of its true value. But much of what I have said I regard as merely tentative, for alas! we know only too well that—

> 'The best laid schemes o' mice an' men
> Gang aft a-gley.'

If, however, we work in a noble spirit enlightened by careful thought, we may at least hope that all our labour will not be thrown away. But I am very glad to have reached an end, however poor the sum total may be, and I can only thank you for listening so long and so acquiescingly to the dreamings of one who finds practice very hard."

IX

HERE I paused and waited for some one else to speak. At last Mrs. Hindley laid down her fan and turning to me said slowly:—

"I am sure, Mr. Trelawney, no one can think your time ill spent, if it has been so productive of suggestions as those you have just laid before us. But you see that flower-bed out there, how carefully the gardener has cleared it of weeds and stones and fenced it in, and yet there is nothing growing there. Now, if it is not cruel to say so, your scheme seems to me somewhat like that bed or the action of the gardener. You take most excellent measures to keep out weeds and anything that may obstruct the growth of the moral flowers, but I do not see that you have planted the other seeds which should occupy the spare ground. And yet if the soil is left unoccupied, may it not be the case of the man who turned out one devil only to have his empty breast occupied later with seven worse than the first? Do not think me hard in criticising you thus, for I am indeed grateful for what you have said; but it does seem to me that we want something more positive, and as I cannot supply it, I should be glad to hear suggestions from some one who can."

I was beginning to say that I was really disappointed after all my efforts at being told that I had merely taken the preliminary steps, when Dr. Hindley intervened, and turning to his wife said:—

"I think you forget, my dear, two things. The first is that morality has two distinct sides, one an avoidance of evil, whether temptation or action, the other a positive doing of good. Now I cannot help feeling that the latter is to a great extent a late development, and that to guard from evil, so as to kill bad tendencies by want of exercise and nourishment, must be our first step. The avoidance of evil is after all but the negative way of describing the choice of good. And secondly, I think you have quite forgotten that we discussed at some length Professor Adler's method of instruction in morality, and that all that Mr. Trelawney proposed to do was to supplement that by pointing out various particulars in which our school arrangements might help our efforts directly."

"But still his recommendations were largely negative."

"I think," said Mr. Reynolds, "that is almost unavoidable. It can hardly be possible to draw up a scheme of cases for action and then say what is to be done in each case. But surely after all, if you think over what was said, you will admit there was a great deal in the way of positive suggestion, such as the seizure of every chance of letting a boy act for himself, the effect of monitorships and similar positions of trust, the direct inculcation of habits of charity and forbearance, the control of the temper and the like; surely you would admit these to be positive."

"Yes," said Mrs. Hindley; "but if I may shift my ground a little, they seem to me desultory, and not a real scheme."

"Ah," I said, "there I quite admit what you say. But I do not see how it is possible to draw up an actual scheme. We have discussed at great length the pros and cons of so arranging matters as to present cases of conflict to children, in fact to tempt them, and I thought we were unanimous in condemning the practice. But if we are to wait for ordinary life to give us chances to show our moral strength, then I do not understand how any one can hope to draw up a scheme of any kind. Of course in some cases of moral action, such as the support of a charitable institution—a work now so common with our public schools—we do get a chance of practising morality; but after all that is as a corporate body more than as individuals, and besides has the advantage of not necessarily leading to great moral harm supposing a boy refuses to help. I do not think I mentioned that as one of the matters in which I should certainly support current practice. If I omitted it, I should like to make good the omission now. But that is comparatively a slight test of any boy's power of withstanding temptation on any large and personal scale; and how you are going to provide such tests I do not see. *I* certainly cannot do so. After all morality is a matter primarily of the will, if we are to go into the psychology of it, from which we have hitherto kept aloof; and the will is affected partly by natural inclinations,—if philosophers will permit such an unphilosophical statement,—partly by the reason and partly by the feelings. Now taking these three elements separately, I think that the first, the natural tendency, must be mainly controlled by negative influences if bad, by positive opportunities of practice if good. So far then—and I am not sure that this element perhaps is not more important than either of the other two—it seems to me that what you, Mrs. Hindley, call my negative regulations are precisely what is required. Opportunities for the development of good tendencies are sure to occur of themselves sufficiently often to leave us in no fear that these tendencies will be starved or die from want of exercise, at least in any school which can pretend to anything like a good moral tone at all. But the only effective way of getting over evil tendencies is to atrophy them by cutting off all chances of nourishment: and it was at that result the precautions I laid down were aimed. So far then I do not think my method was so bad. But then on the second element, the reason—the enlightener and trainer of conscience we might call it—there, it seems to me, Professor Adler's method comes in. I have suggested supplementing it by set discourses and essays occasionally, but in the matter of the reason actual cases for practice are comparatively unimportant. There remains the third element which enters into morality as affecting more or less directly the volitional powers, I mean the feelings. Now these I should say are the real motors in morals. I should rather like to adapt a well-known simile to explain exactly what I conceive to be the relation between the three elements in question. Imagine three boys playing at horses, two of them the horses and one the driver. One of the horses we will suppose has much more speed than the other, though not necessarily more strength, but is unable to get on as fast as he wishes because of his companion. The slower one also has wishes about the direction in which they should go, which do not always coincide with the wishes of the other. What happens? The faster one, who here represents the emotions and desire, supplies the motive power which keeps all three going. He would rush on just wherever he likes and as fast as ever he can, were it not that he has to reckon with the other horse, reason, who firstly cannot go at the same speed as his companion, and so is a perpetual curb, and secondly often shows that his aims diverge completely from those of feeling. When the two are in accord, will, who is the driver, does little save follow their lead, perhaps checking them at times, perhaps at other times urging them on. But when the two horses are at variance and want to go different ways, what has the driver, Master Will, to do? Clearly to balance the wishes of the two and take perhaps a middle course, perhaps go wholly with the one leader or the other. I do not pretend that the analogy is perfect, analogies rarely if ever are: the chief defect lies in the fact that one is bound to represent will as something outside of and independent of reason and the emotions and desire, whereas there can be no will without emotions and perhaps none without reason. The three from this point of view are in fact indissolubly connected. Now these feelings, which to me seem to give the motive power, being in fact the mothers of desire, what is the proper method of training them? Surely by appealing to them directly, by presenting enticing pictures of all that is good and keeping far off the pictures of all that is bad. We have, in fact, to make virtue attractive, and this it seems to me my proposed course of action does; for I try to keep out of sight all that may tempt in vice, and if vice is not known, but admiration for the good cherished in its place, this love will prevent the other assuming sway: two contradictory affections cannot occupy the same ground at once. Where chances of moral choice come in, I have already said we must be ready to help, and we should do so by stirring the emotions to feel that moral goodness is lovable in itself: if then we bear in mind this amount of positive injunction which I have already laid down, and if, above all, we show by our own example that we feel the attractiveness of virtue, I do not think that the various negative requirements which I have given in some detail ought to lay me open to the charge of having done nothing direct. All I fear is that we may have seemed to overweight the intellectual side of the matter, as if reason were predominant: for my own part I should say that of the three factors which enter into the determination of character, the most important are the feelings, and it is to their right culture that our efforts must be in their final aim directed. Let the feelings be right and volition will seldom fail to concur; and in those comparatively rare cases where flabbiness of will is attached to apparent depth of feeling —though I fear if analysed this would often prove to be nothing but mawkish sentimentality—we must attack the will, as I have already shown, in other ways, by making the child decide in cases where it is absolutely necessary that some decision or other should be taken. Moreover, we can work upon the moral reason of children and show them that deep feeling that does not lead to action is itself a defect; it is little better I should say than deliberate hypocrisy."

"Well, Mr. Trelawney, perhaps you are right," Mrs. Hindley replied; "at all events I admit you have made an ingenious defence. And it may be, after all, that the discussion of such a subject as ours must of necessity appear rather negative than positive; but for my own part I cannot help longing for positive instruction, though I feel utterly incapable of supplying it. But I have yet another matter to bring before you. You have acted in the same way as Mrs. Trelawney, and said absolutely nothing about what I fear constitutes the characteristic feature of schools at present—punishment."

"Ah," I replied, "I did not intend to take so strong a line as my wife, and say that punishments were to be non-existent. To that end I grant all our efforts must be directed, for it is the ideal thing, however far from it we may be at present. But I fully admit that though we are sketching an ideal, we are bound to have some consideration for present circumstances, in order to indicate to some extent how it is possible to pass from what Herbert Spencer calls our barbarous condition to the higher and nobler state for which we are all striving. Now, the first principle I should lay down would be this, that you must make your punishments as light and infrequent as possible, and drop them always when you think that by a word or two of advice—in private it may be—or a little extra pressure upon the boy's good feeling and regard for you, you can attain your end without direct punishment. Lightness and infrequency should be our first aim : let moral persuasion take their place. A hardened offender, if we should unhappily meet with any, is far more likely to be influenced by novel treatment and recognition of his position as a responsible being than if we simply handle him as an inanimate object or as a being who cannot grow callous to suffering. Much of our punishment is effectless because it is so habitual. I grant that in many cases a boy will strive to avoid what is with him a common punishment for which he does not really care; but there are cases where a kind of despair springs up, and the offender will offend from mere perversity and annoyance. Can any system be worse? Variation of punishment must therefore be our second aim, and for the third, I should say, take care to choose a punishment which, if possible, is natural; if not possible, shall at least do the boy actual good in itself though not as a punishment. My reason for adding such a proviso is this, that our school arrangements being largely artificial and meant to provide for work being done with the least trespassing achievable upon the claims of others to freedom from interruption, it is not always possible so to treat an offender as to let him merely suffer the natural result of his misdeed. Take, for instance, such a case as that of a boy forgetting to bring his book or his pen. You will say that the natural punishment is for him to do without it. True, but in most cases I fear that would to him be no punishment at all, apart from the fact that his dropping behind will in most cases hamper the class for the future: so part of his penalty falls upon others."

Here my wife interposed. "I think," she said, "it is not quite accurate to say that girls, at all events, and I imagine boys are the same, would not feel it as a punishment to be left without their books. It is one of the leading features in a child's composition that she cannot bear to be unique. I have before now adopted that method of punishing, and I find that a child grows positively angry at being, as it were, left out in the cold, and seldom offends in the same way again. Moreover, you must insist on the offender taking part quite as much in the lesson without her book as the others with. And further, I should, in the case of any delay arising, point out most carefully the wrong the offender was doing to others as well as herself; and by emphasizing this point, especially in the minds of those who suffer unjustly, you can bring the whole weight of their indignation to bear upon the wrong-doer, who will scarcely dare to face that formidable opposition again. It is not difficult to work the children up to the point of driving others in this way, especially if it means that you have been prevented getting through the set amount of work in the time, and so have to take some minutes out of school."

"Don't you think," said Mrs. Reynolds, "considering how rigid children are in enforcing their views upon others, that it is rather an unmerciful engine to use?"

"It may be so to some extent, yet I think it is justifiable. They will probably merely express their feelings violently, and the sense that she has offended against public opinion will probably cure the offender of that terrible social fault, a careless disregard of the interests of others."

"Your position, my dear," I said, "is no doubt the correct one; the only difficulty is that it seems so unjust to deliberately punish others for the sake of the one."

"I do not think it unjust; indeed, it seems to me one of the main incentives to the progress of the world. If the punishment for sins fell upon the sinner alone, morality would be a matter of purely personal interest. But it is precisely because almost every wrong deed affects others perhaps even more than ourselves that we are enabled to bring strong pressure to bear upon those who would live only at their own sweet will to abstain from acts which are injurious not merely to themselves. And of all lessons of morality I look upon this as one of the most valuable to be taught to a child. It was Dr. Hindley, I think, who laid down the admirable principle that one of our lodestars must be the development of a sense of unending responsibility. If we are able to show children by a practical object-lesson in such a small point as that we have just been considering, how every act has its bearing upon the happiness of others, we have a far greater chance of leading them to realize this most vital principle in the more serious acts of their after-life. Man cannot live alone: our every act therefore must be influenced by a consideration of the bearing it will have upon the happiness of others. Children, after all, must be prepared for life, and we can easily show them that what happens at school is but the counterpart of what happens hereafter."

"I still feel the difficulty; I am not at all sure that we ought to make others suffer because they will do so in after-life."

"I differ from you, Mr. Trelawney," said Mrs. Hindley, "and agree with your wife. After all, we must take the world as it stands. It is impossible to imagine what would be the state of morality—indeed, I rather think the term would have no meaning—if each of us were an isolated being with no bearings at all upon the rest of the world; and what we have to do is so to train the child that he shall understand the principles upon which his conduct has to be guided through all his days. When the world has reached such a stage that society exercises no pressure, direct or indirect, to keep men from wrongdoing, then human nature will be perfect, and there will be no need to consider the best means of training the young to morality. But till that welcome stranger shall have arrived—and I hardly think he is knocking at our doors just yet—I should do as Mrs. Trelawney advocates —take suggestions from the world of life.

"But to return to the point from which we diverged. You said that in some cases punishment could not be natural. Does not that rather show that your school arrangements are unnatural? Such a feeling ought to throw you back upon criticism and to suggest that there is some defect you can remedy. And it certainly seems to me that if we were to carry out in its full extent the principle my husband enunciated as cardinal, which in our hearts we have all, I believe, accepted as the ideal, that school should be based entirely upon love, it would be impossible to urge that punishments could not be natural; there would always be the one, the master's displeasure, which even now under proper conditions acts as a deterrent—often a powerful one—and under better conditions still would not need reinforcing."

"I am afraid, Mrs. Hindley," I said, "you are very sanguine, though I admit some truth in what you say, even at present."

"And then there is another point," Mrs. Hindley went on. "You said that where punishments could not be natural, it was desirable the punishment should be good in itself apart from the fact of its being a punishment. What did you exactly mean?"

"I meant that at present so many of our punishments are absolutely without colour as moral agents, save in so far as they are just. To keep a boy in with nothing to do may, so far from being a moral measure, be exactly the reverse. Now I would always take care to set some task which, though not perhaps bearing itself a moral character, yet should be the means of doing the boy some good. I would set him, for instance, to a piece of good writing, or to learn a poem or do a sum, or to take a punishment of a different kind. I would give him some drill or other physical exercise, of as stiff a nature as possible, for I am a great believer in the value of physical exertion, especially for idleness. Of course I am aware that convict labour is not very productive, and that punishment drill will not do the good that may be expected from volunteering; but I have found it an advantage, and at all events it secures that a boy gets fresh air, and does not continue his state of brain exhaustion, which in some cases is really at the bottom of his offence.

"The great harm of punishments, however, I am convinced is their frequency, though it is the natural sequence of laying down the law that a given offence shall have a given penalty. But such a position is drawn from the life of a State, which stands on a different footing from the life of an individual. Remembering, as we should do, that at school we are to guide and improve by punishment, and not merely check, we cannot expect the same principles to hold as where we have to do with an established criminal class. Some principles will of course be the same under both conditions, as that the punishment should be proportioned to the offence and its difficulty of detection, but in almost every case there will be a great divergence of detail, and at school in especial we are at liberty to try the effects of mercy much more, as we have some direct knowledge of the offender's general character. For the same reason it is not well to have a fixed scale of punishments; we cannot then remit without seeming unjust. Moreover, such fixity leads to a spirit of calculation, as under strong temptation the boy may reckon up that he is quite willing to purchase the forbidden pleasure at the cost of the established pain. A choice of punishments is sometimes a good thing to adopt, as was the case apparently in the school whose history De Quincey has sketched for us. Punishments there seem to have been few—a strong proof of the goodness of the system he records.

"Another point I would emphasize in considering punishments is the absolute importance of making perfectly clear why a particular punishment is inflicted. I have as head master more than once had boys say that they had no idea why they had been punished. Before punishment a boy must always be induced to admit that he has committed the fault alleged, or else have an opportunity of defending himself from the charge. Few boys, when they see the real aspect of their fault from the point of view of discipline, or of their own moral tone, will resent suffering in consequence of the infringement of rule. But a vast deal of harm is done by leaving boys to think that punishment is due to mere caprice, inflicted often where it is not deserved. Boys do not always see without explanation points that to us seem as clear as day. On the other hand, one must be careful not to allow them to wrangle: if there seems to be a long argument impending—'Answer a fool according to his folly, and he shall be wise in his own conceit'—postpone the matter till afterwards, and talk to him in private. I am a great believer in private talks. Indeed, I would say that the chief punishment should be a report to the head master and a private talk with him. I believe it would be found of far more effect than the stock of punishments now so commonly in vogue. Of course it may occupy a lot of time, but boys dread it more than anything else. They never know what the outcome will be. It would mean, too, that with due caution such reports would be rare; it would never do to cheapen the head master's influence. In a large boarding-school there would be the intermediate step of reporting to the house-master, and so a double check would be kept in reserve.

"But one caution in particular I would lay down—never threaten. That follows naturally from the feeling of trust which we wish to develop throughout the school. It also depends on another principle, which I will enunciate in the clearest terms—avoid absolutely the use of fear. Kindliness must prevail even under severity. Fear, it has been said, is a very hot-bed of lying, and apart altogether from that serious moral danger, it throws a boy's mind off its balance, and acts, I am afraid, often as a kind of fascination—attracts the boy to the very fault forbidden as a bird is attracted by a cat or a snake. It paralyses the will, and that alone is sufficient to condemn its use as a moral agent."

"Then I suppose, Trelawney," said Dr. Hindley, "you would have nothing to say to corporal punishment. I remember Herbert Spencer picks that out in particular as a clear proof of the fact that we are still living in a barbarous state; personally, I detest it utterly, and I imagine you would do the same."

"Detest it, yes; but I am not sure that there is not something to be said for the view of which Herbert Spencer shows himself conscious, that it is perhaps a means well suited to our barbarous condition, barbarous though it be in itself. As a matter of fact, I have not been able to fix my opinions quite firmly on the point. I certainly loathe it, and try to avoid it as much as I can, and if any one says I ought not to use it at all, I am not prepared to defend myself on moral grounds. It seems to me the ultimate reason for its maintenance has simply been laziness or incompetence on the part of the masters. It is so much easier to keep, as it were, a running account, so much wrong on one side, so much punishment on the other, and then what does it matter whether each separate item corresponds to another item on the other side, provided the sum-totals seem evenly balanced? So much easier is it, but how utterly unjust! It never seems to strike those who tacitly act upon this principle, that there is no common measure between a misdeed and its punishment, unless the punishment is the natural outcome of the misdeed. There are only two cases where corporal punishment seems to me justifiable, and even in one of those I cannot defend my view on the ground of its being the natural result; one is the case of gross impurity, the other the case of gross cruelty. In the former case I might hesitate about using the cane; in the latter I think I never should. But I should not be sorry if its use were abandoned altogether, for, apart from the fact that it may in some cases harden, it is a very unequal punishment: to one boy it will be the keenest suffering, to another little more than a passing inconvenience. The point that is so often urged of its being such an indignity to a rational being, I do not think, as the world goes, is of much weight. I always am most careful to put that point of view whenever I do have recourse to caning. The disgrace, I say, is worse than the pain, and some boys certainly feel it so; but after all most of them look upon what seems inevitable as a thing to be endured without remonstrance, and I certainly do not hold that the average boy who has looked upon caning as one of the regular features of school is likely of himself to develop the view that it is an insult to his dignity as a human being. We must not read into the boy's mind the late reflections of philosophers.

"We have already considered the dangers of shame, and it follows from what we then said that all punishment in public is wrong. I never allow another boy to be present when I administer the cane, partly because one can reach a boy's conscience more readily when he is taken alone, partly because the sight of another suffering in this way is apt, I think, instead of developing sympathy, to brutalize. Sympathy is better fostered by other boys knowing what is being done, but not being allowed to see it. And similarly I do not think it is right to administer serious punishment, or perhaps any punishment at all, at the time of the committal of the offence. If we postpone the sentence, we have more chance of taking a dispassionate view, and the boy will realize we are not then likely to be actuated by passion. The difficulty is that the master is in many cases both accuser and judge: we have therefore to guard against the least appearance of heat.

In the case of caning it is well to postpone sentence even till the next day. Let the boy know that you are considering his case : he will pay more attention when called up for sentence.

"Such a matter as striking a boy on the ear or any such form of physical attack I condemn utterly as being not merely the result of passion or want of moral power, but as being in itself of the essence of cowardice. No doubt Dr. Hindley could tell us of the physical harm done, of which I have heard most painful cases ; but a truly moral man who has considered the question, would not, I imagine, stand up for one moment to defend so ignoble and brutal a proceeding. If we treat boys with passion we shall do one of two things—turn them out weak-spirited and feeble specimens of humanity, or engender angry passions in them as well : and then where is the use of our elaborate scheme of moral education ?

"If corporal punishment is to be used either not at all or most sparingly, and our hopes of influencing children through their affections break down, it follows that our only resource is the last one, that of expelling the boy from the school. Now I agree with Dr. Arnold that expulsion is a remedy it is our duty to use more frequently than is often the case. Unfortunately there attaches to it such a social stigma that its effect is likely to last through life. But if it were more frequent that misjudgment would be corrected, and the measure would be sufficient to bring a boy to his senses. But the step is now reserved as a remedy for moral offences of the gravest character : hence it suggests that a boy falls so far short of current standards of morality that he will never be able in after-life to correct his defects. Now it is unfair to any one that he should have his character fixed without chance of alteration by his school career. For not merely may a boy's failure at school be due to some personal bias not at all to his real discredit, but the weakness of boys' wills may often land them in sins which in after years they would deplore more than any one. Not always as the boy is, so is the man. Hence if we could establish a more rational feeling on the matter of expulsion from school, I think we should have done a not small service. But even apart from that argument, we have to balance our duty to an individual boy against our duty to the school as a whole. Now there is no doubt that persistent idleness or impertinence or disobedience, even in minor matters, is a serious moral offence when committed under such circumstances that its influence may spread and hamper the progress of the whole school. Arnold was prepared to use the knife freely and I think he was right: we have more duties to some hundreds of boys than to one. And if that one will not make serious efforts to rise to the level of the others, he must go, lest he bring down others to himself. I am speaking now, be it understood, of comparatively light but persistent offences,—which I would not treat, as Locke does, with the cane,—not of those more grave cases where no one, I suppose, would say that expulsion is not the right course. And even in the interests of the individual himself, I think the course I am advocating is the wisest. He will receive a warning before the step is taken, and the stigma of expulsion may be averted by asking his father to remove him quietly; so far then the boy will have received no harm. What should be done next? Clearly the best course is to bring personal influence to bear: it has failed, it may be, in a school of one hundred or of three or four hundred; it does not follow that it will fail in a school of twenty. I know that of late there has been started a school with the express intention of receiving only those boys who have had to be removed from a public school. Often, as the head of this school maintains, the failure is due as much to the unsuitability of the original school to the peculiar character in question, as to any real defect in the boy's disposition; hence it is but right, he says, that a boy should have a chance of making a fresh start: that chance he gives him, relying in the main upon personal watching and the utmost interest taken in every case. For this reason he sets a limit to his numbers: twenty-four is the number chosen, as many, he thinks, as each master can thoroughly know. He rightly insists on the importance of the personal element from the teachers' side taking a very large share in the discipline of the school: with that view none of us are likely to quarrel. He deserves to succeed in so noble an effort, and should he fail, I think we may conclude that he has really got hold of some of those strange anomalies thrown up occasionally in the history of civilization—reversions to a savage type whom nothing could affect.

"I should like before I close to make one other suggestion on the matter of punishments—a suggestion due to a boyish experience of my own. On one occasion soon after I entered a large school as a child of eleven years, my brother and I were found by one of the masters throwing bread at each other across the dinner-table. The master, who was rather a peppery individual, did not deal with the case at once, but sent for us later on. He pointed out the gravity of the breach of manners involved, which we, I suppose, realized, as I remember it to this day, and then said that if we had not been new boys, he would have caned us. But instead he had determined on another punishment, which was to keep us in, and for what purpose do you suppose? To let us do our night-work; we were not to go until we had finished it! Well do I remember how much amused we were at the idea that such detention was punishment; but as I look back now I see the wisdom of the man, which was quite lost upon the perception of a boy. He knew that he had gained his end, which was to get us to avoid such conduct in future; he knew also, or thought, that he was bound to do something; so he chose a punishment which might seem at first a punishment, but was really not so at all. I have no doubt that instead of feeling grateful to him, we thought him a great fool; but he was willing to forego his reputation for wisdom if only he might be wise in reality. And so I would say now: if you have to punish, choose as often as you can those forms of punishment which seem punishment outside, but are not at all a punishment in reality. You need have no fear that your leniency will be abused; if it were you could soon correct it; all that will happen will be that the boys will think you blind, as they call it,—a great fool; but I do not know that you will be any the worse for that if your character is really a strong one, and the boys, consciously or unconsciously, are alive to the fact."

X.

HERE once more I stopped, having reached my long journey's end, and I could not help heaving a sigh of relief. Mrs. Hindley looked amused and said: "Doubtless you are weary, but we will give your voice a little rest now. And for a time I imagine you will not be prepared to support the character your wife gave you the other day, of never being willing that any one should talk, if you could not lead the way. Truly it is an instance of a natural punishment."

At this sally there was a laugh, and I could only say: "I am afraid that for a week to come my voice will be little heard. However, my boys to-morrow will probably not be sorry, and I shall have a splendid chance of testing the power of mind in moral government."

"But now," said Mrs. Hindley, "who is to proceed? We have still to discuss the University and to give the final wind-up. Who is the best suited for the task?"

Here the Doctor interposed. "Before we pass on to that new branch, I should like to refer to one matter which I hoped to hear either the schoolmaster or his wife discuss; but as they have not done so, I will introduce it myself here, as it affects home and school life rather than the Universities. The question of which I am thinking is the indulgence in unusual pleasures during school time, or when they in any way interfere with a child's regular routine. Is it wise to allow that or not?"

"Certainly," said Reynolds; "it adds a fresh impetus to work, and brightens a child. A little stimulus is always good."

"But how far would you go? Would you let a child stop away from school to make an excursion into the country?"

"I think so; more good may be got from such an excursion than from that particular day's work."

"But what about regularity? Is it not fatal to that?"

"Not once in a way."

"But where would you draw the line?"

"I should only allow such a treat to be very occasional."

"Even occasionally I think it harmful. But take another instance. You remember the case I mentioned before of a father wanting to take his son to Rome for Easter, and the head master refusing leave; do you think the head master right or wrong?"

"Most certainly injudicious; though I can understand his action. Why, you yourself said you held him to be wrong!"

"Well, I will give yet another case. Suppose a brother is returning home after a long absence, would you take your boy to meet him at the station during school hours?"

"Yes, I think so; he need not be away long."

"But how often would you allow such treats?"

"Oh, the chance would not be likely to occur often. I certainly would only permit them very occasionally."

"But you are acting upon no principle."

"No. Each case must be decided on its merits."

"True; but you surely want a principle behind."

"No harm would be done by such occasional treats. I do not think there is any fear of general regularity being broken by such rare occurrences. And beyond regularity what else is there to consider? The child can easily make up what he misses at school."

"Reynolds!" I exclaimed, "I am really surprised. I can tell you of one piece of harm that is done, and that is interruption to the work of the whole class to which belongs the child who is absent for trifling causes. That appeals strongly to me as a schoolmaster, and I really think you will yourself admit that it is a breach of our duty to others to treat them in such a way."

"Yes, I had not thought of that."

"I," said the Doctor, "object entirely to any absence from school at all. Apart from the point which Mr. Trelawney has naturally, as a schoolmaster, just urged, there is the very, very serious moral objection that the child never learns the supremacy of law. I really think, Mr. Reynolds, when you consider the case, you will see how grave a matter this is."

"I admit its gravity, but I only urged an occasional relaxation."

"I would have no relaxation at all. The child's first duty is to learn order, and to do his regular work despite temptations. This duty he never will learn if we do not keep him strictly at his school routine. Duty first and pleasure afterwards is the motto I always quote to my own children when the question turns up; I say they get their relaxations in the holidays, during term time they must earn them."

"I would not be quite as absolute as you are," said my wife. "I have no scruple, for instance, in letting a child stay away for an exceptional family event, such as a marriage; nor do I mind them going out in the evening, provided they can get their work done, and the pleasure will not take too long a time, or upset them for the next day. And your own view on the Rome case seemed the same."

"In the latter of your two instances," said the Doctor, "I am not sure I should agree with you. Steady uniformity of life from day to day is of very great value, morally, intellectually and physically. But in the case of going to Rome, as I indicated before, I probably should have stretched a point, and for a marriage, though I should, I suppose, consent to absence, it would be with considerable reluctance."

"What a Spartan you are, Doctor," I said. "But I am very glad to hear you so emphatic, though I am not sure I should be quite so stringent. Certainly, if all parents were as strict as you desire, day-schools would be free from half their difficulties."

"But," went on Reynolds, "don't you think such a relaxation would be a very fitting reward for previous good work?"

"Virtue should be its own reward. But if that doctrine is too rigid, then let the schoolmaster give a holiday, not the parent steal one. A worse example I cannot imagine. Absence from school ought only to be for the very gravest reasons. I have known parents allow their children to stay up late for the purpose of going to concerts or dances or theatres; with what result on their next day's work, I should not like to think. I remember once being shown by a friend a printed address from the head master of a large day-school to the parents of all his boys, in which he specially urged the wrongness of any such interruption to the steady school routine as theatre-going. My friend thought he was exorbitant in his demands; I, on the contrary, thoroughly approved. It is often quite as easy for parents to arrange the pleasures so that they will not clash with school; and even if that is impossible, surely the discipline of self-denial has its value for the child. During school years, and during the time when regular instruction is given at home, nothing ought to interfere. I hoped to have heard the matter considered by the last two speakers, or by one of them; but as they passed it over, I felt bound to raise a protest. It is a question of vital importance, if the child is to become orderly and possessed of a due sense of the claims which others have upon him. The gospel is one to be preached to parents; we cannot proclaim it too loudly. Most people when the crisis comes urge, as Mr. Reynolds did, that it is only for once; I say, let it not be for even only once, else when you refuse another indulgence, your child will say you are inconsistent and capricious, deciding just as pleases you from the whim of the moment. That too is a danger to consider. If once a child is embarked on an orderly life, let nothing interfere so far as we can help; interferences enough will come from outside, let us do nothing to further them.

"But now having made my protest I am happy, and quite ready, if no one has any other objection to raise, to proceed to the discussion of the Universities. My wife, I remember, was just asking who was to handle the subject."

"Yes," said Mrs. Hindley, "who is to give the finishing touch to this long discussion?"

"I was going to say, Mrs. Hindley," said my wife, "when you asked the question before, that my husband, the Doctor and I have all done our parts, and I think it would be interesting to hear you with your levelling opinions upon those hotbeds of luxury, as I have no doubt you would call them, the Universities."

"That would be all right enough," Mrs. Hindley replied, "if we were discussing a purely social question and the value and use of the Universities to society at large. But for the present we are accepting them as an essential part of a complete scheme of national education, and all we have to do is to lay down the ways in which they can most advantage moral education. For this purpose it seems desirable that the matter should be handled by one who has actual knowledge and experience of them. But as we have not here a University don, we must be content with smaller fry. Mr. Reynolds and Mr. Trelawney are the only members of our party who have actually been at our two older Universities; naturally therefore it should be one of them who should expound to us the position and functions of a University in moral education; and as Mr. Trelawney has already had his share of work, and has pleaded that he is tired, not, mark you, incapable, I propose we ask Mr. Reynolds to take the question—what part should a University play in a system of moral education?"

The proposition met with general assent, and Mr. Reynolds at once began:—

"I will not plead that I am not specially fitted for the task you have put into my hands, for though it is true, yet I think it possible I may be as well fitted as any one here present. Granted that I am not and never have been a don, yet I keep myself in fairly close touch with the University, and it has not unfrequently happened that when I have been dining at high table, or have been staying with dons in their private houses, I have heard our present subject handled at some length. Since we first started the topic of moral education, I have been trying to collect what sentiments I had heard; and though I cannot say how much of what I shall propound is the opinion expressed by others and how much my own elaboration therefrom, I will give it you just for what it is worth.

"To begin with, I shall assume that a boy when entering the University has been under the training we have already sketched for securing a good moral development. If this be so, he will start his new life with quite a different character from what has been styled the nerveless condition in which the mass of undergraduates at present appear. Granted that he has been taught to stand on his own legs, and that he could give reasons for the greater part of his conduct, and has been in the habit of judging, not by conventional codes, but by an abstract rule of right and wrong, what has the University got to do? It is evident, comparatively little, save to extend his knowledge and capacities for action, and to give him more chance of proving his power to rise to a high level from a plain sense of duty and not from any fear of external pressure. I think, therefore, you will see that I am going to be brief, and I do not fancy you will wish anything else.

"Yet before I actually begin, I should like to say one word on the question of religion. We set out to discuss the possibility of a moral education apart from the sanctions of religion, and I at first demurred on the ground that such a morality would be at best a lifeless thing. I am now free to admit that I think I was wrong. Not that for one moment I do not consider that in the ultimate resort all true morality must rest upon religion, and that the morality of the world as it now is, so far as it is good, is a direct growth from Christianity; but I see more clearly than I did that in education it is possible to treat the subjects separately, and that something will be gained thereby, as we shall separate the real essence of religious truths from all that is accidental or peculiar to certain sects. Still I cannot but hold that in treating morality alone, if religious lessons, that is, are not to be given parallel to the others, we are throwing away the strongest support we can have; and if it could be supposed that all religion were to disappear for ever from the world, morality I am sure would not survive it long. However much morality may try to separate herself from her mother, religion, I am certain the study of the former alone leads by an inevitable sequence of thought to the demonstration of the necessity of the latter. All our talk has proved it, though the name of religion has hardly been mentioned."

"On your two propositions just enunciated," said the Doctor, "I should say that every one may have his own opinion."

"Certainly, replied Reynolds, "though I should be really sorry to think that any one here did not recognise in his heart the indissoluble connection of religion and morality. But as we are not treating of religious education at present—though if you were to ask me, I should say that no scheme of moral education could be complete in practice which did not include it—I will say no more about the matter, but pass on at once to consider ethical training as best given in the Universities.

"Now granted, as I have said, that boys leaving school at about eighteen or nineteen are to have behind them the careful moral training we have already sketched, together with the habit of thinking about morals and the knowledge of their great responsibility in the matter, I think the first principle I should lay down would be this, that at the University there should be no restraints at all except those of the young man's own conscience and public opinion. His conscience, though we have scarcely mentioned the term, will have been sufficiently enlightened to act as a safe guide: if it does not do so by now, I fear it never will."

"I am afraid," I said, "that among the many awful proposals we have had to make in the course of our discussion, none is more awful, at least to the experts, than your proposal to sweep away all the restraints. What about the elaborate paraphernalia of gowns and gatings, chapels and roll-calls? And how, pray, are the poor proctors to live, to say nothing of their more unfortunate bull-dogs? Why, I can see in my mind's eye the dean of my college with hair turned white with horror, and as for the Head, I am sure, if he heard it, he would die in an apoplectic fit."

"To shock the world, Trelawney, is often the only way to procure a reform. But is it not ridiculous that we should have to keep so close a watch upon responsible beings, supposed the best products of our boasted public schools, when they have come to such years that they must, whether we wish it or no, be largely treated as men? There must be something rotten, both probably at the schools and at the Universities, when such a system has to be pursued."

"But what would you do," I asked, "in the case of offenders?"

"Send them down."

"That would surely be rather hard."

"No harder—nay, not so hard as your expulsion system at school. And there is even more reason for such a course at the University, inasmuch as the subjects are so much older. If at nineteen a man does not know how to employ himself reasonably, it is as well to teach him by setting him to earn his own living as speedily as possible. For my part, I would be far more stringent than is usually the case on the matter of wasting time. I would not have the University regarded as a place where men can spend three or four years in nothing but racing and athletics, card-playing and entertainments. I would have it a home of serious work, a fitting crown to all the past education. You may say that colleges must have money to live. I say in reply, that if such a standard were maintained as I suggest, the cost of living at the University would decrease so much, and the middle classes would have so much higher an idea of the value of a University course—at present I know many of them regard it as merely a scene of dissipation—that the colleges would be in no dread of being bankrupt, and the influences of the University would have far more chance than now of touching those who are most in need of them. Too often now the leaders of thought, especially of scientific thought, are utterly unconnected with, nay, even hostile to, our older Universities. Matters, I grant, have improved immensely, but still not enough; and if the reform does not come more quickly still, I fear we shall find it forced upon us from without. When once the democracy realizes the wealth and possibilities of good in the Universities, it is not likely to leave them alone. Primary education has been reformed, secondary is on the eve of undergoing the same process; the only hope for the Universities is to reform themselves. True, intellectual reform is wanted; but in the main, I believe, it is the moral side that is urgent. This must be my excuse if I have seemed hot on the matter, and if I have run away or seemed to run away from what is our immediate subject.

"Discipline, then, I say, should be unnecessary at the University: expulsion should be the only course. But there are two respects in which I hold that the University affords us an excellent ground for training in morals: first, in direct exposition of the theory; and secondly, in unique opportunities of practice. These two points seem to me to sum up the whole duty of a University as regards moral training, and these are the points I shall proceed to elaborate.

"First, then, I will treat of the exposition of the theory. Now it was one of the points which I was sorry that Mr. Trelawney did not make quite clear—the actual extent of knowledge of moral philosophy proper with which a boy on his system was supposed to leave school."

" My own feeling," I said, " is that it is better not to touch the subject at all at school. After all, a child trained, as we have proposed, will have got the habit of mind suited for discussing the problems of ethics: he will recognise the difficulties in the conflict of duties, and so, if thoughtful, will have come to see that we may want eventually some ultimate canon to guide our decision. This, I think, is as far as it is desirable to go. If a boy happens to get on to the subject in his private reading, I do not know that I should discourage him, but I would never invite him to treat the matter in school. My objection is chiefly this: that I think in many cases the beginnings of moral philosophy have an unsettling effect; and if there is any tendency in this direction, it is better that it should manifest itself when the student is living among those who have passed beyond this stage, rather than when he is still with those who have not yet arrived at the difficulties, from whom, therefore, he can gain no help, and to whom he may himself suggest doubts which they will never have the means of settling."

" Yes," said Reynolds, " that is the best plan to adopt, though I fear that if our training has been at all systematic, the difficulties will arise long before a boy leaves school. But, after all, I am not sure whether the difficulties he may feel would not be quite as great whether he knew or did not know moral philosophy. For it seems to me that the schemes of moral philosophers, when regarded as means of furnishing us with a master-key to our duties, are extremely unsatisfactory. I do not know that they are any the worse for that, for not merely are they meant to cover a much wider ground, but the philosophers would be the first to confess that a satisfactory conclusion, apart from religion, has not yet been reached. But one thing happily we may note—that amid all the varieties of principle which have been laid down as the ultimate sanctions of morality, there is scarcely one which leads to a serious difference in code from the rest, when we attempt to apply them in actual practice.

"Now, moral philosophy is an abstract science, and therefore it is not to be expected that in itself it will have any bearing upon character. It is really when we apply its conclusions to practice that it becomes an art, and as such important to us here. Now, as I have already said, the various principles which have been propounded as the ultimate sources of moral obligation do not often lead to serious practical divergencies, if indeed they do in any one case. What, then, is the use of studying the science? It is useful, apart from its mental discipline, as leading us to see that after all morality is founded in the nature of man, and that every moral act is connected with every other as an inseparable part of one great whole. It teaches us, moreover, that there are certain parts of the mind which touch morality more closely than others, and hence it shows us that if we desire to influence another character, we must attack it in certain ways. Moreover, it co-ordinates all the disjointed knowledge we have already obtained on the several duties, and so we come to see that morality is not haphazard, but has a logical order, and can be based upon logical principles. No one indeed, I should say, can be considered a master of his subject till he is capable of teaching it; and no one can be secure in teaching morality till he has studied moral philosophy. It will be seldom, perhaps, that he will be forced back to first principles, but occasions may arise. And similarly no one can be sure of his conduct till he can give reasons for each act; if he has not the reason behind him, he is at the mercy of every quibbler, and woe to the man whose moral principles are questioned, if he cannot go back to his ultimate foundation! But, above all, I would say it is the study of ethics that enables us to train the conscience to a higher level than that suggested by the unthinking rules which get heaped upon it as the ages pass; it is only by understanding the theory of morals, in a more or less complete form, that we can disentangle morality and religion from the meshes in which they get caught and set them free to pursue their own way. Moral education, in short, depends on moral instruction, moral knowledge, and moral thought.

"But there is a great deal included in moral philosophy that has but a very slight and indirect bearing upon moral practice. And here we have to be on our guard. It is quite possible to be a thorough student of ethics and yet be an immoral man. For moral philosophy appeals chiefly to the intellect; hence if what is called in popular parlance the heart, in more strict language the emotions and the will, be not right, then we cannot expect that moral philosophy will lead of itself to moral life. It may be the old, old story:—

> ' Video meliora proboque,
> Deteriora sequor.'

—I see the good and choose the bad. St. Paul dwelt upon the danger long since in emphatic terms. Do not let us cheat ourselves then with words. It would be the same thing as saying that a man who knew the whole theory of music was therefore a capable musician. Valuable, then, as I hold the study of morals to be when the character has already been well-shaped towards a moral life, I do not claim that it alone can have any direct influence in producing morality. When, however, there is a leaning towards morality, even though it be comparatively slight, I believe that the deeper knowledge which the study of ethics gives, the realization which it brings of the inherent necessity of morality and of its indissoluble connection with the progress of the world, tends, by this greater breadth of view imparted and the stimulus to thought before action is taken, to strengthen and secure what may previously have been but feeble aspirations to a moral life, resting perhaps as much on the fear of public opinion as upon any really moral base. I certainly found it so in my own earlier days."

"Dear me, Reynolds," I said, "I should never have thought that your morality was so weak as to have required the study of ethics to prop it securely."

Reynolds laughed and said:—

"No; I did not quite mean that it was unstable in itself, though I should think it presumptuous to claim that it was very strong; I do not imagine I was worse, and certainly not better, than the average undergraduate of my day and class. What I meant was that I found the study clinch my theory of morals and set in a clear light some duties which hitherto I had grounded upon empirical considerations and had not been able to completely justify in the abstract. But my position generally is this: that it would be hardly desirable for the world at large to study ethics, as it requires great grasp of mind to follow out all the bearings of the theory, and I fear that, where the intellectual powers are not sufficient to carry the arguments to their logical conclusion, the study might have merely an upsetting effect; but, on the other hand, I hold that it is very desirable, nay, absolutely imperative for the good of the world, that some men should devote themselves to this pursuit, and popularize by degrees the results of their studies in a practical shape, so that we may have a gradual infiltration of the best thought and the highest motives from the thinking classes downwards through society at large.

"I do not think I need say more on the first of the two aims which I laid down as a chief object for a University to pursue in moral instruction as a whole; but there are two particular departments to which it would be well to refer, though I do not hold that instruction under these heads should be entirely confined to the University stage. I was hoping to hear them handled by Mr. Trelawney, but as he said nothing about them, I will try to supply his place. The two matters I refer to are the duties which fall upon us, first as parents, secondly as members of a State."

I was going to defend myself, when Mrs. Hindley said:—

"I am glad, Mr. Reynolds, you propose to treat these subjects, and especially the former. I know my husband declared he would dwell upon the matter, but he wickedly forgot all about his promise. So we shall all, I am sure, be the more grateful to you for any help you may give. Without a consideration of parental duty the rest of our scheme would be almost futile, for unless we train parents in the way to train others, we can only rely upon their usual vague guesses, and leave matters to be regulated by their own whims; how fatal a course that is, the history of nearly every home is sufficient to prove. The training of parents in their specific duties, I regard even more than the training of schoolmasters, as the source whence will come the regeneration of the world. And if it is combined with training in citizenship, we shall have covered the whole ground so far as the individual is concerned. Citizenship consists partly of a man's duty to himself, partly of his duty to others, while parental duty is concerned with our duty to others from a rather different point of view; when once the whole man is guided by reason in both these points, then we may look upon our task as achieved. Of course practice will not rise to the height of theory all at once, but at least we shall have an ideal for which to struggle, and that surely must be the first advance before we can hope to make steady progress. Failures in actual practice we condone, if only we know an effort is being made."

"It is amazing," said the Doctor, "how much instruction is wanted in the matter of our ordinary parental duties. The way children are maltreated is a horror and a disgrace. We doctors see more of it than any one else, but there is enough to convince any one who will choose to have open eyes. I am only thinking now of physical mismanagement —neglect of duty from the doctor's point of view. Rousseau, I am told, long since made an attack upon the system of swaddling children, and trying to force them to walk before their legs are strong enough, but since I have been in this big town, where—I suppose from its comparatively rapid growth—ideas have not had such an opportunity of spreading as they do in smaller places which develop less fast, it has made my heart bleed to see how children are forced to keep themselves erect, or at least to try, long before their legs are anything but cartilage. What is the consequence? For the time they suffer agony, and for the rest of their days are afflicted with misshapen limbs. I never in the whole of my life put together saw so many people with bandy legs as I have seen since I came here. This I give as one instance, and but a simple one, of the harm that may be done by parental ignorance, and, if in what seems so obvious a matter, parents are so utterly incapable of thought, what do we suppose is likely to happen in the graver and less obvious sphere of pure morality? I think you clergymen, Mr. Reynolds, might do much to stop the evil, if in your sermons sometimes you would condescend to such small every-day duties, quitting the high altitudes, where so many of you live, of the dogmas and theories of religious thought."

"I do not think, Dr. Hindley," Reynolds replied, "if you looked into the case at all narrowly, you would find us so heedless as you suppose. A clergyman's influence is not limited to his pulpit. There is not one of us probably who, in visiting his parishioners, does not give words of advice on such matters as these. But for the present that is neither here nor there; let us return to consider the training of parents.

"We all admit its imperative necessity; how is it to be carried out? Now the training of parents, it seems to me, differs little from complete instruction in precisely that somewhat elaborate scheme we have been considering for so long a time past. Instruction in parental duty is instruction in education—its proper methods and its proper aims. Hence it follows we must instruct our future parents in the scheme of morality we have here propounded. Parts of it may, it is true, be dropped, or only just lightly touched—in particular, those which specially concern school; but the main principles must be well fixed in the mind, and, with home education, even the details. And, of course, as we are to train for a duty which covers more than the merely moral sphere, we shall have in regard to this branch of our subject to give specific instruction in the best methods, not merely of imparting moral training, but also of training the intellect and even the body. You see the question becomes one of a knowledge of education, at least from the theoretical side. In fact, training in education must be the final end of all other moral training whatever."

"Herbert Spencer's position very nearly," I said.

"Dear me," said Mr. Reynolds, "I did not know I was trenching upon his preserves. I do not suppose I should often agree with him; but I am glad if I am supported by so great a thinker. However, you see what a vast work we have undertaken, unless indeed, you deny—and I sincerely hope you will not—that such is in reality the proper end of our moral training. The only question is—when can this last point be tackled? Now much of the work, it seems to me, falls properly within the sphere of the school, and that for two reasons: one, that as we are at school instilling moral principles, coupled more and more with the foundation on which they rest, it will hardly be going out of our way to show that the rules we are then formulating will admit of application by the children themselves to those whom, when they have reached maturity, it will fall to their lot to direct; the other, that so few will ever proceed to the University that, if we postpone the matter till then, we shall give no instruction to the vast majority at all. Hence, I certainly think it would have been well had Mr. Trelawney treated the subject when discussing the work to be done at school."

"The reason," I said, "why I did not do so was that I thought we had agreed to accept all that Professor Adler proposed unless we specifically notified dissent. Now Professor Adler does treat of parental duty, though not, perhaps, at great length; hence, I thought myself justified in disregarding the topic, or rather, I should say, in not specially mentioning it."

"Does he elaborate a scheme?"

"No; he treats it as arising out of filial duty—I do not mean in the natural order of things, but in his order of treatment. It is true it is a very short discussion which he gives, but it seems to me on the right lines, and enough to remind his readers that it is an essential part of moral instruction."

"I see; but I must confess I think it rather awkward if we are to be constantly referring to him to supplement our own scheme."

"If we are to repeat all that is good in others," I said, "we shall never end."

"True, no doubt; but what if we have not read the book?"

"Get it, and read it; seldom would money be better invested."

"Well, I will do so, but meantime will just finish what I had to say about this particular point. Granted then that much may be done at school towards giving that instruction in parental duty which we desire,—and I should like to say in passing that such instruction is sure to be popular as it makes children look ahead and realize their responsibilities, and if there is one thing children like it is having the sense of their own importance recognised, and being treated as capable of managing others,—it will only remain for the University to carry further the somewhat piecemeal knowledge of the subject that has been gained at school, and to organize it into a scientific whole. In this sphere, in fact, the work of the University will be much the same as in ethical investigation. The University will reduce to a science what were previously scattered thoughts; it will bring order into what may have been more or less chaos.

"Before I leave this topic I should like to say how great will be our difficulty, a difficulty we have, I think, mentioned before, in securing any great advance in current morality for a long time to come, owing to the unfortunate circumstance that it is precisely those who need such instruction most who leave school earliest, and are, therefore, least likely to get it systematically. Perhaps as the world grows older school time may be extended, till every one is kept so long under control that he has reached years of comparative discretion before he is allowed to shift for himself. But that result I fear will not be just yet, and will in itself imply a great advance in the moral tone of the world at large. Meantime, I am afraid the elementary schoolmasters have thrust upon them the heaviest burden of all instructors—the effort to make some lasting impression in the direction of sound morality by the time the children are twelve or thirteen, which impression shall continue to grow and bear fruit increasingly from generation to generation. Let us only pray that their efforts may be successful.

"Instruction in civic duty I still have to tackle. I do not intend to lay down a scheme of actual instruction. I am regarding the question solely from the moral point of view, and in this way it seems to me it is simply an extension of that duty towards our neighbour, which is one of the leading features in any system of morality. For the same reason, I think, it would have been well if Mr. Trelawney had discussed the subject and not I; though the University stage may give a broader and more living aspect to the matter, I do not see how it can be passed over at school. Indeed, I think it springs naturally from two sets of lessons—those on morality and those on history. It is the final summary of our duty towards our neighbour, and the more to be emphasized, because in this case our neighbour is not an individual able to make known the wrong he has suffered, but a body, to whom if harm is done, it will often be spread over so wide an area as to lead us to think, as Mr. Trelawney has shown, that no harm has been done at all. But I suppose, Trelawney, you said nothing about it, because it is treated by Adler, eh?"

"Yes, precisely."

"Oh well, it is a pity then that you have not given us a complete statement of what on the one hand we shall find in that book, and what on the other we have to supply ourselves."

"I think, if you remember, Reynolds," I said, "I last time gave you an outline sketch of the subjects treated, and one of them certainly was civic duty."

"I must have forgotten then, and can only apologise. But in the matter of civic duty I should like to lay down a caution similar to that which I gave about ethics; it is that any amount of knowledge and instruction in our duty will not make us do it, unless the will is right. And next appears another difficulty: the term civic duty has a double meaning which I think is likely to lead to disappointment for those who are so keen on introducing the subject into our schools and continuation classes—I mean that it may cover a consideration of two distinct things: our moral duties simply as duties, and the practical aspect of the different functions of the various members of the body politic and the place we ourselves have to fill among them. The instruction, that is, may consist simply of an intellectual side, giving the knowledge, for instance, of the duties of a policeman, or of a mayor, it may be, or board of guardians. Now that is practically nothing to morality; it is not that we want now. Our business here in treating of civic duty is to show what it is right for a citizen to do—to vote, for instance, at elections, not to be led astray by claptrap, to think out problems for himself, to actively strive to prevent official jobbery, and a thousand other points of a similar kind—a matter very different, I rather fancy, from what some who have advocated the subject so strongly have really had in view. These are topics which clearly come under the heading of morals, and it will be the duty of the trainers in morals at the University to take up the threads on these points where they have been dropped at school, and connect them together in such a way as to lead to the fundamental principles on which all such duties rest. The intellectual instruction on the subject will, no doubt, take precedence —that is to a large extent inevitable; but so far as our present purpose is concerned, we shall have to cut out much of what is called civic duty from the other point of view, and above all things bear in mind that our aim is morality, not acquaintance with practical business.

"And the University has one special advantage in dealing with this particular subject. I have already said that at the University there should be no discipline save the discipline of conscience. Now I believe it is a rule at our two great Universities that undergraduates are not allowed to attend political meetings;—I am not quite sure, because at the time I was up there was no political election on;— all I can say is, that if the facts are really so, there has been a serious error of judgment, leading to the neglect of one of the finest opportunities a young man could possibly have of applying the principles he has learnt in theory to real practice. For consider the state of things as we would have them be. A young man comes up on our system with his heart and mind full of a sense of duty, and the principles which are to be his guide throughout life. At an election while he is still an undergraduate and a student, he has a chance of seeing the difference between the usual morality of political life, and that nobler standard to which he has been led to aspire. He is still undergoing ethical instruction, and if he feels tempted to side with a party to the neglect of his own loftier principles, he has at least the chance of having his errors pointed out to him and redeeming his mistakes by being helped to think out questions in a more dispassionate and scientific spirit than will in any likelihood ever be the case hereafter. If he has strong prejudices, as most young men have, founded upon no sort of decent reason, then he can, perhaps, be guided to see wherein his error lies. But in after-life where can he look for such help? It should be part of the duty of moral instructors at the University to discuss all political questions from the purely moral standpoint, throwing aside, so far as possible, all personal bias, and to not merely encourage, but even command their pupils to go to political meetings and report on the way in which the arguments advanced disregarded true morality. I can imagine no method better calculated to check sophisms, and do something to raise the tone of political life. I know that people would say it is utterly impracticable, but I do not think so, if only two conditions were realized : first, an honest attempt in this direction, and secondly, the existence of the kind of undergraduate whom we are supposing our system to produce.

"This consideration, indeed, has brought me to the great advantage which I consider the University has in the matter of moral training—the opportunity of direct practice, especially in those larger social virtues which a boy's age, and the conditions of school prevent him from directly touching before. In fact, I should say of the University that it is, or should be, the practising school of social ethics, giving the final burnishing touches before the finished product is turned out into the world to show by wear and tear of what value it is. It is like what a training college should be; the knowledge should be largely possessed before entrance, and then the University should provide incessant opening for applying rules to practice under guidance and correction. Of course the more elementary virtues, and especially the self-regarding ones, will in most cases have had ample means of practice afforded them both at school and at home; but with the political and social virtues on a great scale it is not so, and I would have the University largely turned into a field for practice in these particulars. Not merely such matters as political elections can be brought within the sphere of morality in some such way as I have suggested, but all branches of philanthropy can be carefully studied, not in the abstract and from books merely, but by taking actual part in philanthropic work, seeing the true condition of the poor, collecting statistics, and trying remedies on a small scale, all under the guidance of those who have longer experience, and are able to keep clearly burning before them the bright light of pure morality. If the University would devote itself to some such work as this, a vast deal might be done to check vague vapourings about the condition of the poor; as it is now, instead of having the thousands of undergradutes all brought into personal contact with their poorer brethren and learning to know the realities of life, we have to content ourselves with the few dozen who touch the subject practically at the University, and those, I fear fewer still, who after going down can and do reside for a time in some University settlement, where, good as the work is, it is so far at a disadvantage, that it is often difficult to find time to discuss the questions in the abstract, and where in any case we are no longer in a little oasis, as it were, cut off from the world, with our sole or main duty to treat all such questions from the purely moral point of view. To couple the practice with the final stage of instruction seems to me natural, and the culminating point of our whole scheme; I can but hope therefore that you will approve of my proposals, for one and all of us are agreed that morality must be our main aim, and that without morality—to which I would also join religion—life would be an impossibility, nothing less than a hell upon earth. This danger it is our duty to do our utmost to remove further and further into regions of banishment, till that great time shall at last come when sin shall be no more, and the bright light of heaven shall shine over all even here upon this our weary earth."

Butler & Tanner, The Selwood Printing Works, Frome, and London.

www.ingramcontent.com/pod-product-compliance
Lightning Source LLC
Chambersburg PA
CBHW032221230426
43666CB00033B/446